SKYSCRAPERS_GRATTE-CIEL_WOLKENKRATZER

SKYSCRAPERS_GRATTE-CIEL_WOLKENKRATZER

Editor • Éditrice • Autorin
Ariadna Àlvarez Garreta (architect • architecte • Architekt)

Publishing Director • Directeur Éditorial • Verlagsleiter
Nacho Asensio

Texts • Textes • Texte
Ariadna Àlvarez Garreta
Joaquim Ballarín Bargalló (architect • architecte • architekt)

Translation • Traduction • Übersetzung
Peter Miller (English)
Julian Bermejo (Français)
Sabine Schaub (Deutsch)

Design and layout • Conception et maquettage • Design und Grafik
BOOKS FACTORY

Production • Production • Produktion
Juanjo Rodríguez Novel

Copyright © 2002 Atrium Group
Publishing project: Books Factory, S.L.
e-mail: books@booksfactory.org

Published by: Atrium Internacional
de México, S.A. de C.V.
Fresas nº 60 (Colonia del Valle)
03200 México D.F. MÉXICO

Tel: +525 575 90 94
Fax: +525 559 21 52
e-mail: atriumex@prodigy.net.mx
www.atriumbooks.com

ISBN: 84-95692-25-2
National Book Catalogue Number
B-36453-2002

Printed in Spain
Grabasa, S.L.

Copyright © 2002 Atrium Group
Projet éditorial: Books Factory, S.L.
e-mail: books@booksfactory.org

Publié par: Atrium Internacional
de México, S.A. de C.V.
Fresas nº 60 (Colonia del Valle)
03200 México D.F. MÉXICO

Tél: +525 575 90 94
Fax: +525 559 21 52
e-mail: atriumex@prodigy.net.mx
www.atriumbooks.com

ISBN: 84-95692-25-2
Dépôt Légal:
B-36453-2002

Imprimé en Espagne
Grabasa, S.L.

Copyright © 2002 Atrium Group
Ausgabeleitung: Books Factory, S.L.
Email: books@booksfactory.org

Originalverlag: Atrium Internacional
de México, S.A. de C.V.
Fresas nº 60 (Colonia del Valle)
03200 México D.F. MÉXICO

Tel.: +525 575 90 94
Fax: +525 559 21 52
Email: atriumex@prodigy.net.mx
www.atriumbooks.com

ISBN: 84-95692-25-2
Verlagsnummer:
B-36453-2002

Druck in Spanien
Grabasa, S.L.

INDEX-INDEX-INHALT

INTRODUCTION

This book proposes a non-historical vision of the most representative tall buildings of the last decade of the 20th Century reflecting current architecture in different realities, cultures and cities throughout the world, from twenty-floor buildings to the utopian eighty meter-tall skyscrapers.

The choice has been made to include some emblematic buildings from the second half of the last century, taking architecture to be an artistic discipline tied to history. Going through the book chronologically, we observe that the starting point is established in the fifties as a reference to the technical and formal evolution of skyscrapers. Between the 80s and the 90s we find a greater number of examples to reach the central axis of the book, the 90s. As its character is not historical, the buildings have been ordered alphabetically with the intention of facilitating an efficient form of consultation and handling of the information for the reader. Each reader will be able to plan routes, according to their interests, through an ample and objective vision, leaving the more technical analysis and information to other publications.

Following a geographic trajectory, we can see how the period established in this volume coincides in many cases with the economic and constructive expansion of the Asian continent. These cities, over a period of ten years, have seen their traditional silhouette transformed by big towers in a vertiginous race lacking in town planning to regulate their implantation on urban land. The relationship between man and architecture has been the greatest preoccupation of the architect, but in the case of tall buildings this goes beyond the human dimension, establishing a level of relationship at city scale. In this case, the problem of representation covers the relationship between the public space/constructed space, the contact of the building with the ground, the volumetry and choice of materials. How to make compatible the scale of skyscrapers with the traditional city is the architectural investigation proposed by this compilation.

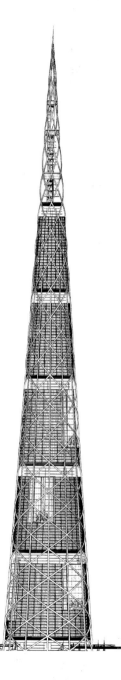

The date of each project corresponds to the year in the period of construction comes to an end, which could be past, present or future with the incorporation of proposals for buildings for the cities of the new millennium.

This book is dedicated to all those people who perished in the attacks of September 11th 2001 which destroyed the Twin Towers of New York and part of the Pentagon building in Washington. We also want to remember all those who lost their lives in the rescue tasks and those who die on a daily basis all over the world as victims of economic avarice and the intolerance of some governments.

Ariadna Àlvarez Garreta

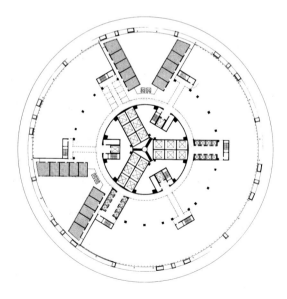

INTRODUCTION

Ce livre propose une vision non historique des gratte-ciel les plus représentatifs de la dernière décade du XXème siècle. Il présente l'actualité architectonique sur des réalités différentes, des cultures et des villes du monde entier, des bâtiments de vingt étages aux gratte-ciel utopiques d'une hauteur de huit cent mètres.

L'on a considéré qu'il était convenable de citer certains bâtiments emblématiques de la seconde moitié du siècle passé, l'architecture est comprise comme une discipline artistique liée à l'histoire. Lorsque l'on suit le livre chronologiquement, on se rend compte que le point de départ établi correspond aux années 50 en tant que référence de l'évolution technique et formelle du gratte-ciel. Entre les années 80 et 90 nous trouvons déjà plus d'exemples afin d'arriver à l'axe central du livre, les années 90. Puisque la caractéristique n'est pas historique, les bâtiments ont été classés par ordre alphabétique pour ainsi faciliter au lecteur une consultation et un emploi efficace de l'information. Chaque lecteur pourra programmer des parcours en fonction de ses inquiétudes, la vision sera ample et objective; l'analyse et l'information, plus techniques, sont réservées à d'autres publications.

Si l'on effectue un parcours géographique, l'on peut observer que la période établie dans ce volume coïncide dans plusieurs cas avec l'essor économique et du bâtiment du continent asiatique. Pendant dix ans, le profil traditionnel de ces villes a tout à fait changé à cause des grandes tours; il s'agit d'une course terrible dépourvue du contenu urbanistique qui aurait permis de contrôler leur implantation sur le sol urbain. Le rapport entre l'homme et l'architecture a été le souci le plus important de l'architecte, mais dans le cas du gratte-ciel, celui-ci dépasse la dimension humaine; il établit un niveau de rapport sur l'échelle de la ville. Dans ce cas, le problème de la représentation englobe le rapport entre l'espace public/espace construit, le contact du bâtiment avec le sol, la volumétrie et le choix des matériaux. Comment rendre compatible l'échelle des gratte-ciel avec la ville traditionnelle? Ceci correspond à la recherche architectonique proposée dans ce recueil.

La date de chacun des projets correspond à l'année de l'achèvement de la période de la construction, celle-ci peut être passée, présente ou future. L'on a aussi inclus des propositions de bâtiments pour les villes du nouveau millénaire.

Ce livre est dédicacé à toutes les personnes qui sont mortes lors de l'attentat du 11 de septembre 2001 qui a détruit les Twin Towers de New York et une partie du bâtiment du Pentagone à Washington. Nous voulons aussi nous rappeler de tous ceux qui ont perdu leur vie lors des travaux de secours et de ceux qui meurent chaque jour dans le monde entier, les victimes de l'avarice économique et de l'intolérance de certains gouvernements.

Ariadna Àlvarez Garreta

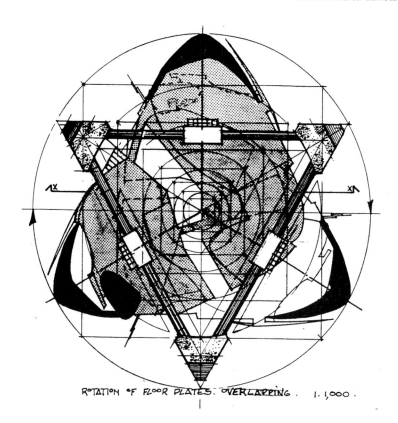

ROTATION OF FLOOR PLATES. OVERLAPPING . 1. 1,000 .

EINLEITUNG

Dieses Buch beabsichtigt, einen Überblick über die markantesten Hochhäuser der letzten Dekade des 20. Jahrhunderts sowie deren architektonische Aktualität in unterschiedlichen Landschaften, Kulturen und Städten in aller Welt - von 20stöckigen Gebäuden bis hin zu utopischen 800 Meter hohen Wolkenkratzern - zu geben.

Ebenso ist es zweckmäßig, einige emblematische Gebäude der zweiten Hälfte des vergangenen Jahrhunderts anzuführen, denn der Architektur wird neben Kunst auch eine geschichtliche Aufgabe zugeschrieben. Geht man dieses Buch in chronologischer Reihenfolge durch, stellt man fest, daß hierzu die 50iger Jahre Ausgangspunkt der technischen und gestalterischen Entwicklung von Wolkenkratzern sind. Zwischen den 80igern und 90igern gibt es bereits eine größere Anzahl von Wolkenkratzern und als Hauptteil dieser Ausgabe werden diejenigen Gebäude vorgestellt, die in den 90iger Jahren entstanden sind. Da es sich hier nicht um eine geschichtliche Aufstellung handelt, werden die Bauten alphabetisch aufgeführt und zwar mit der Absicht, dem Leser die Suche und die Handhabung von Informationen zu erleichtern. Jeder Leser kann sich je nach Wunsch einen umfassenden und objektiven

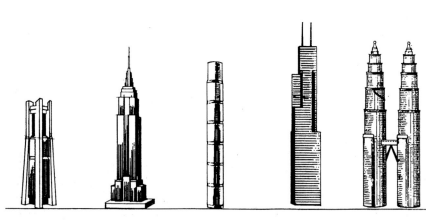

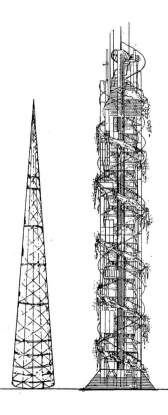

Überblick verschaffen, wobei Analysen und tiefer-gehende technische Informationen zusätzlichen Veröffentlichungen überlassen werden.

Bei dieser geographischen Rundreise stellen wir fest, daß der in diesem Buch behandelte Zeitabschnitt in vielen Fällen mit dem des wirt-schaftlichen und baulichen Wachstums auf dem asiatischen Kontinent übereingeht. Innerhalb einer Periode von 10 Jahren mußten diese Orte mitan-sehen, wie sich ihre traditionellen Silhouetten in rasanter Geschwindigkeit und ohne jegliche Urbanisierungsplanung durch Wolkenratzer drastisch verändert haben. Die Beziehung Mensch/Bau hat Architekten immer am meisten beschäftigt, Aber was die Entstehung von Wolkenkratzer anbelangt, übersteigen diese Dimensionen, die für den Menschen begreiflich sind und verändern so ihren Beziehungsgrad zur Stadt. In unserem Fall möch-ten wir das Verhältnis zwischen öffentlichem Raum/ bebautem Raum, Bodenkontakt des Gebäudes, räumlichen Umfang und Wahl der Baumaterialien behandeln. Wie verträglich das Höhenverhältnis von Wolkenkratzern zur traditionellen Stadt sein kann, stellt diese Zusammenstellung als eine Art archi-tektonischer Investigation dar.

Die bei jedem Gebäude angegebene Jahreszahl entspricht dem Jahr der Fertigstellung. Das kann bereits zurückliegen oder ist aktuell, kann aber auch zukünftig sein, womit gleichzeitig Bebauungsvorschläge für Städte im neuen Millenium gemacht werden.

Dieses Buch ist allen denjenigen Personen gewid-met, die durch das Attentat am 11. September 2001 ihr Leben verloren haben und bei dem die Twin Towers von New York sowie Teil des Pentagongebäudes in Washington zerstört wurden. Auch möchten wir an diejenigen erinnern, die bei den Bergungsarbeiten verstarben und an die Menschen, die täglich in aller Welt zu Opfern der Geldgier und der Intoleranz eini-ger Regierungen werden.

Ariadna Àlvarez Garreta

5 3 ʳᵈ AT THIRD

PHILIP JONSON & JOHN BURGEE ARCHITECTS

CLIENT / CLIENT / AUFTRAGGEBER: GERLAD D.HINES INTERESTS	**1986**
TOTAL AREA / SURFACE TOTALE / GES/ • TOBERFLÄCHE: 54.495 m²	
FLOORS / PLANS / STOCKWERKE - HEIGHT / HAUTEUR / HÖHE: 34 fl / 138 m	

Also known as Lipstick, this is an emblematic building in the city because of its characterstic volumetry and architectural quality which was projected for the company Revlon. The contact with the ground on pillars provides a porch on the ground floor and the triple staggering with which it rises is the result of the urban planning rule which characterizes the speculative buildings of New York offices. The eliptical form of the ground plan (and the location of the structure) gives a spatial distribution which is more interesting with respect to a traditional office building, guaranteeing total views of the exterior. The facade is treated like a luxurious skin in bands of polished Imperial Swedish red granite, stainless steel and glass.

Connu aussi comme Lipstick, il s'agit d'un bâtiment emblématique de la ville à cause de sa volumétrie caractéristique et de sa qualité architectonique, il fut conçu par la société Revlon. Le contact avec le sol sur piliers proportionne un porche au rez-de-chaussée et l'échelonnement triple sur lequel il s'élève est le résultat de la norme urbanistique qui caractérise les immeubles spéculatifs de bureaux de New York. La forme elliptique de l'étage (et l'emplacement de la structure) offre une distribution spatiale plus intéressante par rapport à un immeuble de bureaux traditionnel, ceci garantit tout à fait les vues à l'extérieur. La façade est traitée comme une peau luxueuse, avec des franges rouges en granite Impérial Suédois poli, en acier inoxydable et en verre.

Für die Firma Revlon entworfen und auch bekannt als Lipstick gilt dieses Gebäude aufgrund seiner charakteristischen Volumetrie und Bauqualität, als eines der emblematischen Bauten der Stadt. Das Gebäude steht auf Säulen, die im Erdgeschoss eine überdachten Vorhalle ergeben. Die dreifache Gebäudeabstufung ist Ergebnis einer Städtbaunorm, die die spektakulären Bürotürme New York´s charakterisieren. Durch den elipsenförmige Grund-riss (und die Lage des Baues) erreicht man eine interessantere räumliche Auflösung als in einem üblichen Bürohaus und rundherum freie Aussicht nach außen ist garantiert.Die Fassadenverblendung – ähnlich einer Luxushaut –in roten Streifen aus poliertem schwedischem Granit, Edelstahl und Glas.

The elliptical shape of the ground plan (atypical in the city's architecture) rising from the ground floor with a porch and the desire to distinguish itself from neighbouring buildings allows it to gain public space. The corners on the block are enlarged where there is more pedestrian traffic.

La forme elliptique de l'étage (si atypique dans l'architecture de la ville) qui s'élève en rez-de-chaussée avec un porche et la volonté de se démarquer des bâtiments avoisinants, permettent un gain d'espace publique. Les coins du pâté sont plus amples sur le point le plus fréquenté par les piétons.

Zusätzlicher Freiraum wird durch die elliptische Geschoßform (so untypisch in der Stadtarchitektur) gewonnen, die in der unteren Etage mit einem überdachten Eingang beginnt und sich auf diese Weise von den Nachbargebäuden unterscheiden möchte. Die Ecken des Gebäudeblocks weitern sich, dort wo der Fußgängerverkehr am größten ist.

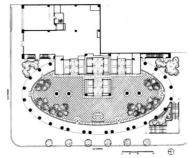

The two-storey foyer was decorated with great sobriety. The façades are made up of two strips of reflecting glass, polished red granite and aluminium. The elliptical curve is tangent to the pavement at its centre and creates an illusion of spatial continuity.

Le hall d'une hauteur de deux étages fut décoré très sobrement, les façades sont composées de deux franges en verre réfléchissant, en granite rouge poli et en aluminium. La courbe elliptique est tangente, du centre, au trottoir, elle crée une sensation spatiale de continuité.

Das 2stöckige Vestibül ist in eleganter Schlichtheit ausgestattet. Über die Aussenfassaden ziehen sich zwei Spiegelblenden sowie roter geschliffener Granit und Aluminium. Die elliptische Kurve berührt mit ihrer Mitte den Bürgersteig und vermittelt das Gefühl einer Raumkontinuität.

Projected for a well-known American brand of cosmetics, the shape of this building recalls a tube of lipstick. The architects used pop iconography to reflect their idea of an American city, made up of a mixture of buildings and styles, images, people, shapes and colours.

La forme de ce bâtiment, conçu pour une firme de produits cosmétiques américaine connue, ressemble à un rouge à lèvres. Les architectes ont employé une iconographie pop pour reproduire leur idée de la ville américaine, composée par le mélange de bâtiments et de typologies, d'images, de gens, de formes et de couleurs.

Die Bauform des Gebäudes, welches für ein bekanntes amerikanisches Kosmetikunternehmen entworfen wurde, erinnert an einen Lippenstift. Die Architekten verwandten eine Pop-Darstellung, die ihre Idee der amerikanischen Stadt transportiert. Diese Darstellung ist eine Mischung von Gebäude- und Menschenbildern, Formen und Farben.

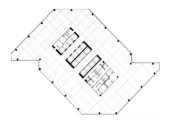

101 PARK AVENUE

ELI ATTIA ARCHITECTS

CLIENT / CLIENT / AUFTRAGGEBER: H.J KALIKOW & CO. INC.

1982

TOTAL AREA / SURFACE TOTALE / GESAMTOBERFLÄCHE: 111.524 m²

FLOORS / PLANS / STOCKWERKE - HEIGHT / HAUTEUR / HÖHE: 50 fl / 183 m

Designed as an efficient office building destined to attract high level clients, its shape and orientation are a direct answer to the conditioning factors of its location, pre-existing factors and planning conditions of the city. The building is oriented diagonally to allow access through the lots only point of contact with Park Avenue. To respect the schematic continuity and that of adjacent buildings, the lines which limit the streets and other existing buildings were maintained, creating a podium upon which the structure of the tower is raised. The building's shape reduces the visual mass of the construction.

Il a été conçu comme un immeuble de bureaux efficient destiné à attirer des clients à haut niveau, sa forme et son orientation représente une réponse directe aux conditions de l'emplacement, aux préexistences et aux conditions urbanistiques de la ville. Le bâtiment est orienté en diagonal afin de permettre l'accès par le seul point de contact du terrain avec Park Avenue. Afin de respecter la continuité de la trame et des bâtiments adjacents, l'on a gardé les alignements qui délimitent les rues et d'autres bâtiments déjà présents, créant ainsi un podium sur lequel s'élève la structure de la tour. La forme du bâtiment réduit la masse visuelle de la construction.

Als modernes Bürogebäude entworfen, um Kunden des gehobenen Niveaus zu erreichen. Sein Baustil und Orientierung passen sich bestens dem Standort, der bereits vorhandenen Bebauung und den urbanistischen Bedingungen der Stadt an. Das Gebäude steht diagonal zu der Ecke Park Avenue, an der sich auch der einzige Eingang zum Gebäude befindet. Um trotzdem die Linie der Straßen und der Nachbargebäude beizubehalten, wurde die Turmstruktur auf einem podiumartigen Unterbau errichtet. Die Bauart reduziert die sichtbare Konstruktionsmasse.

The location of the public squares related to the access and the section of the project in this area help the transition between interior and exterior.

L'emplacement des places publiques relatives à l'accès et la section du projet sur cette zone favorisent le transit intérieur-extérieur.

Die Straßenlage und anliegende Plätze sowie die Ausrichtung des Gebäudes in diesem Stadtviertel erleichtern den Durchgangsverkehr von innen nach außen.

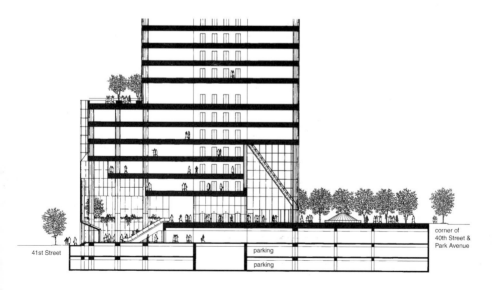

41st Street

parking

parking

corner of
40th Street &
Park Avenue

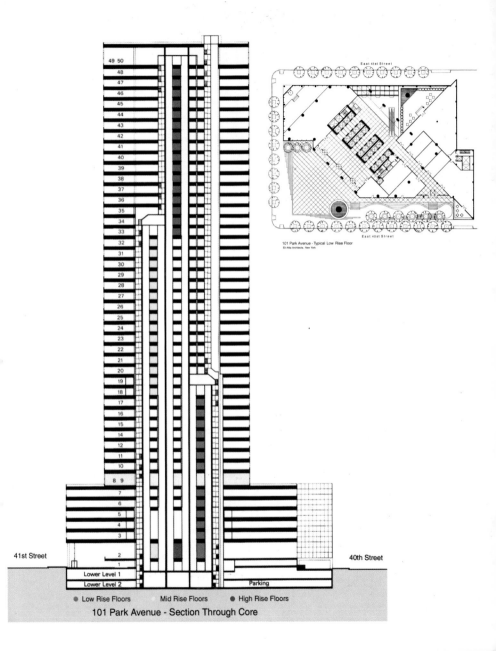

49 50
48
47
46
45
44
43
42
41
40
39
38
37
36
35
34
33
32
31
30
29
28
27
26
25
24
23
22
21
20
19
18
17
16
15
14
12
11
10
8 9
7
6
5
4
3
2
1

Lower Level 1
Lower Level 2

41st Street

40th Street

Parking

East 41st Street

East 40th Street

101 Park Avenue - Typical Low Rise Floor
Eli Attia Architects, New York

● Low Rise Floors   ○ Mid Rise Floors   ● High Rise Floors

101 Park Avenue - Section Through Core

The fragmented façade helps break up the shape and widens visuals, making the building lighter and less imposing.

La façade fragmentée contribue à casser la forme et à amplifier la vision, elle rend le bâtiment moins imposant et plus léger.

Die fragmentierte Fassade lockert die Form und erweitert das Blickfeld; läßt das Gebäude weniger mächtig aber auch leichter wirken.

The project emphasizes the singularity of the meeting between Park
Avenue and 44th Street, drawing back the building by means of the
chamfered facade and locating the access and a public square.

*Le projet souligne la singularité de la rencontre entre Park Avenue
et la rue 44; le bâtiment est déplacé grâce au chanfreinage de la
façade et nous y trouvons l'accès et une place publique.*

Einzigartiges Zusammentreffen an der Ecke Park Avenue und der 44.
Straße. Durch die abgeschrägte Fassade wird das Gebäude
zurückgesetzt. Davor liegt ein Vorplatz mit Eingang zum Gebäude.

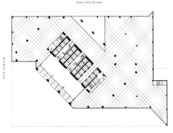

101 Park Avenue – 2nd Floor
Eli Attia Architects, New York

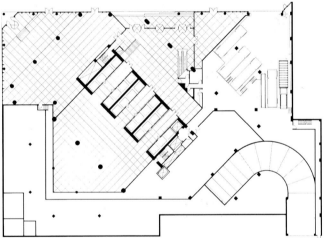

The project places great importance on its effect on the surroundings, attempting to control its areas of shadow and creating free spaces.

Le projet accorde une grande importance à l'effet sur l'environnement, il essaie de contrôler ses surfaces d'ombre et il crée des espaces libres.

Das Gebäude hat in seiner Umgebung eine besondere Wirkung. Weitestgehend wird der Gebäudeschatten vermieden und es ergeben sich ausreichend Freiflächen.

181 WEST MADISON

CESAR PELLI & ASSOCIATES INC.

CLIENT / CLIENT / AUFTRAGGEBER: MIGLIN-BEITLER DEVELOPMENTS	**1990**
TOTAL AREA / SURFACE TOTALE / GESAMTOBERFLÄCHE: 97.370 m²	
FLOORS / PLANS / STOCKWERKE - HEIGHT / HAUTEUR / HÖHE: 50 fl / 184 m	

This office tower found on the Chicago Loop was designed with the style of those sculptural skyscrapers of the 20s in the city where these buildings were constructed for the first time. With a square plan, it rises describing an elegant silhouette which, when it reaches the upper part, is breeched, thus losing part of its volume, and is topped with an elegant crown which distinguishes it from the city skyline. The vertical rhythm of the façade is made up of strips of granite combined with the glass of the windows, and the stainless steel mullions which reinforce the ascending character of the building.

Cette tour de bureaux qui se trouve au Loop de Chicago a été conçue selon le style des gratteciel sculpturaux des années 20 dans la ville où l'on a commencé à construire ces bâtiments. La vue en plan est carrée, elle s'élève et représente une silhouette élégante qui se déplace lorsque au niveau de la partie supérieure, elle perd ainsi un peu de volume. Elle est finie par une couronne élégante qui la distingue du skyline de la ville. Le rythme vertical de la façade est composé de franges en granite combinées avec le verre des vitres et de montants en acier inoxydable qui renforcent le caractère ascendant du bâtiment.

Dieser Büroturm befindet sich im Loop von Chicago und wurde im Stil der 20iger Jahre entworfen, so wie diejenigen Wolkenkratzer, die anfänglich in dieser Stadt errichtet wurden. Auf quadratischem Grundriß erhebt sich diese elegante Silhouette bis das Gebäude im oberen Bereich durch mehrere stufenartigen Absätze leicht an Umfang verliert und schließlich mit einer eleganten Dachkrone endet, so daß das Gebäude an der Skyline der Stadt leicht auffällt. Der gleichmässige Rhythmus der Fassade erfolgt abwechselnd zwischen Granitblenden kombiniert mit dem Glas der Fenster und den Edelstahlträgern, die den aufsteigenden Charakter des Gebäudes besonders betonen.

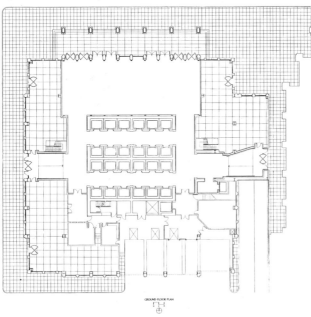

GROUND FLOOR PLAN

Above, main access to the building marked by a metallic pergola. Below, ground floor of the building. The structure of the tower responds to a central core of vertical communications and services, thus freeing the perimeter for office space.

En haut, accès principal du bâtiment prononcé par une pergola en métal.
En bas, rez-de-chaussée du bâtiment. La structure de la tour dispose d'un noyau central de communications verticales et de services, ce qui libère ainsi le périmètre réservé à l'espace des bureaux.

Oben: Haupteingang mit vorgebauter Metallüberdachung.
Unten: untere Etage. Durch zentral ausgerichtete Fahrstühle und weitere Versorgungseinrichtungen ist genügend Platz für Büroräumlickeiten.

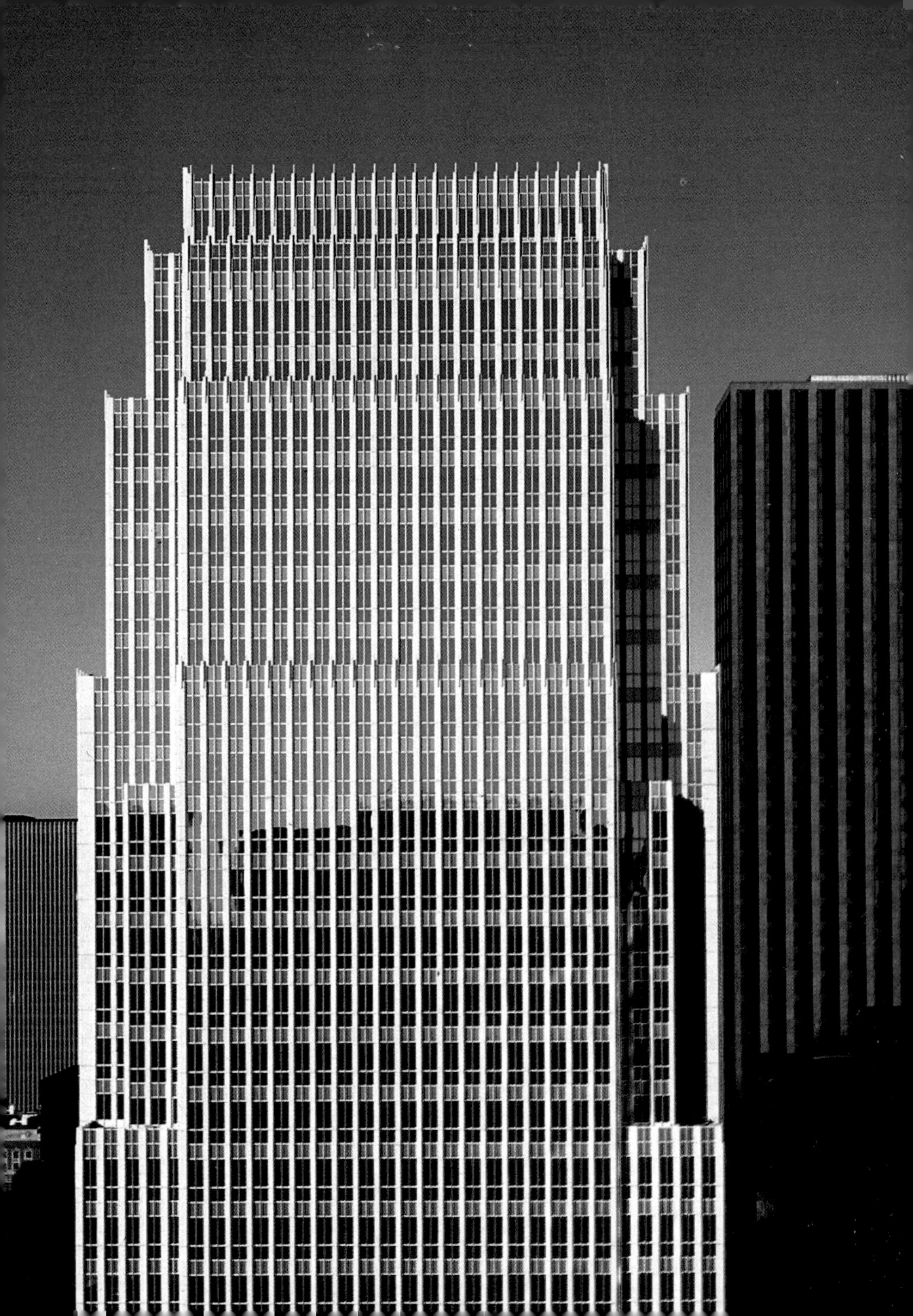

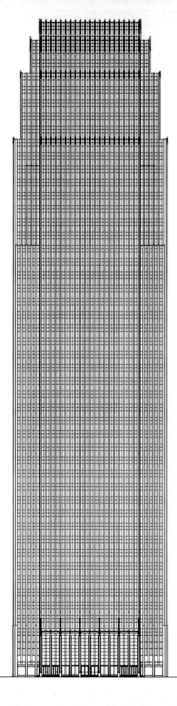

The interior lobby is a four-floor high loggia (it forms part of the base of the building) with large windows. It was thought of as a space which would receive a lot of light from outside which was decorated with gray and green marble.

Le hall intérieur est une loggia d'une hauteur de quatre étages (elle appartient à la base du bâtiment) avec de grandes fenêtres; il a été conçu comme un espace très illuminé de l'extérieur et il a été décoré avec des marbres gris et verts.

Innenansicht der 4 Stockwerke hohen Eingangshalle (Teil des Bausockels) mit hohen Fenstern, durch die das Tageslicht einfällt und ist mit grauem und grünen Marmor dekoriert.

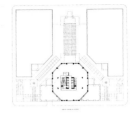

CHICAGO

311 SOUTH WACKER DRIVE

KOHN PEDERSEN FOX ASSOCIATES PC (KPF)

CLIENT / CLIENT / AUFTRAGGEBER: LINCOLN PROPERTY COMPANY	**1991**
TOTAL AREA / SURFACE TOTALE / GESAMTOBERFLÄCHE: 130.000 m²	
FLOORS / PLANS / STOCKWERKE - HEIGHT / HAUTEUR / HÖHE: 65 fl / 293 m	

This building, contiguous to the well-known Sears Tower, was the first of a group of three towers situated around a winter garden, conceived as pedestrian core and linked with different systems of transport concentrated in this area. The large public space is organized by means of two large squares crossed by a covered pedestrian area. The winter garden is also the lobby through which the octagonal office tower is accessed. Its bulky volume is decomposed in different elements. It culminates with a large translucent glass cylinder which is lit up at night, making the building stand out from the Chicago landscape.

Ce bâtiment avoisinant la fameuse Sears Tower fut le premier des trois tours situées autour d'un jardin d'hiver, qui fut conçu comme le noyau piéton et la liaison avec plusieurs systèmes de transport concentrés dans cette zone. Le grand espace publique est organisé avec deux grandes places coupées par une zone piétonne couverte. Le jardin d'hiver est aussi un hall d'accès à la tour octogonale de bureaux. Son volume massif est divisé en plusieurs éléments. Le sommet est un grand cylindre en verre translucide qui s'illumine le soir et distingue le bâtiment dans le paysage de Chicago.

Dieses Nachbargebäude des bekannten Sears Tower war der erste von drei geplanten Türmen umgeben von einem Wintergarten, der als Fußgängerbereich und gleichzeitig als Anbindung an unterschiedliche Transportsysteme dieses Stadtviertels gedacht war. Das große Freigelände besteht aus zwei großen Plätzen, die von einer überdachten Fußgängerzone durchquert werden. Der Wintergarten ist gleichzeitig auch der Haupteingang zum achteckigen Büroturms. Bauteile unterschiedlicher Höhe lockern das Gesamtbild auf. Das Gebäude endet mit einem riesigen durchsichtigen Glaszylinder, der nachts beleuchtet wird. So fällt der Bau am Nachthimmel über Chicago besonders auf.

The treatment of the façades is horizontal with vertical stripes which mark the concrete structure. The most stand out material is the red granite from Texas which forms a contrast with the neighboring Sears Tower.

Le traitement de la façade se compose de franges horizontales et verticales qui marquent la structure en béton. Le matériau le plus remarquable est le granite Rouge de Texas, ce qui contraste avec le bâtiment de la Sears Tower avoisinante.

Längst- und Querverblendungen an der Fassade, die die Betonstruktur betonen. Auffallendes Material ist der rote texanische Granit, der besonderes mit dem Nachbargebäude, dem Sears Tower, konstrastiert.

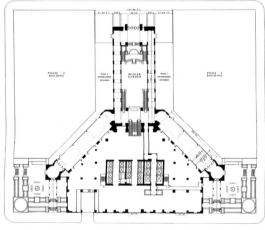

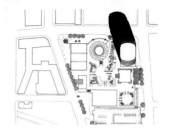

777 TOWER

CESAR PELLI & ASSOCIATES INC.

1990

CLIENT / CLIENT / AUFTRAGGEBER: SOUTH FIGUEROA PLAZA ASSOCIATES

TOTAL AREA / SURFACE TOTALE / GESAMTOBERFLÄCHE: 102.200 m²

FLOORS / PLANS / STOCKWERKE - HEIGHT / HAUTEUR / HÖHE: 53 fl / 221 m

Located in the business area of Los Angeles, it is one of the most graceful buildings in the area and a landmark in the city. The building, a square prism with the corners rounded, diminishes arching towards the east and west, maintaining the same façade plan towards the south and north. This is covered with lightly colored metal, with special attention to the treatment of the details, generating shadows and volumes which break up the monotony of the plan. The building's access lobby, at triple space, leaves its east and south façades completely glass-covered, so that the building is arrived at through an area bathed in sunlight.

Elle se trouve dans la zone des affaires de Los Angeles, elle est un des bâtiments les plus graciles de la zone et un signe de la ville. Le bâtiment, un prisme carré aux las coins arrondis, décroît et s'arque vers l'est et l'ouest, et maintient les mêmes surfaces sur la façade sud et nord. Celle-ci est recouverte de métal légèrement coloré, les détails ont reçu un traitement spécial, ce qui produit des ombres et des volumes qui cassent la monotonie de la surface. Les façades est et sud du hall d'accès au bâtiment, à trois espaces, sont complètement vitrées; l'accès au bâtiment reçoit ainsi un bain de lumière solaire.

Im Businessviertel von Los Angeles gelegen, gilt er als eines der elegantesten Gebäude des Viertels und Zielpunkt in der Stadt. Quadratischer Grundriß mit abgerundeten Gebäudeecken. Auf der Ost/Westseite sowie auf der Nord/Südseite verjüngt sich das Gebäude mit leicht nach innen geschwungener Fassade. Diese ist mit leicht choloriertem Metall überzogen, wobei besonders auf Details wie Schattierungen geachtet wurde, um somit die Monotonie der Flächen zu brechen. Durch die 3stöckige Eingangshalle des Gebäudes ist die Süd/Ostfassade vollständig verglast, so daß der Zugang zum Gebäude völlig in Sonne gebadet ist.

The bulky zones of the façade develop a volumetric capacity which breaks up the monotony of the curtain wall.

Les zones pleines de la façade développent une capacité volumétrique qui casse la monotonie du mur rideau.

Die massiven Fassadenbereiche verleihen dem Gebäude Volumen und unterbrechen die Monotonie der Außenhaut.

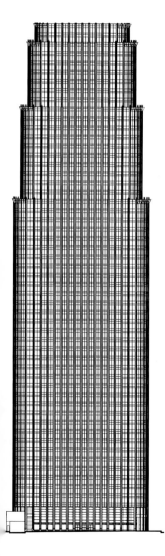

The lobby, at triple height, is bathed in sunlight thanks to the liberation of the façade, completely glass-covered.

Le hall, à trois hauteurs est inondé de lumière solaire car la façade, qui est tout à fait vitrée, est dégagée.

Dank verglaster Fassadenöffnungen versinkt die 3stöckige Eingangshalle im Sonnenlicht.

ABN-AMRO BANK WORLD HQTRS.

PEI COBB FREED & PARTNERS

CLIENT / CLIENT / AUFTRAGGEBER: ABN-AMRO BANK N.V	**1999**

TOTAL AREA / SURFACE TOTALE / GESAMTOBERFLÄCHE: 105.000 m²

FLOORS / PLANS / STOCKWERKE - HEIGHT / HAUTEUR / HÖHE: 24 fl / 96 m

Located next to an important communications junction in the southern sector of the center of Amsterdam, the building aims to be representative, providing an image for the firm. The project folds out in three directions: the 24-floor building, which contains offices and marks the importance of the urban axis, a 7-floor building, which contains the areas of relation – central lobby, auditorium, conference hall, center and meeting halls and a restaurant for 500 diners surrounding a garden park, and finally a 17-floor building which has an employees canteen on the top floor. In the basement there is a large car park and the plumbing and electrical systems areas.

Le bâtiment qui est situé près d'un noyau de communications très important du secteur sud du centre de Amsterdam, recherche la représentativité et l'image de la marque. Le projet se développe dans trois sens: le bâtiment à 24 étages, qui comporte des bureaux et qui remarque l'importance de l'axe urbain; un bâtiment à 7 étages, qui comporte les espaces des relations -hall central, auditorium, sale de conférences, centre et salles de réunions et un restaurant pour 500 commensaux, il entoure un jardin de loisirs, et, enfin, un bâtiment à 17 étages qui dispose d'un restaurant pour les employés au dernier étage. Au sous-sol nous trouvons un grand parking et les zones des installations.

An einem wichtigen Verkehrsknotenpunkt im Südteil des Zentrums von Amsterdam steht dieses imageträchtige Gebäude des Bankunternehmens. Die Anlage verläuft in 3 Himmelsrichtungen. Ein 24 stöckiges Bürogebäude als bedeutender Dreh– und Angelpunkt der Stadt. Ein 7 stöckiges Gebäude mit Haupteingangshalle, Auditorium, Konferenzsaal, Tagungszentrum, Sitzungsräumen und Restaurant mit 500 Plätzen. Alles ist von einer Parkanlage umgeben. Hinzu kommt ein weiteres 17stöckiges Gebäude mit Restaurant im oberen Stockwerk für die Angestellten. Weitreichende Parkmöglichkeiten sowie Versorgungsanlagen befinden sich unterirdisch.

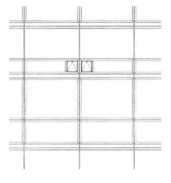
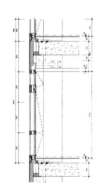
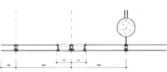

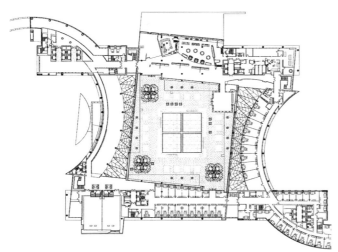

The general plan combines an orthogonal organization with circular forms.
High up, some blocks form a slight incline in its façade.

Le plan général combine une organisation octogonale avec des formes circulaires.
En hauteur, certains blocs inclinent un peu leur façade.

Der Gesamtgrundriß der Anlage ist eine Kombination aus rechten Winkeln sowie Halbkreisen.
Einige Gebäude neigen sich leicht voneinander ab.

The façade presents differently paced gaps and colored finishes in the different projected volumes.

La façade présente plusieurs vides rythmés et des couleurs de finissage sur les différents volumes projetés.

Die Aussenseiten der Anlage präsentieren unterschiedliche Ausführung und Farbgebung.

Despite the extension and magnitude of the complex, the design has been kept in the scale closest to the users.

Malgré l'envergure et la grandeur du complexe, la conception a maintenu une échelle plus proche aux utilisateurs.

Trotz der Ausdehnung und Größenordnung dieses Komplexes ist die Gestaltung der Flächen sehr benutzerfreundlich ausgefallen.

The interior decoration of the building, sober and contemporary, expresses the power and dynamism of the bank.

Le décor intérieur du bâtiment, sobre et contemporain, exprime le pouvoir et le dynamisme de la banque.

Die schlichte und kontemporäre Innenausstattung des Gebäudes drücken die Macht und Dynamik der Bank aus.

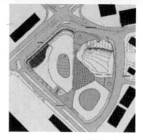

AL ASIMA SHOPPING VILLAGE

T.R. HAMZAH & YEAN SDN BHD

CLIENT / CLIENT / AUFTRAGGEBER: SALHIA REAL ESTATE COMPANY K.S.C.

2000

TOTAL AREA / SURFACE TOTALE / GESAMTOBERFLÄCHE: 44.000 m²

FLOORS / PLANS / STOCKWERKE - HEIGHT / HAUTEUR / HÖHE: 40 fl / 157,5 m

The client for this building wanted a shopping and office complex which proposed a different concept from the American classic, the concept drifts towards a "Retail Village" characterized by the incorporation of vernacular elements. Organized starting out from three units, each of them organized starting out from a ring around a core, they are inter-related by means of another larger core. The result is an entity formed by a tower and a four-floor building of offices and a three-floor shopping base which, like a jellyfish, absorbs and unifies the surface area of the complex. The formal result and the bioclimatic design of the building have turned it into a reference point in the city.

Le client de ce bâtiment désirait un complexe commercial et de bureaux dont le concept serait différent de celui de l'américain classique, le concept vise un "Retail Village" qui a pour caractéristique l'incorporation d'éléments vernaculaires. Il est organisé à partir de trois unités, chacune de celles-ci est organisée à partir d'un anneau autour d'un noyau, elles sont interconnectées par un autre noyau qui est plus grand. Le résultat est un établissement composé d'une tour et d'un immeuble de bureaux à 4 étages et d'un socle commercial d'une hauteur de 3 étages qui absorbe et unifie toute la surface du complexe comme une méduse. Grâce au résultat quant à la forme et à la conception bioclimatique du bâtiment, il est devenu une référence de la ville.

Wunsch des Bauherrn dieses Gebäudes war, ein vom klassischen amerkanischen Konzept abweichendes Shopping- und Bürocenter zu errichten. Die Idee tendierte zu einem "Retail Village", das sich durch das Einfliessen einheimischer Elemente charakterisiert. Drei Baueinheiten sind Bestandteil des Komplexes. Jeder einzelne Bau ist ringförmig um einen Kernbereich angelegt, der sich wiederum mit dem nächsten größeren Kernbereich vereinigt. Das Ergebnis ist eine Anlage bestehend aus einem Turm, einem 4 stöckigen Bürogebäude und einem dreigeschössigen Unterbau mit Shoppingcenter, der ähnlich einer Krake, den gesamten Komplex um spannt und unter sich vereint. Gestaltung und bioklimatisches Design führten dazu, daß dieser Bau zum Anziehungspunkt in der Stadt wurde.

The part of the building complex at ground level establishes a connection with the exterior, and the shopping plaza ceilings are immense skylights, giving shoppers the feeling of walking on a street rather than the inside of a building.

La partie du complexe qui se trouve dans le bâtiment socle est en relation avec l'extérieur, et les toits des places sont recouverts avec des grandes lucarnes, ce qui permet que le promeneur ait la sensation de se trouver dans une rue et non pas à l'intérieur d'un bâtiment.

Der Teil des Komplexes, der sich im Unterbau befindet, ist besonders großzügig mit außen verbunden. Die Überdachung der Plätze ist mit großen Oberlichtern versehen und verleihen einem das Gefühl, sich auf der Straße zu befinden, nicht aber im Innern eines Gebäudes.

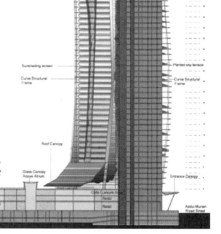

The tower consists of a series of membranes that envelop the structure, which is the skeleton of the building, and protect it from the exterior.

La tour fonctionne à partir de membranes qui recouvrent la structure, elles sont le squelette du bâtiment et le protègent de l'extérieur.

Der Turm funktioniert wie eine strukturumhüllende (das Gebäudeskelett) Membrane und schützt sie vor Einflüssen von außen.

AL FAISALIAH COMPLEX

FOSTER & PARTNERS

CLIENT / CLIENT / AUFTRAGGEBER: KING FAISAL FOUNDATION	**2000**
TOTAL AREA / SURFACE TOTALE / GESAMTOBERFLÄCHE: 240.000 m²	
FLOORS / PLANS / STOCKWERKE - HEIGHT / HAUTEUR / HÖHE: 40 fl / 267m	

This office tower is a key point in the planning development of the city, because it is also the first skyscraper in Saudi Arabia. Stands out because of a profile that rises gently towards the sky, containing the golden sphere where an exclusive restaurant offers views of the city and environs. The complex also houses a luxury hotel, a banquet and conference center, up-market apartments and three commercial floors. The project, which aspires to a balance between the cost of the building and its effectiveness, flexibility, environmental and architectural harmony, develops interesting proposals in the treatment of façades and layout of the building.

Cette tour de bureaux est un des points principaux du développement urbanistique de la ville, car il est aussi le premier gratte-ciel en Arabie Saoudite. Le profil qui s'élève doucement vers le ciel le distingue et il garde la sphère dorée à l'intérieur, dans celle-ci un restaurant exclusif offre des vues de la ville et des alentours. Le complexe auberge aussi un hôtel de luxe, un centre pour banquets et conférences, des appartements grand standing et trois étages commerciaux. Le projet qui prétend l'équilibre entre le coût du bâtiment et l'efficacité, la flexibilité, l'harmonie environnementale et architectonique, développe des propositions intéressantes quant au traitement des façades et à la distribution du bâtiment.

Dieser Büroturm ist ein Schlüsselpunkt in der städtbaulichen Entwicklung dieser Stadt, zumal es auch der erste Wolkenkratzer Saudi Arabiens ist. Sein sanfter, zum Himmel aufsteigender Umriß fällt besonders ins Auge. In der goldfarbenen Kugel unter der Gebäudespitze liegt ein exklusives Restaurant mit Ausblick über Stadt und Umgebung. Der Komplex beherbergt neben einem Luxushotel, ein Zentrum für Bankette und Konferenzen, Apartments für gehobene Ansprüche und drei Geschäftsetagen. Der Bau beabsichtigt, das Gleichgewicht zwischen Kosten und Nutzen, Flexibilität, Harmonie von Umwelt und Architektur herzustellen und entwickelt dabei interessante Denkanstösse hinsichtlich Aussenflächenbehandlung und Gebäudegliederung.

Above, in the base of the tower, a five-floor high lobby links towards the north with the hotel and towards the south with the apartments and the shopping area. On the left, detail of the façade of the tower where it meets the base. Panels of aluminum regulate the solar radiation of the façade and prevent its reflection.

En haut, sur la base de la tour, un hall d'une hauteur de cinq étages communique, au nord, avec l'hôtel et, au sud, avec les appartements et la zone des boutiques. À gauche, détail de la façade de la tour au point de coïncidence avec la base. Des panneaux en aluminium régulent la radiation solaire de la façade et évitent les reflets.

Oben: untere Etage des Turmes mit Eingangshalle, die sich über eine Höhe von 5 Stockwerken erstreckt und sich auf der Nordseite mit dem Hotel und im Südteil mit den Apartments und der Ladenpassage verbindet.
Links: Detail der Außenfassade an der Stoßlinie zwischen Turm und Unterbau. Aluminiumpanele regulieren die Sonneneinstrahlung auf die Fassade und vermeiden die Rückstrahlung.

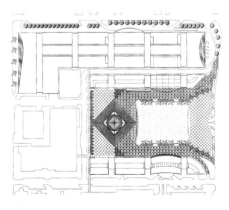

The square plan is laid out from a central structural core of vertical communications and services. The rest of the structure is located in the corners tethering the building.

La vue en plan carrée est distribuée à partir d'un noyau structurel central de communications verticales et de services. Le reste de la structure se trouve sur les coins, elle attache le bâtiment.

In dem quadratischer Grundriß befinden sich als Zentralstruktur Aufzüge und Versorgungseinrichtungen. Das restliche Baugefüge wird von vier Gebäudeecken zusammengehalten.

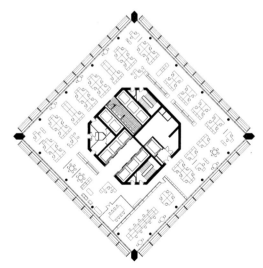

AURORA PLACE

RENZO PIANO BUILDING WORKSHOP

CLIENT / CLIENT / AUFTRAGGEBER: LEND LEASE DEVELOPMENT	**1996**
TOTAL AREA / SURFACE TOTALE / GESAMTOBERFLÄCHE: 49.000 m²	
FLOORS / PLANS / STOCKWERKE - HEIGHT / HAUTEUR / HÖHE: 44 fl / 200 m	

Built to coincide with the Sydney Olympics, its program combines residential use, in a 17-floor building and the office tower, of 44 floors. Its location in a district whose origin dates back to the mid-19th century, with all the contextual weight that this implies, its proximity to the Sydney Opera House by Jorn Urzon, with which it does not shy away from dialogue, the social intention of provoking the relationship between the work and residential areas, by means of shared public leisure areas and special attention to the climatic conditions and the physical environment in which it is located, constitute the bases of the development of the project.

Construit pour coincider avec les Jeux Olympiques de Sydney, son programme combine l'usage résidentiel dans l'immeuble de 17 étages, et celui de bureaux dans la tour de 44.Son emplacement dans un quartier dont les origines remontent au XIX siècle, avec toute la charge de contexte que cela represente, la proximité de l'Opéra de Sidney de Jorn Urzon, avec lequel il ne réfute pas dialogue, la préocupation sociale de provoquer une relation entre les zones de travail et celles résidentielles grâce à des zones publiques de loisirs en comun et, une attention particulière aux conditions climatiques et à l'entourage physique oú il se trouve, sont les éléments de base du développement de ce projet.

Wurde anlässlich der Olympiade in Sydney errichtet. In einem 17stöckigen Bau befinden sich Wohnungen und Büros in einem 44 Stockwerke hohem Turm. Diese Anlage befindet sich in einem Stadtviertel, das im 19. Jahrhun-dert entstand und liegt in der Nähe der Oper von Sydney, die von Jorn Urzon entworfen wurde. Das Aurora Place lehnt aber nicht den Dialog mit dem Operngebäude ab, sondern möchte sich eingliedern und beabsichtigt ebenso, mittels gemeinsamer öffentlicher Freizeitzonen eine soziale Beziehung zwischen den Arbeits– und Wohnbereichen herzustellen. Gleichzeitig ist auch Basis für diese Projektbearbeitung die besondere Beachtung klimatischer und umfeldbestimmender Bedingungen.

The project emphasizes the delicate and free aspects of
the form, as shown by the closures of the main façades.

*Le projet met en valeur la forme libre et délicate, tel
que l'illustrent les fermetures des façades principales.*

Der Bau vermittelt nachdrücklich eine delikate freie Form.
Dies wird insbesonders durch die Einfassung der
Hauptfassaden ausgedrückt.

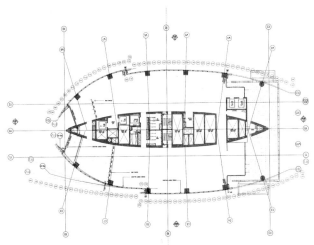

The design of the building has an ethereal quality, to diminish its capacity to impose itself on the built-up surroundings.

Le design de l'édifice est d'une qualité subtile, permettant de réduire sa capacité d'imposition sur les édifices alentours.

Das Design des Gebäudes hat eine besonders ätherische Qualität, um auf diese Weise seine Behauptung gegenüber dem bebauten Umfeld etwas zu reduzieren.

The glass skin of the building regulates the rays of the sun and the temperature of the walls, at the same time as it confers a misty tonality.

La surface cristaline de l'édifice regule les rayons de soleil et la température des murs en même temps qu'elle lui donne une tonalité nébuleuse.

Der matte Ton der Außenverglasung des Gebäudes reguliert den Einfall der Sonneneinstrahlung sowie die Temperatur der Außenmauern.

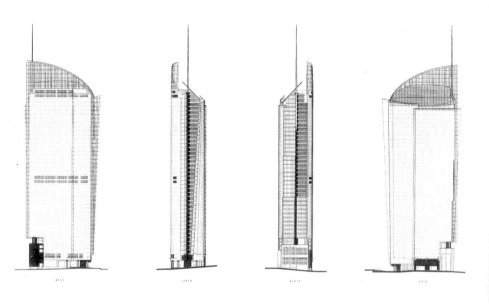

The curtain wall spreads beyond the volume of the building, dissolving its limits and accentuating its light appearance.

Le mur rideau s'étend au delà du volume de l'édifice, atténuant ses limites et mettant l'accent sur son aspect de légèreté.

Die Außenhaut geht über den Gebäudeumfang hinaus, lockert seine Begrenzungsflächen und akzentuiert seine Leichtigkeit.

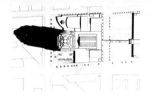

BANK OF AMERICA CORPORATE CENTER

CESAR PELLI & ASSOCIATES INC.

1992

CLIENT / CLIENT / AUFTRAGGEBER: NATIONSBANK CORPORATION, CHARTER PROPIERTIES & LINCOLN PROPERTY CO.
TOTAL AREA / SURFACE TOTALE / GESAMTOBERFLÄCHE: 126.000 m²
FLOORS / PLANS / STOCKWERKE - HEIGHT / HAUTEUR / HÖHE: 60 fl / 265,5 m

Known as NationsBank, this building, which houses the central offices of the bank, is found in the geographical, historical and economic center of Charlotte. Its construction responded to both the economic profitability of the promoter and the possibility of culturally and economically revitalizing the city center, forming part of the public complex. Two garden squares and the Founders Hall (a civic and shopping center) are found in the base of the tower. Its silhouette, which is characterized by the breeching towards the interior in ascending direction of the curved façades, is a landmark in the cityscape.

Connu comme NationsBank, ce bâtiment qui auberge les bureaux centraux de la banque, se trouve au centre géographique, historique et économique de Charlotte. Sa construction respecte aussi bien la rentabilité économique du promoteur que la possibilité de revitaliser culturellement et économiquement le centre urbain, il appartient au complexe public. Deux places avec des jardins et le Founders Hall, (un centre commercial et civique) se trouvent sur la base de la tour. Sa silhouette, dont la caractéristique est le déplacement vers l'intérieur, en ascendant, des façades courbées, est une référence du paysage urbain.

Als NationsBank bekannt, beherbergt dieses Gebäude die Zentralverwaltung der Bank. Sie liegt geografisch zentral in der historischen und wirtschaftlichen Mitte von Charlotte. Mit seiner Entstehung, die ebenso das wirtschaftliche Potential seines Auftraggebers widerspiegelt, ergab sich auch die Möglichkeit einer kulturellen und wirtschaftlichen Wiederbelebung der Stadtmitte und verwandelte sich zu einem öffent– lichem Teilbereich. Am Fuß des Gebäudes liegen zwei Grünanlagen und die Founders Hall (ein Einkaufs– und Bürgerzentrum). Seine Silhouette charakterisiert sich durch zurücksetzte, leicht nach innen geschwungene aufsteigende Aussenseite und gilt als Blickpunkt im Stadtpanorama.

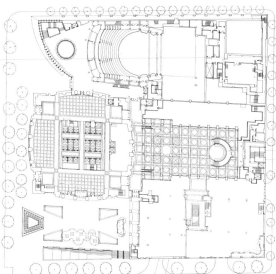

Above, one of the accesses to the tower next to the waterfall which opens out on the squares. The base is cased in dark granite with marble columns at the entrances.

En haut, un des accès à la tour près de la cascade qui s'ouvre vers les places. La base est recouverte de granite foncé, les colonnes des accès sont en marbre.

Oben: einer der Gebäudezugänge mit Wasserkaskade, die sich zu den Plätzen hin öffnet. Der Gebäudesockel ist an den Eingängen mit dunklem Granit und Marmorsäulen versehen.

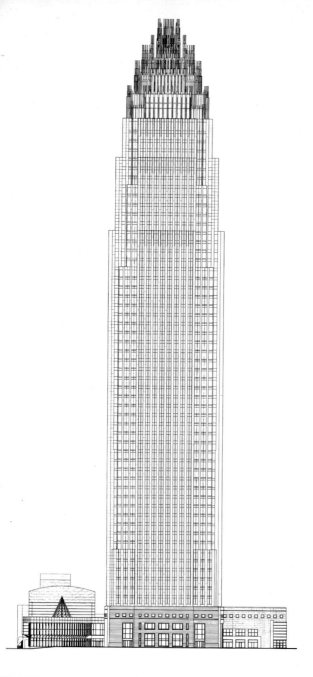

The composition of the façades is based on horizontal and vertical bands where granite predominates over the windows.

Les façades se composent de franges horizontales et verticales, le granite prédomine sur les fenêtres.

Aussenseite mit waagerechten und senkrechten Blenden, wobei Granit bei der Einfassung von Fenstern hervorherrscht.

Above, view of the main lobby from which the elevator lobbies open out, also shown in detail on the left.

En haut, vue du hall principal d'où émergent les halls des ascenseurs, ils figurent aussi à gauche.

Oben: Blick in die Haupteingangshalle mit den Fluren zu den Liftanlagen, auch links noch einmal detaillierter zu sehen.

BIONIC TOWER

CERVERA-PIOZ & CELAYA

CLIENT / CLIENT / AUFTRAGGEBER: THE CHINESE GOVERNMENT	**1992**
TOTAL AREA / SURFACE TOTALE / GESAMTOBERFLÄCHE: 275.000.000 m²	
FLOORS / PLANS / STOCKWERKE - HEIGHT / HAUTEUR / HÖHE: 300 fl / 1.230 m	

Based on the development of Bionic Architecture, a science which unites Architecture with Engineering and Biology, proposes the use of a highly resistant reinforced concrete microstructure capable of supporting 2,000 Kg/cm² (currently 250 Kg/cm2 is in use), a floating foundation (which maintains the weight of the building isolated from contact with the earth by means of plastic fluids) and a structure which imitates the internal formation of trees, with multiple vertical capillary vessels which complete a building with a stylized cereal shape whose elliptical floors have an area of 223,450 m² (45 soccer pitches).

Dérivant du développement de l'Architecture Bionique, une science qui unit l'Architecture et le Génie et la Biologie, propose l'emploi d'un béton armé micro-structuré à grande résistance, capable de supporter 2.000 Kg / cm² (actuellement on utilise celui de 250 Kg / cm²), une cimentation flottante (qui maintient le poids du bâtiment isolé du contact au sol avec des fluides plastiques) et une structure qui imite le développement interne des arbres, plusieurs vaisseaux capillaires verticaux finissent un bâtiment qui ressemble à une céréale stylisée dont les étages elliptiques peuvent mesurer 223.450 m² (45 terrains de football).

Basierend auf der Bionik– architektur, die Biologie und Engineering vereint. Dazu verwandte man einen höchst widerstandsfähigen Mikrostructurstahl-beton mit einer Tragkraft von 2000 Kg/cm² (gegenwärtig verwendet man 250 Kg/cm2), Schwimmfundament (hält das Gewicht des Gebäudes über dem Boden mittels Druckmitteln) und einer Struktur, die an einen gewundenen Baumstamm erinnert und das Gebäude endet in Form einer stilisierten Getreideähre. Die elliptischen Stockwerke ergeben eine Gesamtfläche von 223.450 m² (das entspricht dem Ausmaß von 45 Fußballfeldern).

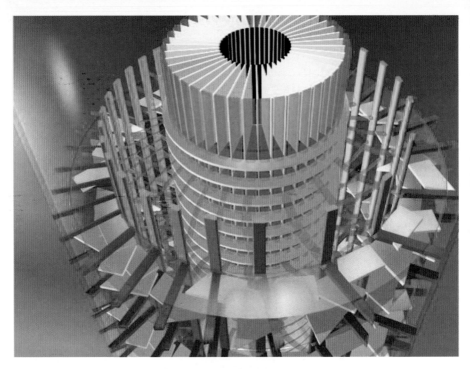

Typical section of the Bionic city, commercial, cultural and leisure uses in the interior, offices and residences in the exterior. Below, the floor structural concept.

Section typique de la ville Bionique; usages commerciaux, culturels et de loisirs à l'intérieur, bureaux et résidences à l'extérieur. En bas, le concept structurel de l'étage.

Typischer Querschnitt der binomischen Stadt. Geschäfts- kultur und Freizeitanlagen in der Mitte, Büros und Wohnungen am Aussenkern. Unten: Konzept der Gebäudestruktur.

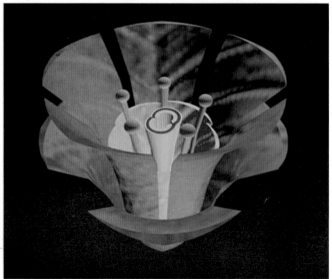

Section of a tree showing the micro-fragmented structure which gives rigidity
to the conducts which transport fluids.

Section d'un arbre, elle montre la structure micro fragmentée qui apporte une rigidité aux conduites qui transportent des fluides.

Querschnitt eines Stammes, der die mikrofragmentierte Struktur zeigt und den Gefäßen Halt gibt.

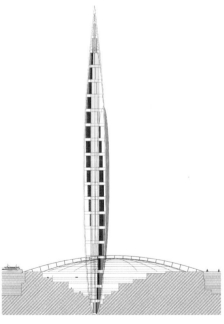

Figurative elevation locating the building in Hong Kong and section showing the heliocoidal distribution of levels and anchorage of the tower.

Élévation figurée, le bâtiment est placé à Hong Kong et section qui offre la distribution hélicoïdale des niveaux et l'ancrage de la tour.

Simulierte Ansicht auf das Gebäude in Hongkong und Skizze mit Darstellung der schraubenförmigen Anordnung der Ebenen und der Verankerung des Turms mit dem Boden.

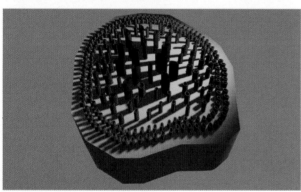

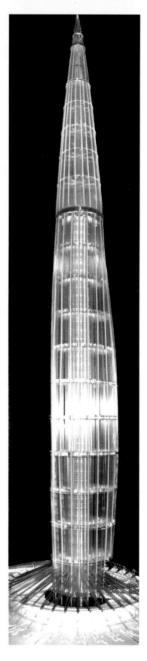

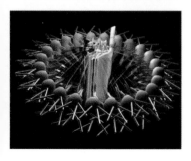

Structural and mock-up
representations of the
completed building.

*Représentations structurelles
et maquette du bâtiment
terminé.*

Darstellung von Strukturen
und Modell des
Gesamtgebäudes.

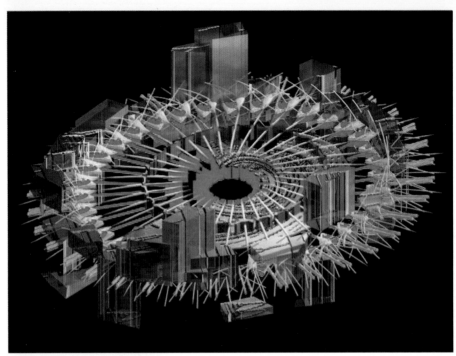

Representation of the fractal layout
of the vertical quarters and structural
schemes.

*Représentation de la distribution
fractale des quartiers verticaux et
schémas structurels.*

Darstellung über querschnittliche
Anordnung der Vertikaltrakte und
Strukturschemen.

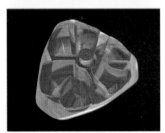

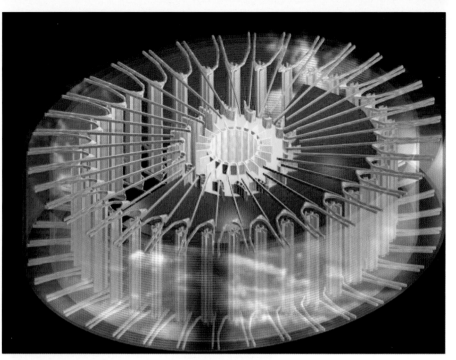

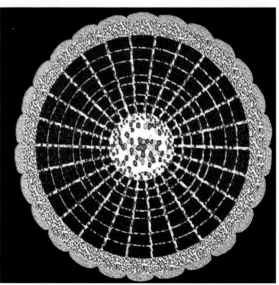

Sketch of the "multi-radial flotation system" earthquake resistant foundations.

Schémas du système de cimentation qui résiste aux tremblements de terre, «système de flottation multiradiale».

Schema des erdbebensicheren Fundaments "Multiradiales Schwimmsystem".

BNI CITY

ZEIDNER GRINNELL PARTNERSHIP

CLIENT / CLIENT / AUFTRAGGEBER: PT LYMAN INVESTINDO	**1996**

TOTAL AREA / SURFACE TOTALE / GESAMTOBERFLÄCHE: 522.000 m²

FLOORS / PLANS / STOCKWERKE - HEIGHT / HAUTEUR / HÖHE: 46 fl / 250 m

The firm of architects conceived the general plan of the project for this mixed use superblock, situated in a lot of 15 hectares in the center of Jakarta and later developed the 46 floor office tower, currently the highest in Indonesia. With its characteristic deck topped with a mast and its volumetry of light granite and the blue reflective curtain wall, this building is the most significant landmark of the Jakarta skyline. The regular shape of the plan, which introduces the solid façade treatment, complements the design of the coronation of the building.

La firme des architectes conçut le plan général du projet de ce super bloc à usages mixtes, situé sur un emplacement de 15 hectares au centre de Jakarta et développa ensuite la tour de bureaux à 46 étages –de nos jours, la plus haute en Indonésie–. Ce bâtiment, au chapeau caractéristique couronné d'un mât, dont la volumétrie est en granite claire et dont le mur rideau réfléchissant est bleu, représente le signe le plus représentatif du skyline de Yakarta. La forme régulière de la vue en plan, qui introduit le traitement de façade pleine, complète la conception du couronnement du bâtiment.

Dieser Superblock wurden von den Architekten als Multifunktionsgebäude konzipiert und befindet sich auf einem 15 Hektar großem Gelände im Zentrum von Jakarta. Danach entstand der Büroturm mit 46 Stockwerken –derzeitig der höchste Indonesiens–.

Dieses Gebäude hebt sich durch seinen hohen Masten als Gebäudespitze und durch das hellen Blau des Himmels reflektierenden Granitaussenhaut an der Skyline von Jakarta ab. Die regelmäßige Bauform und die massive Aussenseite des Gebäudes werden durch den Gebäudeabschluß ergänzt.

The volumetry of the building is divided into three zones; a stone base, a square tower which combines stone with glass, and a glass-covered coronation.

La volumétríe du bâtiment est divisée en trois zones; une base en pierre, une tour carrée qui combine la pierre et le verre et un couronnement vitré.

Die Volumetrie teilt sich in 3 Bereiche: ein Unterbau aus Stein, ein quadratischer Turm, der Stein mit Glas kombiniert und ein gläserner Aufbau als Abschluß.

The use of materials and the design of the building suggest that as it gains height, the construction evolves towards lightness and freedom of form.

L'emploi des matériaux et la conception du bâtiment évoquent, plus on augmente la hauteur, une évolution de la construction vers le léger et la liberté de la forme.

Angewandte Materialien und die sich bei wachsender Höhe ändernde Formgebung, lassen das Gebäude leicht und freizügig wirken.

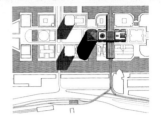

CANARY WHARF

CESAR PELLI & ASSOCIATES INC.

CLIENT / CLIENT / AUFTRAGGEBER: OLIMPIA & YORK	**1991**
TOTAL AREA / SURFACE TOTALE / GESAMTOBERFLÄCHE: 167.200 m²	
FLOORS / PLANS / STOCKWERKE - HEIGHT / HAUTEUR / HÖHE: 48 fl / 236,2 m	

Planned within the re-conversion of the Thames docks. The development of the project also includes the Retail and Assembly building and the light railway station; both buildings are connected by an avenue, and the station receives an average of 60,000 travelers a day. The building, technologically designed for the 21st Century, takes the shape of a great square prism with breeched corners – they give slenderness and emphasize the height – crowned by a pyramid. The surfaces of the exterior walls are covered in stainless steel, reflecting and adopting the coloring and changes in the London sky.

Sa planification correspond aux opérations de reconversion des quais de la Tamise. Le développement du projet inclut aussi le bâtiment Retail and Assembly et une gare; les deux bâtiments sont connectés par une avenue, et la gare reçoit, en moyenne, 60.000 voyageurs par jour. Le bâtiment, conçu technologiquement pour le XXIème siècle, adopte la forme d'un grand prisme carré aux coins déplacés –ils apportent de la sveltesse et accentuent la hauteur– couronné d'une pyramide. Les surfaces des murs extérieurs sont recouvertes en acier inoxydable, elles réfléchissent et adoptent la couleur et les variations du ciel de Londres.

Dieses Gebäude war Teil des Wiederherstellungsplans der Themse–Piers. Die Projektentwicklung umfaßt auch das Gebäude Retail and Assembly und eine Bahnstation. Diese Bauten sind durch eine breite Straße verbunden; die Bahnstation empfängt täglich durchschnittlich 60.000 Reisende. Das Gebäude, technisch für das 21. Jahrhundert entwickelt, hat die Form eines großen quadratischen Prismas –von eleganter Schlichtheit und aufragend– mit zurückgesetzten Gebäudekan-tenund endet in einer Pyramide als Dachabschluß. Die Außenwände sind mit Edelstahl verkleidet, die das Farbenspiel des Londoner Himmels aufnehmen und reflektieren.

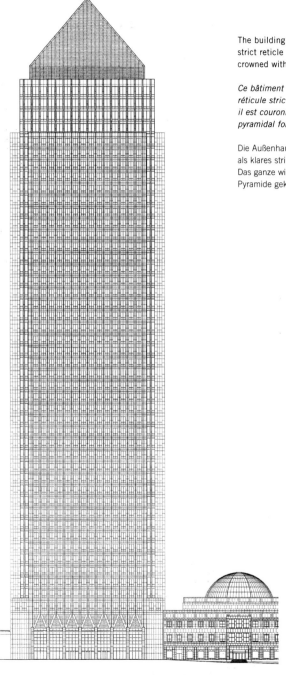

The building has been designed as a strict reticle of gaps and solids, crowned with a dark pyramid deck.

Ce bâtiment a été conçu comme un réticule strict de vides et de pleins, il est couronné d'un chapeau pyramidal foncé.

Die Außenhaut des Gebäudes wurde als klares striktes Gitternetz gestaltet. Das ganze wird von einer dunklen Pyramide gekrönt.

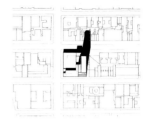

CARNEGIE HALL TOWER

CESAR PELLI & ASSOCIATES INC.

CLIENT / CLIENT / AUFTRAGGEBER: ROCKROSE DEVELOPMENT CORPORATION

TOTAL AREA / SURFACE TOTALE / GESAMTOBERFLÄCHE: 49.000 m²

FLOORS / PLANS / STOCKWERKE - HEIGHT / HAUTEUR / HÖHE: 60 fl / 230,7 m

1991

This slender tower is a reference point in Manhattan as it forms part of the historic Music Hall group of buildings, to which part of its surface is incorporated as an annex. It rises in a narrow lot between the Carnegie Hall building and the Russian Tea Salon. The base follows the line and height of the Music Hall cornice and above it rises the tower, only 15 meters wide, withdrawn from the façade. This works by means of two interwoven pieces of wrought iron integrating into the walls the wind resistance elements. The final design is in harmony with its surroundings.

Cette tour svelte est un point de référence de Manhattan, car elle appartient à l'ensemble historique des bâtiments du Music Hall, elle y incorpore une partie de sa surface comme annexe. Elle s'élève sur un terrain étroit entre le bâtiment du Carnegie Hall et le Salon de Thé Russe. La base suit l'alignement et la hauteur de la corniche du Music Hall et la tour s'élève en amont, elle fait 15 mètres de large et prend du recul face à la façade. Celle-ci fonctionne avec deux hourdis connectés et intègre les éléments de résistance au vent sur les murs. La conception finale est en harmonie avec son environnement.

Dieser schlanke Gebäudeturm ist einer der Referenzpunkte Manhattans, gehört zum historischen Music Hall-Komplex und fügt sich mit einem Teil seiner Oberfläche in dieses Ensemble. Der Bau steht auf einem schmalen Gelände zwi- schen der Carnegie Hall und dem Russischen Teesalon. Der Gebäudesockel verläuft in gerade Linie und der Turm erhebt sich mit zurückgesetzter nur 15 m breiter Fassade über dem Dachsims der Music Hall. Zwei ineinandergreifende Armierungen machen das Gebäude windfest. Die Gesamtgestaltung harmonisiert mit seiner Umgebung.

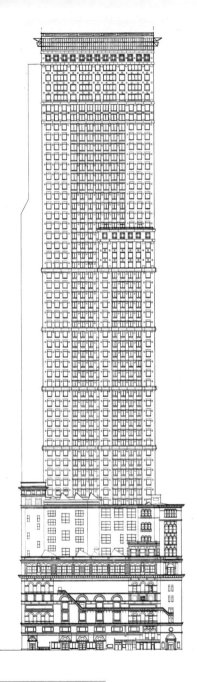

The design of the tower was supervised by the council because the Music Hall group of buildings forms part of the city's architectural heritage.

La conception de la tour a été supervisée par la mairie, car l'ensemble des bâtiments du Music Hall appartient au patrimoine architectonique de la ville.

Die Stadtverwaltung überwachte den Entwurf des Gebäudes, zumal der Music Hall-Komplex Teil des architektonischen Erbes der Stadt ist.

Above, main entrance to the tower. The base, six meters tall, is conditioned by the cornice of the Music Hall building situated on its left.

En haut, accès principal à la tour. La base, six mètres de haut, est conditionnée par la corniche du bâtiment du Music Hall situé à gauche.

Oben: Haupteingang. Die 6 m hohe Eingangshalle wird von dem Sims der Music Hall auf der linken Seite bestimmt.

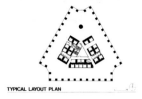

TYPICAL LAYOUT PLAN

CENTRAL PLAZA

DENNIS LAU & N.G. CHUN MAN
ARCHITECTS & ENGINEERS (H.K) LTD

CLIENT / CLIENT / AUFTRAGGEBER: SUN HUNG KAI REAL ESTATE AGENCY LTD SINO LAND CO. LTD & RYODEN (HOLDINGS) LTD	**1992**

TOTAL AREA / SURFACE TOTALE / GESAMTOBERFLÄCHE: 130.140 m²

FLOORS / PLANS / STOCKWERKE - HEIGHT / HAUTEUR / HÖHE: 78 fl / 375 m

This building is still currently the tallest in Hong Kong. When it was finished, it was the tallest of the skyscrapers of reinforced concrete structure and the tallest in the world outside the United States. Elegantly designed in the form of a triangular prism, the tower has a pyramidal deck crowned with a 60 meter mast, illuminated at night with golden neon on the glass pyramid of its base, which shines with different colors. The building gives a new dimension to the concept of high level offices, developing high quality connection areas, a swimming pool, a luxurious club and social and leisure facilities.

Ce bâtiment est encore aujourd'hui le plus haut de Hong Kong, et fut lors de son achèvement le plus haut des gratte-ciel à structure en béton armé et le plus haut du monde, hormis les Etats-Unis. La tour, conçue élégamment, a l'aspect d'un prisme triangulaire, elle adopte un chapeau pyramidal couronné d'un mát de 60 mètres, illuminé le soir avec un néon doré, sur la pyramide en verre de la base, avec plusieurs couleurs qui brillent. Le bâtiment apporte une nouvelle dimension au concept de bureaux grand standing, il développe des espaces de relations de grande qualité; une piscine, un club de luxe et une offre sociale et de loisir.

Noch ist dieser Bau gegenwärtig der höchste von Hong Kong. Zur Zeit seiner Fertigstellung war es das höchste Stahlbetongebäude und der höchster Wolkenkratzer außerhalb von USA. Elegante Gestaltung in Form eines dreieckigen Prismas. Das Gebäude endet mit einem pyramidenartigen Aufbau, der von einem 60 m hohen Mast gekrönt wird. Nachts wird das Gebäude in goldfarbenes Neonlicht gehüllt und läßt die Fassade in allen Schattierungen glänzen. Das Gebäude stellt eine neue Dimension für Bürogebäude des gehobenen Standards dar, das über ein exzellentes Angebot wie Swimming Pool, luxuriösem Club, Gesellschaftsräume und Freizeitmöglichkeiten verfügt.

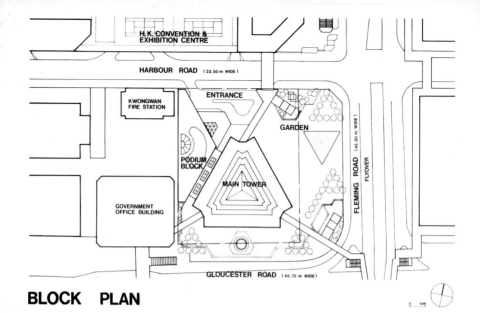

**H.K. CONVENTION &
EXHIBITION CENTRE**

HARBOUR ROAD (22.50 m WIDE)

ENTRANCE

**KWONGWAN
FIRE STATION**

GARDEN

FLEMING ROAD (45.20 m WIDE)

FLYOVER

**PODIUM
BLOCK**

MAIN TOWER

**GOVERNMENT
OFFICE BUILDING**

GLOUCESTER ROAD (45.72 m WIDE)

BLOCK PLAN

An equilateral triangle,
elegantly breeched at its
vertexes, forms the plan of
the building, culminating
with a gradually withdrawn
deck.

*Un triangle équilatéral
élégamment déplacé sur les
bords correspond au plan du
bâtiment, un chapeau
graduellement décalé le
couronne.*

Eine elegante dreieckige
Anordnung mit nach innen
gekehrten Ecken bilden den
Grundriß des Gebäudes,
welches von einer leicht
zurückgesetzten Dachhaut
gekrönt wird.

Its size and purity of form confer on the building an ample capacity for domination of the built-up surroundings.

Le volume et la pureté de la forme confèrent au bâtiment une grande capacité pour dominer l'environnement bâti.

Dieses Gebäude dominiert absolut durch seine Größenordnung und die klare Formgebung die Bebauung seines Umfelds.

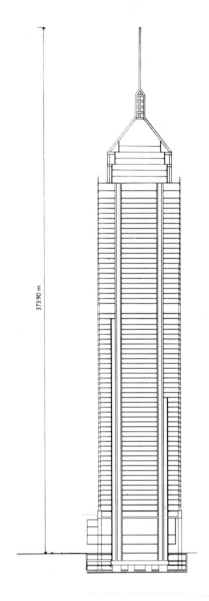

373.90 m

0 ___ 10M

The curtain wall of the façade of the skyscraper combines white, black and golden tonalities of reflective glass.

Le mur rideau de la façade du gratte-ciel combine des tonalités blanches, noires et dorées en verre réfléchissant.

Die Außenhautverglasung des Wolkenkratzers spiegelt in weißen, schwarzen und goldfarbenen Tönen.

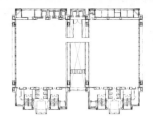

CENTURY TOWER

FOSTER & PARTNERS

1991

CLIENT / CLIENT / AUFTRAGGEBER: OBUNSHA CORPORATION

TOTAL AREA / SURFACE TOTALE / GESAMTOBERFLÄCHE: 26.590 m²

FLOORS / PLANS / STOCKWERKE - HEIGHT / HAUTEUR / HÖHE: 21 fl / 104 m

This office building continues developing the ideas of the Hong Kong and Shanghai Bank. It responds to the necessities of the client, who wants the greatest economic performance from the building, and the architect's necessities with a quality design. Located in the city center, the volume of the building is divided into two bodies united by the lower floor, so that by having narrower spaces, a greater quantity of light penetrates. If, in addition, the structural and communications core is moved towards the façades, the plan is freed from obstacles, which allows any kind of layout.

Cet immeuble de bureaux développe encore les idées du Hong Kong & Shanghai Bank. Il répond aux besoins du client qui recherche le meilleur rendement économique du bâtiment, et aussi à l'architecte avec une conception de qualité. Le bâtiment se trouve au centre de la ville, son volume est divisé en deux corps communiqués par le rez-de-chaussée, de façon à ce qu'il pénètre plus de lumière car ses coursives sont plus étroites et aussi, si l'on déplace le noyau central et de communications, la surface d'obstacles qui permettent tout type de distribution est libérée.

Dieses Bürogebäude ist eine Verkörperung der Ideen der Hong Kong & Shanghai Bank. Es ent- spricht der Anforderungen der Auftraggeber, die größtmöglichen wirtschaftlichen Nutzen des Gebäudes suchen und die des Architekten, der ein Qualitätsdesign präsentiert. Der in der Stadtmitte gelegene Bau verteilt sich auf zwei Gebäudeteile, die durch das Erdgeschoss miteinander verbunden sind. Die Geschossbreite wurde dabei schmal gehalten, sodaß ein hohe Lichteinfall erreicht wird. Außer dem wurde der Strukturkern und die Kommunikationsbereich au die Gebäudeseiten verlagert, sodaß eine hindernissfreie Grundfläche entstand, die alle möglicher Raumverteilungen zuläßt.

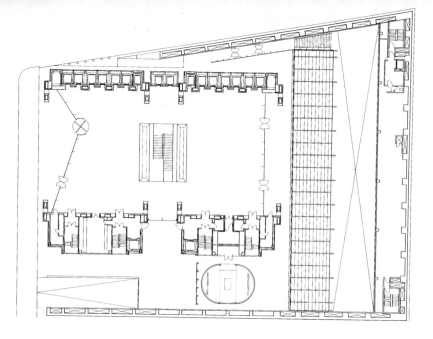

Above, the lower floor of the building where the glass-covered lobby is found, in the central area a vacuum is generated because the building is divided into two parallel bodies. This vacuum is shown in the picture on the right.

En haut, rez-de-chaussée du bâtiment où se trouve le hall couvert en verre, un vide est engendré sur la zone centrale car le bâtiment est divisé en deux corps parallèles. Ce vide est présent sur l'image de la droite.

Oben: untere Etage des Gebäudes mit verglaster Eingangshalle. Da der Bau aus zwei parallel verlaufenden Gebäudeteilen besteht, entstand ein großzügiger offener Zentralbereich. Dieser ist auch auf der rechten Seite zu sehen.

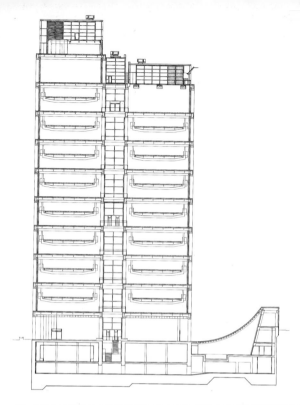

In addition to the offices, the building is equipped with several rest areas, a gymnasium, a swimming pool, a restaurant and a museum. The upper picture shows the swimming pool. The sloping roof, which filters light, and the vegetation create a special atmosphere. It is a place to relax.

Outre les bureaux, le bâtiment dispose de plusieurs équipements comme des zones de repos, un gymnase, une piscine, un restaurant et un musée. Sur l'image du haut on voit la piscine, le toit incliné qui filtre la lumière et la végétation crée une atmosphère spéciale, il s'agit d'un endroit pour le relax.

Neben Büros verfügt das Gebäude über verschiedene Einrichtungen wie Ruhezonen, einem Fitnessraum, Schwimmbad, Restaurant und einem Museum. Im Foto oben das Schwimmbad mit Schrägdach. Der Lichteinfall und die Vegetation vermitteln eine besondere Atmosphäre – ein Bereich zum Relaxen.

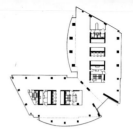

CITYBANK PLAZA

ROCCO SEN KEE YIM

CLIENT / CLIENT / AUFTRAGGEBER: CITYBANK

1992

FLOORS / PLANS / STOCKWERKE - HEIGHT / HAUTEUR / HÖHE: 40 - 50 fl / 120 - 150 m

Located in the center of Hong Kong, it is situated next to the Bank of China, by I.M. Pei, one of the city's most emblematic constructions. Far from competing with it, the new building seeks differentiation. Fruit of the intersection of two towers of different heights that combine straight and curved façades, contrasting with the straight volume of the Bank of China. The towers go straight into the ground, without any base body, and the curtain wall of the façades withdraws to leave the structure bare and provoke the entrance to the building, letting it flow towards the garden and the square which accompany the building.

Situé au centre de Hong Kong, il se trouve juste à côté de la Banque de Chine, de I. M. Pei, une des constructions les plus emblématiques de la ville. Loin d'être en concurrence, le nouveau bâtiment recherche la différenciation. Il est le fruit de l'intersection de deux tours d'une hauteur différente qui combinent des façades droites et courbes, cela contraste avec le volume droit de la Banque de Chine. Les tours reposent directement sur le sol, sans aucun corps de base, et le mur rideau des façades s'enlève afin que la structure soit décharnée et pour provoquer l'accès au bâtiment, cela permet la fluidité vers le jardin et la place qui joints au bâtiment.

Im Zentrum von Hong Kong neben einer der emblematischsten Konstruktionen der Stadt, der Bank of China vom Architekten I.M. Pei gelegen.Das Citybank Plaza ist weit davon entfernt mit diesem Gebäude konkurrieren zu wollen, sondern möchte sich differenzieren. Zwei unterschiedlich hohe Türme kombinieren flache und geschwungene Fassaden und bilden einen Kontrast zum gerade gestreckten Bau der Bank of China. Ohne irgendeinen Unterbau stehen die Türme direkt auf dem Boden. Die Aussenseite ist im unteren Teil zurückversetzt und bildet dort den Zugangsbereich zum Gebäude, der sich zur vorgelagerten Parkanlage und einem Platz hin öffnet.

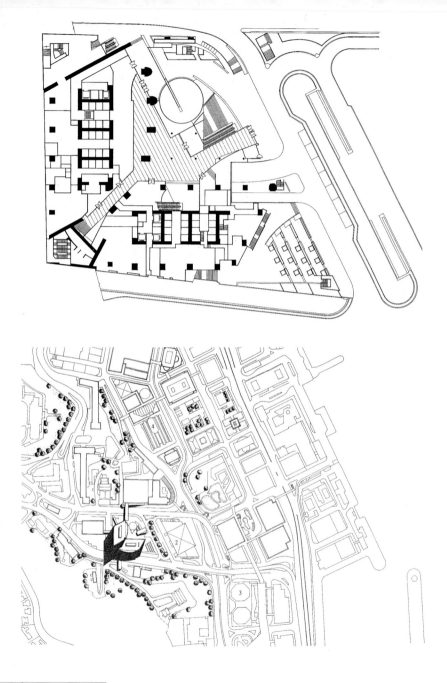

Interior and exterior views of the pedestrian entrance
from the street to the lobby, in the area of intersection
of the two towers.

*Vues, intérieur et extérieur, de l'accès pour piétons de la
rue vers le hall, sur la zone de rencontre des deux tours.*

Innen- und Aussenansicht des Fußgängerzugangs von der
Straße in die Eingangshalle an der Schnittstelle, wo beiden
Türme aufeinander treffen.

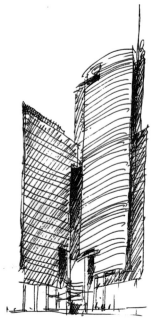

Interior escalators between the entrance at street level and the raised square which is developed in the lobby.

Escaliers mécaniques intérieurs entre l'accès à la cote de la rue et la place élevée qui se développe dans le hall.

Rolltreppen verbinden innen den Zugang von der Straße mit der höherliegenden Eingangshalle.

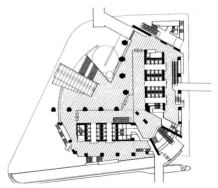

Picture of the view pedestrians have when entering the lobby and looking upwards.

Image de la vue des piétons lorsqu'ils entrent dans le hall et regardent en haut.

Aussicht der Fußgänger, wenn sie bei Betreten des Vestibüls den Blick nach oben richten.

Views of the stairs and distribution hallways of the building's office floors.

Vues des escaliers et des couloirs de distribution des étages des bureaux du bâtiment.

Ansicht des Treppenhauses und Zugangsflure in den Büroetagen.

FRANKFURT

COMMERZBANK HQTRS.

FOSTER & PARTNERS

1997

CLIENT / CLIENT / AUFTRAGGEBER: COMMERZBANK AG	
TOTAL AREA / SURFACE TOTALE / GESAMTOBERFLÄCHE: 100.000 m²	
FLOORS / PLANS / STOCKWERKE - HEIGHT / HAUTEUR / HÖHE: 53 fl / 259 m	

This is the first green skyscraper in Europe. A building that tries to be respectful with the city and the environment. The central concept is based on the natural system of illumination and ventilation instead of the usual mechanical systems in office buildings. Each office allows its user to adjust the environmental conditions, which means a reduction in the energy consumption of the building. The triangular plan allows a central space which illuminates and ventilates the grouped floors, interspersing gardens between them. In addition to the psychological effect created by looking at them, they function as rest areas.

Il s'agit du premier gratte-ciel vert en Europe. Un bâtiment qui désire respecter la ville et l'environnement. Le concept central a pour base les systèmes naturels d'illumination et de ventilation au lieu des systèmes mécaniques usuels des immeubles de bureaux. Chaque bureau permet à son utilisateur de réguler les conditions environnementales, cela suppose aussi la réduction de la consommation d'énergie du bâtiment. La vue en plan triangulaire permet un espace central qui illumine et ventile les appartements, ils sont disposés selon une intercalation de jardins. Outre l'effet psychologique créé par leur vision, ils ont la fonction de zone de repos.

Der erste sogenannte „grüne" Wolkenkratzer Europas, der sowohl die Stadt als auch die Umwelt rücksichtsvoll behandelt. Zentralidee ist, natürliches Tageslicht und Belüftung anstatt der in Bürogebäuden üblichen mechanischen Systeme zu nutzen. In jedem Büro können die Nutzer die klimatischen Bedingungen individuell anpassen, was wiederum zur Reduzierung des Energieverbrauches des Gebäudes führt. Eine dreieckige Anlage mit einem offenen Innenraum spenden in den angrenzenden Etagen Licht und Luft. Dazwischen wurden abwechselnd Gärten angelegt, die als Erholungszonen genutzt werden können.

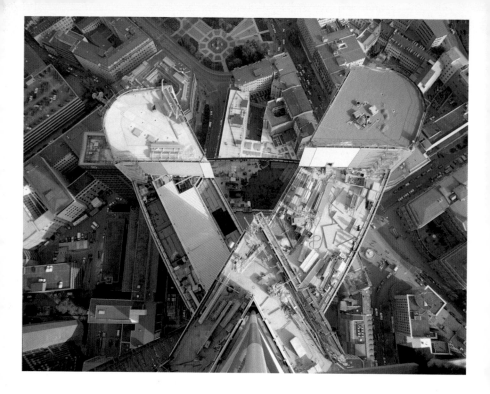

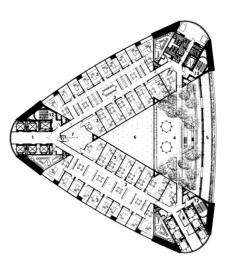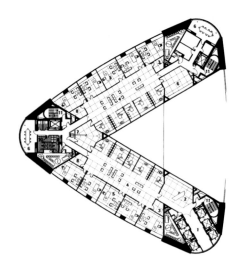

Above, view of the building from the opposite river bank. The interspersed gardens break the continuity of the façade, offering a modern image of transparency and luminosity.

En haut, vue du bâtiment de l'autre bord de la rivière. Les jardins intercalés cassent la continuité de la façade, cela offre une image moderne de transparence et de luminosité.

Oben: Aussicht auf das Gebäudes von der gegenüberliegenden Flußseite. Die eingelassenen Grünanlagen lockern die Fassade auf und vermitteln ein modernes Image der Transparenz und Helligkeit.

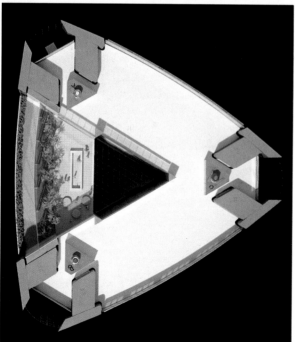

Above, different mock-ups of the phases of the project. On the left, mock-up of the plan which is clearly organized with the structural communications cores in the vertexes of the triangle.

En haut, plusieurs maquettes des phases du projet. À gauche, maquette du plan franchement organisé avec les noyaux de communications structurels sur les bords du triangle.

Oben: unterschiedliche Modellbauten einzelner Projektphasen. Links: Grundrißmodell mit klarer strukturierter Verteilung an den Scheitelpunkten des Dreiecks.

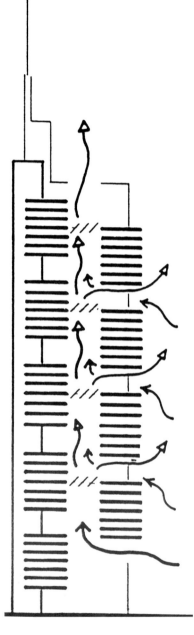

Details of the façade and diagram of the building, where the gardens can be seen interspersed between the floors, and the natural ventilation.

Détails de la façade et schémas du bâtiment, l'on peut apprécier les jardins intercalés entre les appartements et la ventilation naturelle.

Details der Aussenfassade und Gebäudeschema, die zwischen den Stockwerken eingelassene Gärten sowie den natürlichen Belüftungsverlauf darstellen.

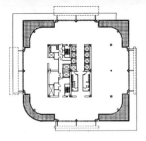

CONDÉ NAST

FOX & FOWLE

1999

CLIENT / CLIENT / AUFTRAGGEBER: THE DURST ORGANIZATION

TOTAL AREA / SURFACE TOTALE / GESAMTOBERFLÄCHE: 154.218 m²

FLOORS / PLANS / STOCKWERKE - HEIGHT / HAUTEUR / HÖHE: 48 fl / 247 m

Located on a corner of Times Square, at the junction between Broadway and 42nd Street and Bryant Park, rises the first building born of a public and private consortium which promotes the development of the traditional center of Manhattan. Its image starts out for tow differentiated readings reflected in the facades. The north and west assume the boisterous character of Times Square, made of metal and glass. The south and east reflect a personality made up of the texture and scale of the treatment of the most appropriate masonry for the midtown Manhattan urban context and the refined style of Bryant Park. The building is born with the vocation to be a new standard of the Manhattan of the 21st Century, capturing the essence of the commercial city and proposing a contemporary corporate image.

Sur un coin de Times Square, au croisement de Broadway, de la rue 42 et du "Bryant Park", s'élève le premier bâtiment dont l'origine est un groupement public et privé qui soutient le développement du centre traditionnel de Manhattan. Le point de départ de son image, ce sont les deux lectures différentes que l'on découvre sur les façades. Celle du nord et celle de l'ouest possèdent le caractère bruyant de Times Square, elles sont en métal et en verre. Celle du sud et celle de l'est présentent une personnalité composée, quant à la texture et à l'échelle du traitement de l'ouvrage plus conforme au contexte urbain du "midtown" de Manhattan et au style raffiné du "Bryant Park". Le bâtiment est né avec une vocation, celle d'être un nouvel étendard du Manhattan du XXIème siècle, il capture l'essence de la ville commerciale et il propose une image corporative contemporaine

An einer Ecke des Times Square gelegen, an der Kreuzung Broadway, der 42. Straße und dem "Bryant Park", erhebt sich das erste Gebäude eines öffentlichen und privaten Konsortiums, welches die Entwicklung des traditionellen Manhattan fördert. Die Fassaden vermitteln zwei unterschiedliche Eindrücke. Nord- und Westseite aus Stahl und Glas übernehmen den belebten Charakter des Times Square. Süd- und Ostseite des Gebäudes spiegeln anhand von Textur und Farbgebung des Mauerwerks, das urbane Umfeld Manhattan's Midtown und die Eleganz des "Bryant Park" wieder. Das Gebäude enstand mit der Absicht, Manhattan's neues Abzeichen des 21. Jahrhunderts zu werden, welches das Wesen einer business town einfängt und sich als Spiegelbild kontemporären Zusammenlebens darzustellen.

The north-west corner of the building, which houses the Nasdaq headquarters, is joined with an eleven-storey high semi-cylinder whose exterior panel emits current stock market quotations for passers-by to observe.

Le coin nord-ouest du bâtiment est fermé par un demi cylindre d'une hauteur de onze étages où se trouve le siège du Nasdaq dont le revêtement est un écran qui dispose de tous les index boursiers, ainsi le passant peut être au courant des derniers mouvements.

Die Nordwestseite des Gebäudes schließt sich in Form eines 11stöckigen Halbzylinders. Darin befindet sich der Hauptsitz der Nasdaq-Börse. Die Außenverkleidung besteht aus einem riesigen Schirm, auf dem die Börsenergebnisse angezeigt sind, sodaß sich die Fußgänger in jedem Moment über den letzten Börsenstand informieren können.

Environment-conscious architects planned a building with an integral energy concept, using recycled waste material in the construction process.

Les architectes sensibles aux facteurs environnementaux conçurent un bâtiment avec un concept d'énergie intégrale et déjà lors du processus de construction furent recyclés les déchets.

Da Architekten immer sensibel auf die Umweltfaktoren reagieren, beinhaltete der Entwurf dieses Gebäudes integrale, energetische Aspekte. Schon während der Bauphase wurden Bauabfälle in das Recycling verbracht.

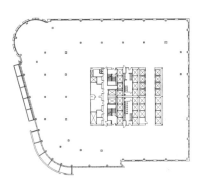

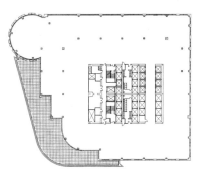

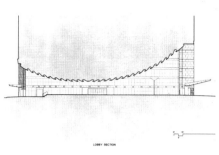

LOBBY SECTION

The multi-level concourse is a walkway that joins 42nd and 43rd street. It is covered by a double ceiling in the shape of an inverted parabola that heightens the feeling of depth of field, which is pierced by two elevator shafts.

Le hall, sur plusieurs hauteurs, joint les rues 42 et 43, il joue le rôle d'un passage. Il est recouvert d'un faux toit en parabole inversée, ce qui accentue la sensation de profondeur du parcours qui est coupé par deux batteries d'ascenseurs.

Das hohe Eingangsvestibül gilt auch als Verbindungsglied zwischen der 42. und 43. Straße. Es ist von einer umgekehrten Paraboldecke überdacht, die der Durchgangsstrecke Tiefe verleiht. Außerdem wird das Ganze durch zwei Aufzugsschächten durchquert.

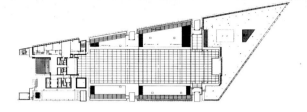

DEBIS HAUS

RENZO PIANO BUILDING WORKSHOP
+ CHRISTOPH KOHLBECKER

CLIENT / CLIENT / AUFTRAGGEBER: DAIMLER-CHRYSLER AG

1999

TOTAL AREA / SURFACE TOTALE / GESAMTOBERFLÄCHE: 45.100 m²

FLOORS / PLANS / STOCKWERKE - HEIGHT / HAUTEUR / HÖHE: 21 fl / 106 m

This is the first skyscraper in Postdammer Platz, which has radically altered the city's skyline. This square, where a railway station was built in 1840, was the biggest in Berlin until the Second World War. Due to the heavy traffic flow, in 1920 a set of traffic lights was installed, the first in Europe. After being sectioned by the construction of a wall in 1961, it became an immense barren lot. After its fall, it was the object in 1992 of an urban planning competition which has returned the place to its condition of urban and social center. The Debis Haus complex is located in the lots which were occupied by the Daimler-Benz factory and comprises several office buildings which form a triangular base topped by a tower.

Il est le premier gratte-ciel de la Postdamer Platz qui a altéré radicalement le skyline de la ville. Cette place où l'on construisit une gare en 1840 fut la plus importante de Berlin jusqu'à la IIème Guerre Mondiale. À cause de la grande circulation, en 1920 fut installé un feu trico-lore, le premier en Europe. Après la coupure due à la construction en 1961 du mur, elle est devenue un immense terrain vague. Après la chute de ce dernier, en 1992 elle a été l'objet d'un plan urbanistique, sous appel d'offres, qui a rendu à cet endroit son rang en tant que centre urbain et social. Le complexe de la Debis Haus se trouve sur les terrains qui étaient occupés par la fabri-que Daimler-Benz et comprend plusieurs immeubles de bureaux qui composent une base trian-gulaire couronnée par une tour.

Der erste Wolkenkratzer am Potsdamer Platz, der radikal die Skyline der Stadt verändert hat. Auf diesem Platz entstand 1840 ein Bahnhof, der bis zum 2. Weltkrieg der grösste Berlin's war. Aufgrund des hohen Verkehrsaufkommens wurde 1920 eine Ampel – die erste in Europa – aufgestellt. Nach Teilung der Stadt 1961 durch den Mauerbau wurde dieses Gelände zu Brachland. Nach dem Mauerfall wurde 1992 ein Stadtbebauungsplan ausgeschrieben, der diesen Ort wieder zum urbanen und sozialen Mittelpunkt werden ließ. Der Debis Haus-Komplex liegt auf dem Gelände der Daimler-Benz AG und besteht aus verschiedenen im Dreieck angeordnete Bürogebäude, die zusammen den Unterbau des Gebäudeturms bilden.

The materials chosen are ceramics, steel and glass. The tower dedicates equal attention to office space and functional aspects (elevators and stairwells), so the façade features stairwells and ventilation ducts.

Les matériaux choisis sont la céramique, l'acier et le verre. La tour combine les espaces de bureaux avec les plus fonctionnels (ascenseurs et escaliers), ils on reçu le même traitement, ainsi, sur la façade, nous trouvons des caissons d'escaliers et des tours de ventilation.

Ausgewählte verwendete Materialien sind Keramik, Stahl und Glas. Neben Büroräumen befinden sich auch im Turm sichtbar die Verbindungeinrichtungen (Aufzüge und Treppen). So sind Treppenhäuser und Klimatisierungsanlagen von außen aus einzusehen.

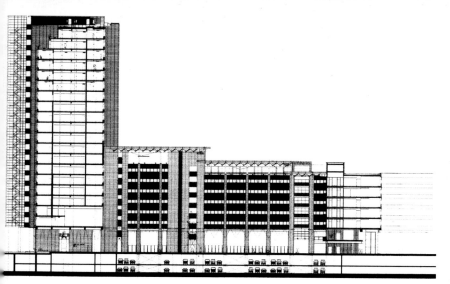

Debis Haus is included in a triangular block 163 metres in length that respects the even height of other historic buildings, except the tower that signals the entrance to the Tiergarten tunnel.

La Debis Haus comprend un pâté triangulaire de 163 mètres de long qui maintient la hauteur régulière des édifices historiques, sauf la tour qui marque l'entrée du tunnel Tiergarten.

Das Debis Haus belegt ein dreieckiges Grundstück mit einer Länge von 163 m und paßt sich in seiner Bauhöhe an die der historischen Gebäude der Umgebung an, mit Ausnahme des Turms, der am Tunneleingang zum Tiergarten steht.

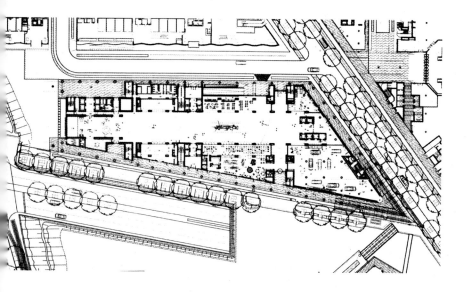

Incoming daylight is controlled by sophisticated filtering systems. The same happens with the building's heating control, which gives energy savings by automatically regulating the interior/exterior temperature and the angle of sunlight using glass panels.

Le contrôle de la lumière solaire s'effectue avec des systèmes sophistiqués qui la filtrent, il en est de même avec le contrôle thermique du bâtiment, on obtient une économie d'énergie avec la régulation automatique de la température intérieure/extérieure et le degré d'incidence des rayons solaires avec des panneaux en verre.

Die Kontrolle des Sonnenlichts erfolgt anhand außergewöhnlicher Filtersysteme. Das gleiche geschieht mit der Wärmetechnik des Hauses. Eine erhebliche Energieeinsparung erlangt man durch die automatische Regulierung der Innen- und Außentemperatur und durch verstellbare Glaspanele an der Außenfront wird der Einfall des Sonnenlichts reguliert.

There are magnificent views from the tower in the former Mitte district city centre of west Berlin and the Kurfürstendamm. Likewise, the new Potsdamer Platz looks radically different from the rest of the city and is injected with new life.

De la tour, on peut jouir des vues magnifiques depuis l'ancien centre de la ville sur le district Mitte vers la partie ouest de Berlin et son Kurfürstendamm. Et aussi, depuis la ville, la nouvelle Postdamer Platz a changé radicalement son image et elle initie une nouvelle vie.

Vom Turm aus hat man einen phantastischen Ausblick hinüber zum alten Teil der Stadt, dem Viertel "Mitte" bis in den Westen Berlins und seinem Kurfürstendamm. Auch hat sich von der Stadt der Blick auf den wiederbelebten Potsdamer Platz radikal verändert .

DEUTSCHE POST AG

MURPHY / JAHN INC. ARCHITECTS

1999

CLIENT / CLIENT / AUFTRAGGEBER: DEUTSCHE POST

FLOORS / PLANS / STOCKWERKE - HEIGHT / HAUTEUR / HÖHE: 44 fl / 162 m

The building is a mixed-use complex of offices, catering area, bars, restaurants, bookstores, conference halls and multi-use halls. Together with the Deutsche Welle and Langer Eugen buildings, it makes up the strip of the city towards the Rheinauenpark. The platform of the tower completes the upper terrace of the park, connected with ramps and stairs towards the lower terraces near to the River Rhine. The oval-shaped plan, separated, is positioned in the direction of the Rhine, opening itself to the city, facilitating its views and minimizing the negative effects of the wind by means of its aerodynamic shape.

Le bâtiment est un complexe à usages mixtes, bureaux, zone de restauration (bars, restaurants), librairie, salles de conférences et salles polyvalentes. Avec les bâtiments du Deutsche Welle et le Langer Eugen, il concrétise la marge de la ville vers le Rheinauenpark. La plate-forme de la tour achève la terrasse supérieure du parc, elle est connectée avec des rampes et des marches vers les terrasses inférieures proches au Rhin. La vue de plan ovale, coupée, est orientée face au Rhin, elle s'ouvre sur la ville, ce qui permet les vues et sa forme aérodynamique minimise les effets négatifs du vent.

Ein Mehrzweckgebäude mit Büros, Bars und Restaurants Bücherei, Konferenzräumen und vielseitig nutzbarer Räumlichkeiten. Gemeinsam mit dem Gebäuden der Deutschen Welle und dem Langen Eugen gestalten sie den Stadtbereich zum angrenzenden Rheinauenpark. Der Turm steht auf der oberen Parkterrasse und ist durch Lauframpen und Treppen mit den tieferliegenden Rheinterrassen verbunden. Der ovale Grundriß des Gebäudes ist zum Rhein ausgerichtet, öffnet sich hin zur Stadt, ermöglicht den freien Ausblick und minimiert durch seine aerodynamische Gebäudeform die negativen Auswirkungen des Windes.

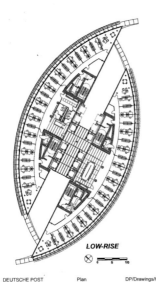

LOW-RISE

⊗ ⊢▬▬⊣
0 5 10

HIGH-RISE

⊗ ⊢▬▬⊣
0 5 10

The project reflects on the tall building through its function, technology and the users' comfort.

Le projet réfléchit sur le bâtiment haut grâce à sa fonction, technologie, et le confort de l'utilisateur.

Beim Entwurf wurden Funktion, Technologie und Benutzerfreundlichkeit des Hochhauses bedacht.

DEUTSCHE POST   Plan   DP/Drawings/HiRes/DP_PLAN_HR

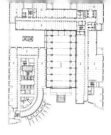

DG BANK HQTRS.

KOHN PEDERSEN FOX ASSOCIATES PC (KPF)

CLIENT / CLIENT / AUFTRAGGEBER: AGIMA	**1993**
TOTAL AREA / SURFACE TOTALE / GESAMTOBERFLÄCHE: 85.000 m²	
FLOORS / PLANS / STOCKWERKE - HEIGHT / HAUTEUR / HÖHE: 54 fl / 208 m	

DG's program includes, in addition to its offices, shopping areas, residential areas, parking and public spaces. It is found in an important shopping avenue near the historical center. The building must create a relationship between these areas. This was the starting point for the architects, against the big two which would have difficulty creating a relationship with the city. The program is organized by levels which respond to volumes and heights, the central offices of the bank in the tower and the other uses in buildings. Also, the entrances and movement had to be separate because of the security measures that the bank required without losing the original idea of a nexus.

Le programme du DG inclut outre ses bureaux, des espaces commerciaux, résidentiels, un parking et un espace publique. Il se trouve sur une avenue commerciale importante près du centre historique. Le bâtiment devait communiquer ces zones. Le programme qui supposa le point de départ des architectes, opposés à la grande tour qui aurait une relation difficile avec la ville, est organisé par des niveaux qui répondent à des volumes et des hauteurs, les bureaux centraux de la banque sur la tour et les autres usages des bâtiments. Il fallait aussi séparer les accès et les passages selon les mesures de sécurité exigés par la banque sans perdre l'idée initiale du nexe.

Das D G-Gebäude weist neben bank- eigenen Büros auch einen Einkaufsbereich, Wohnungen, Parkplätze und öffentliche Bereiche aus. An einer bedeutenden Geschäftsstraße in Altstadtnähe gelegen, wurde mit diesem Bau beabsichtigt, zwischen den Stadtteilen eine Beziehung herzustellen, was anfänglich seitens der Architek-ten – Gegner der Errichtung eines Hochhauses – bezweifelt wurde. Der Bau besteht aus Gebäudeteilen, unterschiedlich in ihren Höhen und ihrer Bauart. Im Gebäudeturm befindet sich die Hauptzentrale der Bank und die anderen Gebäudeteile werden unterschiedlich genutzt. Auch mußten aufgrund von der Bank vorgesehen Sicherheitsgründen Zugangs-und Durchgangsbereiche so getrennt werden, ohne dabei die anfängliche Vorstellung des Nexus zu verlieren.

In Frankfurt, the tall towers stand out from the traditional city. They form part of a concentration of office buildings which exemplify the financial hegemony of the city. On the right, section of the tower through the façade. Technically, its double wall and triple-glazed windows system is the most advanced in the city. It means a saving on energy and responds to the restrictive government ruling on environmental concerns.

Frankfort, les grandes tours dépassent la ville traditionnelle. Elles appartiennent à une concentration d'immeubles de bureaux qui illustrent l'hégémonie financière de la ville. À droite, section de la tour par la façade. Techniquement le système de mur double et de triple vitrage est le plus moderne de la ville. Il suppose une économie d'énergie et répond aux normes gouvernementales sur les restrictions quant à l'environnement.

Frankfurt, die hohen Türme ragen über die traditionelle Stadt hinaus. Eine Ansammlung von Bürogebäuden, die beispielhaft die Bedeutung des Finanzzentrums der Stadt hervorheben. Rechts: Querschnitt der Aussenfasssaden des Turms. Aktuell weist das Gebäude - mit Doppelmauern und dreifacher Fensterverglasung - den höchsten Technikstand in dieser Stadt vor. Es bedeutet Energieeinsparung und entspricht den strikten gesetzlich vorgeschriebenen Umweltnormen.

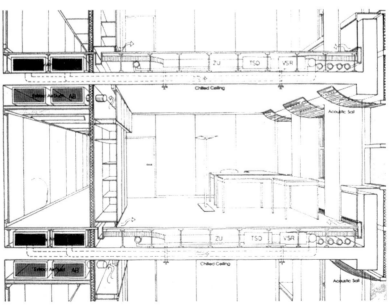

The cornice of the building is a crown, a symbol which identifies the complex from anywhere in the city.

La corniche du bâtiment est une couronne, un symbole qui permet de reconnaître le complexe depuis tous les points de la ville.

Der Obersims des Gebäudes endet mit einer Krone, die von jedem Punkt der Stadt zu erkennen ist.

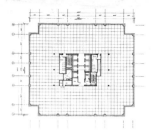
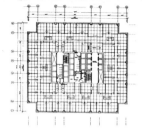

DONNELLEY BUILDING

RICARD BOFILL TALLER D'ARQUITECTURA

1992

CLIENT / CLIENT / AUFTRAGGEBER: THE PRIME GROUP & KEMPER INSURANCE COMPANY

TOTAL AREA / SURFACE TOTALE / GESAMTOBERFLÄCHE: 110.000 m²

FLOORS / PLANS / STOCKWERKE - HEIGHT / HAUTEUR / HÖHE: 50 fl / 247 m

In the project for this office tower, the possibility of a panoramic view over the city was desired, which means that glass is predominant in the façade. In the context of American skyscrapers, especially attractive in Chicago, thought was given to the need to reestablish a dialogue between the classicism of stone (white granite) and the high technology of glass. The façade presents a design of classical proportions with divisions on several levels, united among themselves by columns. The upper part, in the form of a pediment which stands out against the sky, is the distinctive sign of the building in the skyline of Chicago.

Lors du projet de cette tour de bureaux, l'on désira favoriser la possibilité d'une vue panoramique sur la ville grâce à l'emploi de la vitre sur la façade. Dans le contexte des gratte-ciels américains, spécialement attractifs à Chicago, l'on pensa au besoin de rétablir un dialogue entre le classicisme de la pierre (granite blanc) et la grande technologie de la vitre. La façade présente une conception aux proportions classiques, avec des divisions sur plusieurs niveaux unis par des colonnes. La partie supérieure, qui a la forme d'un fronton qui se coupe contre le ciel, est le signe qui distingue le bâtiment sur le skyline de Chicago.

Der Entwurf dieses Büroturms sah vor, hauptsächlich durch eine Fassadenverglasung den Panoramablick über die Stadt herzustellen. Im Kontext amerikanischer Wolkenkratzer, wobei Chicago besonders attraktive Gebäude vorweisen kann, wollte man die Wiederherstellung des Dialoges zwischen klassischem Baustein (weißer Granit) und Hightech-Verglasung erreichen. Die Gestaltung der Fassade zeigt klassische Proportionen mit Querunterteilungen auf unterschiedlichen Höhen, die sich unter- einander wiederum mit Säulen verbinden. Oben endet der Bau mit in den Himmel ragenden Giebeln, die das Gebäude zu einem Erkennungszeichen an der Chicagoer Skyline machen.

The ground floor lobby is 18 meters tall. It is made of gray and white marble. In addition, it is adorned with four sculptures and a mural by the catalan artists Xavier Corberó and Antoni Tàpies.

Le hall du rez-de-chaussée mesure 18 mètres de haut. Il est réalisé en marbre gris et blanc. De plus, il est décoré avec quatre sculptures et un mural des artistes catalans Xavier Corberó et Antoni Tàpies.

18 Meter hohe Eingangshalle in grauem und weißem Marmor. Zudem ist sie mit 4 Skulpturen und einem Wandentwurf der katalanischen Künstler Xavier Corberó und Antoni Tàpies dekoriert.

The building as a whole expresses the will to make an impact on the city's skyline.

Le bâtiment, dans son ensemble, exprime la volonté de s'inscrire sur le skyline de la ville.

Das Gebäude im ganzen gesehen, beabsichtigt Teil der Skyline der Stadt zu sein.

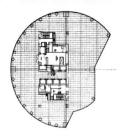

FIRST BANK PLACE

PEI COBB FREED & PARTNERS

CLIENT / CLIENT / AUFTRAGGEBER: IBM ASSOCIATES LTD
PARTNERSHIP & THE OPUS CORPORATION

1992

TOTAL AREA / SURFACE TOTALE / GESAMTOBERFLÄCHE: 140.000 m²

FLOORS / PLANS / STOCKWERKE - HEIGHT / HAUTEUR / HÖHE: 58 fl / 236,2 m

This building, located in central commercial area of the city, was projected attending to three urban conditioners: large skyscrapers, historical buildings of medium height, and a much-loved green space in the congested city center. Thus, the building, which does not occupy the entire lot, rises on an L-shaped plan, in three volumes generated from squares and cylinders in a harmonic succession of materials and heights. Finally, a tower sticks out and is crowned with a semi-circular steel structure.

Ce bâtiment qui se trouve dans un quartier commercial du centre de la ville, fut conçu selon trois conditions urbaines: les grands gratte-ciel, les édifices historiques d'un grandeur moyenne, et une zone verte appréciée dans le centre congestionné de la ville. Ainsi, le bâtiment qui n'occupe pas tout le terrain, s'élève sur une vue du plan en «L», en trois volumes, il est engendré par des carrés et des cylindres sur un enchaînement en harmonie des matériaux et des hauteurs. Enfin, une tour dépasse, elle est couronnée d'une structure demi-circulaire en acier.

Dieses Gebäude steht in einem zentralen Geschäftsviertel der Stadt und wurde entworfen, um sich drei urbanen Situationen anzupassen: den hohen Wolkenkratzern, den mittelhohen historischen Gebäuden und einer beliebten Grünzone im überlaufenen Stadtzentrum. So belegt das Gebäude in L-Form gebaut, nur einen Teil des Grundstücks und setzt sich aus drei Bauteilen - quadratische und zylindrische – zusammen, wobei verwandte Materialien und Höhen miteinander harmonisieren. Als Abschluß ragt ein Turm heraus, der von einer halbkreisförmigen Stahlstruktur gekrönt wird.

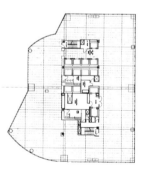

Exterior views of the building, the crown which finishes off the tower characterizes it, making it recognizable from different points of the city.

Vues extérieures du bâtiment, la couronne qui finit la tour le distingue, elle permet de le reconnaître depuis plusieurs points de la ville.

Aussenansichten des Gebäudes. Der Turm charakterisiert sich durch seine Krone als Abschlußteil und ist vòn vielen Punkten der Stadt aus erkennbar.

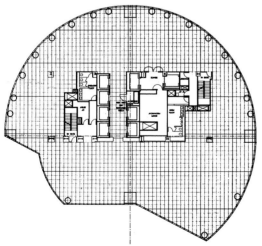

Glass-covered atrium at the corner of the building which opens onto the garden, creating a square at the entrance to the commercial area.

Parvis vitré sur le coin du bâtiment qui s'ouvre sur le jardin, créant une place sur l'accès à l'enceinte commerciale.

Verglastes Atrium gelegen in der Gebäudeecke, die sich zum Park öffnet und die Zugangszone zum Einkaufsbereich bildet.

Inside, a conical rotunda opens out, surrounded by restaurants and commercial spaces.

À l'intérieur, un rond-point conique est ouvert, il est entouré de restaurants et d'espaces commerciaux.

Innen eine konischer Rotunde umgeben von Restaurants und Geschäftsläden.

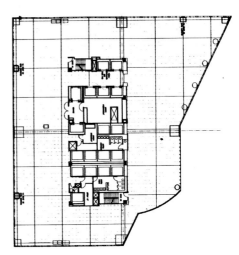

FIRST INTERSTATE WORLD CENTER

PEI COBB FREED & PARTNERS

CLIENT / CLIENT / AUFTRAGGEBER: MAGUIRE THOMAS PARTNERS

1990

TOTAL AREA / SURFACE TOTALE / GESAMTOBERFLÄCHE: 139.000 m²

FLOORS / PLANS / STOCKWERKE - HEIGHT / HAUTEUR / HÖHE: 75 fl / 310,3 m

The design of this tower was inspired by the old Los Angeles Central Library by the architect B. Goodhue. It has light features except for the base and the multiple-faced glass apex. The design of the plan and volumetry divide the articulation between a circle and a square surreptitiously, where the circle ends up dominating the geometric form. The structure of the building is prepared to receive an earthquake of 8·3 on the Richter scale as well as resisting the gusts of wind that a 75 floor tall building suffers.

La conception de cette tour s'est inspirée de la vieille Bibliothèque Centrale de Los Angeles de l'architecte B. Goodhue, elle possède des traits clairs sauf la base et le sommet en verre à plusieurs aspects. La conception de la vue en plana et la volumétrie coupe l'articulation entre un cercle et un carré recouverts, où le cercle s'achève et domine sur la forme géométrique. La structure du bâtiment est adaptée pour recevoir un tremblement de terre de 8,3 sur l'échelle de Richter, elle résiste aussi aux poussées du vent qui affectent une tour à 75 étages de haut.

Der Entwurf dieses Turmes inspirierte sich in der alten Zentralbibliothek von Los Angeles des Architekten B. Goodhue. Außer am Gebäudesockel und dem mehrflächigem Glasaufbau herrschen klare Linien vor. Der Grundriß und der Gebäudeumfang entstehen durch ein inneres Quadrat und einem überlappendem Kreis, wobei dann schließlich der Kreis als geometrische Form dominiert. Die Gebäudestruktur ist für Erdbeben der Stärke 8,3 auf der Richter Skala ausgerichtet und kann außerdem Windstößen widerstehen, denen 75 stöckige Gebäude generell immer ausgesetzt sind.

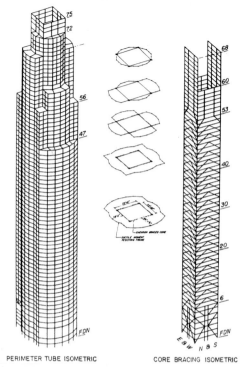

On the left, section, structural diagrams and development of the plan of the tower from the geometric figures of the square and the circle.

À gauche, section, schémas structurels et développement de la vue en plan de la tour à partir des figures géométriques du carré et du cercle.

Links: Querschnitt, Strukturzeichnungen und Entstehung des Turms, ausgehend von den geometrischen Figuren des Quadrates und des Kreises.

PERIMETER TUBE ISOMETRIC   CORE BRACING ISOMETRIC

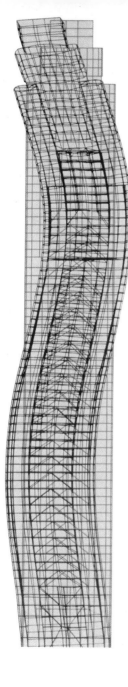

The tower, which is located 42 km away from the San Andrés fault, is currently the tallest building in the world in a seismic zone 4. On the left, the building's response to an earthquake.

La tour, qui est située à 42 Km de la faille de San Andres, est aujourd'hui le bâtiment le plus haut du monde, sur une zone sismique 4. À gauche, réaction du bâtiment face à un tremblement de terre.

Der Turm, der 42 Km vom St. Andreas-Graben entfernt liegt, ist gegenwärtig das höchste Gebäude der Welt, das in einer Zone seismischer Bewegungen der Stärke 4 steht. Links: Gebäudebiegung während eines Erdbebens.

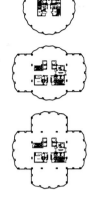

On the next page, views of the monumental colonnade of ground floor pillars, coated with translucent glass dyed green. On this page, different details of the interior of the lobby, the plan of the siting and different plan types.

Sur l'autre page, vues de la colonnade monumentale de piliers, rez-de-chaussée, recouverts de verre translucide, teint vert. Sur cette page, plusieurs détails de l'intérieur du hall, le plan du site et étages types différents.

Auf der anderen Seite: Blick in die untere Etage mit monumentalen Säulen aus lichtdurchlässigem grünlichem Glas. Auf dieser Seite: verschiedene Ansichten der Eingangshalle , Lageplan und unterschiedliche Verteilung.

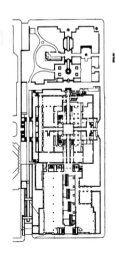

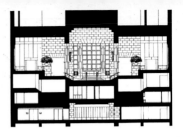

FOUR SEASONS HOTEL

PEI COBB FREED & PARTNERS + FRANK WILLIAMS

CLIENT / CLIENT / AUFTRAGGEBER: EIE REGENT AVENUE CORPORATION.	**1993**
TOTAL AREA / SURFACE TOTALE / GESAMTOBERFLÄCHE: 46.450 m²	
FLOORS / PLANS / STOCKWERKE - HEIGHT / HAUTEUR / HÖHE: 54 fl / 167,65 m.	

This building, designed as a hotel, is sited in one of the most exclusive areas of New York, designed with a classical elegance which transcends time and fashions. The building's program develops beneath street level a gymnasium and meeting halls, the entrance, lobby and public areas in the base, and 372 rooms in the tower. The façade, with plates of high quality limestone, frames large glass windows. The volumetry is defined from a cruciform prism which gradually loses section as it gains great height.

Ce bâtiment, réservé à un hôtel, se trouve sur une des zones les plus exclusives de New York, sa conception propose une élégance classique qui dépasse le concept du temps et des modes. Le programme du bâtiment développe, sous le niveau de la rue, un gymnase et des salles de réunions; l'accès, le hall et les espaces de relations sont sur la base, et les 372 chambres sur la tour. La façade dont le placage est en pierre calcaire de grande qualité, dispose de grandes fenêtres vitrées. La volumétrie est définie à partir d'un prisme en croix qui perd une section par échelon selon l'augmentation en hauteur.

Dieses Hotelgebäude ist in einem der exklusivsten Stadtviertel New Yorks gelegen. Elegantes klassisches Design, das sich über Zeit und Moden hinwegsetzt. Das Gebäude beginnt unterirdisch mit einem Fitnessraum und Versammlungsräumen; im Erdgeschoß befinden sich der Eingang, Vestibül und Empfang, sowie 372 Zimmern in den Obergeschossen. Der mit Kalkstein versehene Aussenfassade wird von großen Fenstern unterbrochen. Die Gebäudeumfang definiert sich ausgehend von einem kreisförmigen Prisma und stuft sich in Höhenrichtung ab.

The tower maintains the domestic scale of the façade by means of the reticle of windows an entire floor high

La tour maintient l'échelle domestique de la façade avec le réticule de fenêtres sur toute la hauteur de l'étage.

Der Turm behält durch die gitterförmige Anordnung der Fensterreihen über sämtliche Etagen sein gleichmäßiges Aussehen.

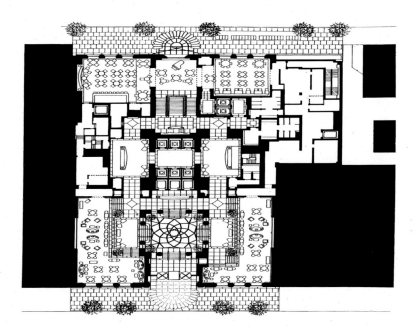

The ground floor is devoted to the public areas of the hotel, regulated by means of a representative luxury entrance.

Le rez-de-chaussée est destiné aux surfaces communes de l'hôtel, il est régulé avec un accès luxueux et représentatif.

Im Erdgeschoß befinden sich verschiedene zum Hotel gehörende Räumlichkeiten, die über den luxuriösen und repräsentativen Eingang erreichbar sind.

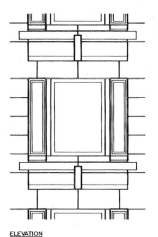

ELEVATION

SECTION

The sumptuous interior decoration in
the public areas is designed as part
of the luxury set design which the
hotel represents.

*La dévoration intérieure somptueuse
des surfaces communes est conçue
en tant que partie de la
scénographie du luxe qui est
représentée dans l'hôtel.*

Die aufwendige Innenausstattung
vermittelt den Luxuscharakter des
Hotels.

GAS NATURAL

ENRIC MIRALLES & BENEDETTA TAGLIABUE ARQ. ASSOCIATS

CLIENT / CLIENT / AUFTRAGGEBER: GAS NATURAL SDG	**1999**
TOTAL AREA / SURFACE TOTALE / GESAMTOBERFLÄCHE: 22.000 m²	
FLOORS / PLANS / STOCKWERKE - HEIGHT / HAUTEUR / HÖHE: 21 fl / 86 m	

This new head office will be situated between the Coastal Ring Road and the old fishermen's quarters of Barceloneta. The architects have described it as a building with a very clear will to be compatible with its urban environment, composed from the small scale of the housing blocks, a park and tall buildings soon to be built. The building responds with the verticality of an office tower at the same time as it is fragmented in smaller scale bodies, which give rise to a projection, which forms a singular public space through an urban landscape of different dimensions, which forms a great bridge towards Barceloneta.

Ce nouveau siège de bureaux se trouvera entre le Cinturó del Litoral et le l'ancien quartier des pêcheurs de la Barceloneta. Les architectes décrivent celui-ci comme un bâtiment dont la volonté très claire est d'être compatible avec l'environnement urbain, composé d'une petite échelle d'appartements, d'un parc et de grands bâtiment en construction imminente. Le bâtiment répond à la verticalité d'une tour de bureaux; il est aussi fragmenté en corps à une échelle plus petite qui engendrent une saillie, celle-ci offre un espace public singulier à travers un paysage urbains à plusieurs dimensions, ce qui représente une grande porte vers la Barceloneta.

Neuer Hauptsitz zwischen dem sogenannten Cinturó del Litoral und dem altem Fischviertel, der Barceloneta gelegen. Die Architekten heben bei diesen Bau den eindeutigen Willen zur Verträglichkeit mit dem städtischen Umfeld bestehend aus niedrigen Wohnhäusern, einem Park und bevorstehenden Hochhauskonstruktionen hervor. Das Gebäude besteht aus einem senkrecht hochragenden Büroturm und tiefer liegender Anbauten, die sich wie Flügel über einen singulären, offenen Raum spannen werden, um im Stadtbild die große Tür zur Barceloneta darzustellen .

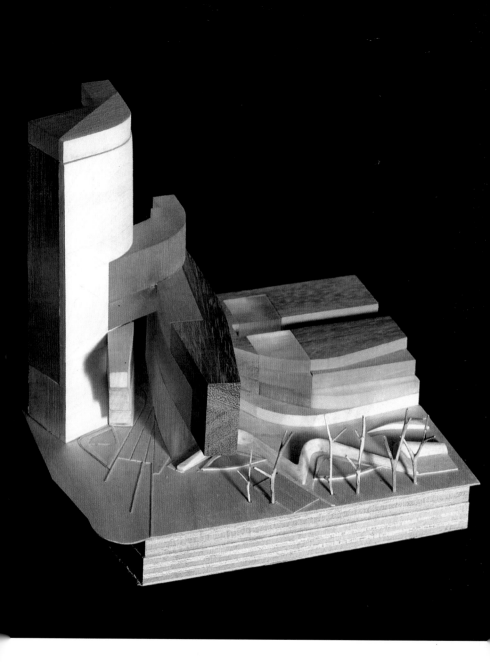

"The treatment of the façades follows similar criteria, a series of large windows give interest from a close-up viewing at the same time as an undifferentiated volumetric treatment...

«Le traitement des façade suit un critère semblable, une série de grandes fenêtres le rendent son aspect intéressant de près tandis que le traitement volumétrique indifférencié...

«Die Behandlung der Fassaden verfolgen ein ähnliches Kriterium aus der Nähe betrachtet, wirkt es durch eine Reihe großer Fenster interessant, während einen die Gesamtaufbereitung eigentlich unberührt läßt...

...which protects the building from the sun and noise, shows some abstract volumes which become confused with the other constructions along the ring road."

...qui protège le bâtiment du sol et du bruit dispose de volumes abstraits que sont confondus avec les autres constructions tout au long du périphérique.»

... das Gebäude vor Sonne und Geräusche schützt, stellt sich mit abstrakten Umrissen dar, die sich mit denen anderer Bauten auf der Länge des Stadtumgehungsrings vermischen.»

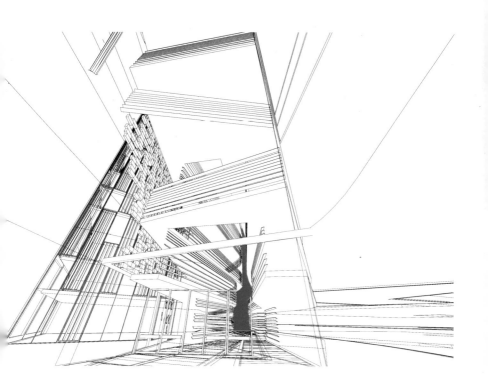

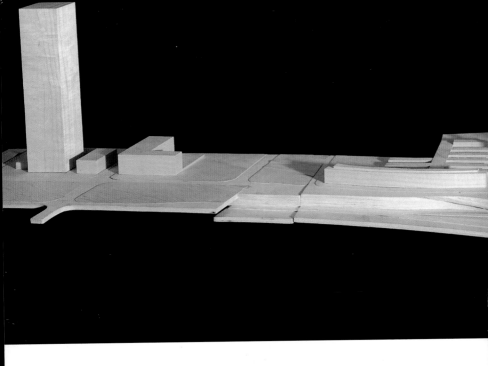

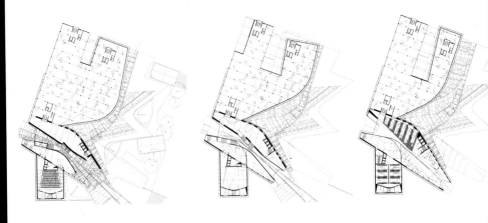

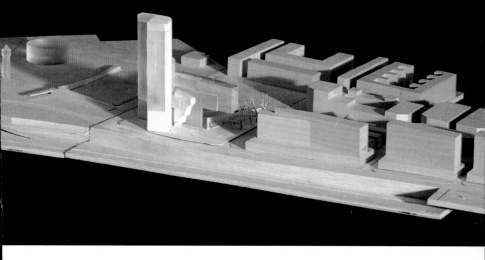

From left to right, the plans of the building in progress are shown.

De gauche à droite nous avons les vues de plan du bâtiment en progression.

Von links nach rechts: Entwicklung jeder einzelnen Bauphase.

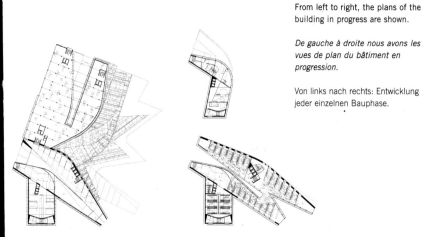

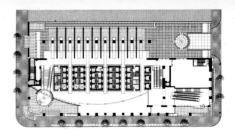

LOS ANGELES

GAS COMPANY TOWER

SKIDMORE, OWINGS & MERILL LLP (SOM)

CLIENT / CLIENT / AUFTRAGGEBER: MAGUIRE THOMAS PARTNERS

1991

TOTAL AREA / SURFACE TOTALE / GESAMTOBERFLÄCHE: 130.000 m²

FLOORS / PLANS / STOCKWERKE - HEIGHT / HAUTEUR / HÖHE: 55 fl / 228,3 m

Central element of the rehabilitation of a downtown area together with the First Interstate World Center, it responds in terms of urban planning and composition as a ball and socket joint between public spaces, historical buildings and modern skyscrapers. It incorporates the volumes and materials that surround it while still representing a corporate image. Its design responds to the neighboring buildings. Starting out from a base which takes its height from the Baltimore Hotel next door, a central trunk of blueish granite rises (like the neighboring Arco Tower) and the sides are wrapped in a metallic cladding (like the First Interstate). A volume of eliptical blue glass which penetrates the granite of the trunk symbolizes a gas flame. As it rises, the trunk shrinks until only the blue glass and the infinite sky are left.

Cet élément central de la réhabilitation d'une zone du downtown avec le First Interstate World Center, est devenu, du point de vue de l'urbanisme et de la composition, la rotule entre les espaces publiques, les bâtiments historiques et les gratte-ciel modernes. Il incorpore les volumes et les matériaux qui l'entourent sans pour autant négliger une image corporative. Sa conception répond au vocabulaire des bâtiments qui l'avoisinent. À partir d'un socle dont la hauteur est celle du proche Baltimore Hotel, il s'élève avec un tronc central en granite bleuâtre (comme son voisin, l'Arco Tower) et les latéraux son recouverts d'un revêtement en métal (comme le First Interstate). Un volume en verre bleu elliptique qui pénètre dans le granite du tronc symbolise une flamme de gaz, plus nous nous élevons, plus le tronc se réduit jusqu'à ce qu'il ne reste plus que du verre bleu et le ciel infini.

Gemeinsam mit dem First Interstate World Center gilt es als Zentralelement eines sanierten Downtownteils, das sich städteplanerisch wie auch gestalterisch als Drehscheibe zwischen öffentlichen Anlagen, historischen Gebäuden und modernen Wolkenkratzern versteht. Der Turm spiegelt Bauarten und Materialien seines Umfeldes wieder, vergißt dabei aber nicht, sich als Firmenabzeichen zu präsentieren. Sein Design entspricht dem der Nachbargebäude. Sein quaderförmiger Unterbau paßt sich der Bauhöhe des nahegelegenen Baltimore Hotel an, darüber erhebt sich der Turm mit einem Zentralkörper aus bläulich schimmerndem Granit (wie der benachbarte Arco Tower) und metallverkleideten Gebäudeseiten (wie das First Interstate). Das elliptische Volumen aus blauem Glas ragt aus dem Granitunterbau und symbolisiert mit wachsender Höhe eine Glasflamme, die sich nach oben hin verjüngt, bis nur noch blaues Glas und der endlose Horizont verbleiben.

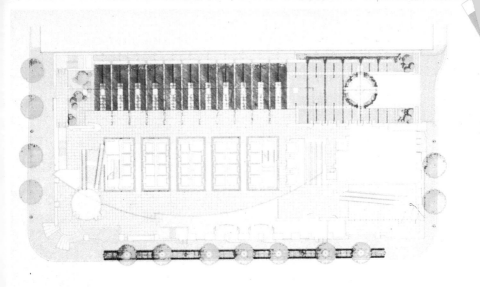

The base of the building, which contains three foyers joined by stairs and elevators, walkways and hanging gardens, is a link between two refurbished public spaces – the Central Library building and Pershing Square. Access to the square is gained from the park and the historic Baltimore Hotel in a sweeping curve.

La base du bâtiment qui dispose de trois halls unis par des escaliers et des ascenseurs, des couloirs internes et des jardins suspendus, est une liaison entre deux espaces publics restaurés: le bâtiment de la Central Library et la place Pershing. L'accès à la place s'ouvre vers le parc et vers un bâtiment historique, le Baltimore Hotel et décrit une courbe.

Drei verschiedene Eingangshallen sind im Erdgeschoss des Gebäudes durch Treppen und Aufzüge, interne Flure und Hängegärten vereint und gelten als Verbindung zu zwei wiederhergestellten öffentlichen Bereichen: dem Central Library Gebäude und dem Pershing Platz. Der Zugang zum Platz öffnet sich mit weitreichender Geste in Richtung des historischen Baltimore Hotel.

The structure is a combination of steel elements that provide the necessary lateral resistance to wind and seismic forces, and carry the vertical gravitational burden.

La structure est une combinaison d'éléments en acier, ce qui garantit la résistance latérale nécessaire face aux forces sismiques et éoliques, elle supporte aussi les charges verticales gravitatoires.

Die Struktur besteht aus einer Kombination von Stahlelementen, die den Seitenteilen des Gebäudes Resistenz gegen seismische Bewegungen und Windstöße verleiht, aber gleichzeitig auch die Vertikallasten der Gravitation aushält.

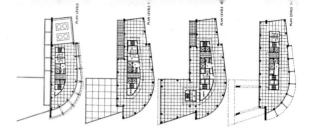

GENERAL BANK TOWER

MURPHY / JAHN INC. ARCHITECTS

CLIENT / CLIENT / AUFTRAGGEBER: GENERAL BANK	**1996**
FLOORS / PLANS / STOCKWERKE- HEIGHT / HAUTEUR / HÖHE: 30fl/ 104 m	

This building is found in an office area. It has the will to respond to the urban context. With a corner lot the encounter and continuity between streets with different buildings had to be resolved. The architects decided to search for partial solutions and instead of projecting a single building they split it up into parts, unifying them with a uniform treatment of the façades. From the location of the bank's offices on the corner, with a curved tower, the lateral encounters are resolved with volumes of forms and heights which adapt to the neighboring buildings. Thus, the building offers three different images.

Ce bâtiment qui se trouve sur une zone de bureaux, désire répondre au contexte urbain. Le terrain en équerre devait résoudre la rencontre et la continuité entre les rues dont les bâtiments sont différents. Les architectes on décidé de trouver des solutions partielles et au lieu de concevoir un bâtiment unique, ils l'ont partagé en plusieurs parties, elles sont unies par un traitement uniforme des façades. À partir de l'emplacement des bureaux de la banque sur le coin, une tour courbée, l'on a résolu les rencontres latérales avec des volumes dont la forme et la hauteur s'adaptent aux bâtiments avoisinants. Ainsi, le bâtiment offre des images différentes.

Dieses Gebäude befindet sich in einem Büroviertel und paßt sich dem städtischen Umfeld an. Da es auf einem Eckgrundstück steht, wurde bei seiner Entstehung für die Lage an der Straßenkreuzung und die Anpassung an bereits bestehende Bebauungen eine Lösung gefunden. Anstatt einer uniformen Baueinheit, entschieden sich die Architekten, das Gebäude auf unterschiedlich hohe Teile zu verteilen , wobei allerdings die Fassade einheitlich gestaltet wurde. Zur Straßenecke hin ist das Bankgebäude ein gebogener Turm, der hintere Gebäudeteil ist kantig und steht niedriger und paßt sich auf diese Weise der Nachbarbebauung an. Auf diese Art vermittelt das Gebäude unterschiedliche Ansichten.

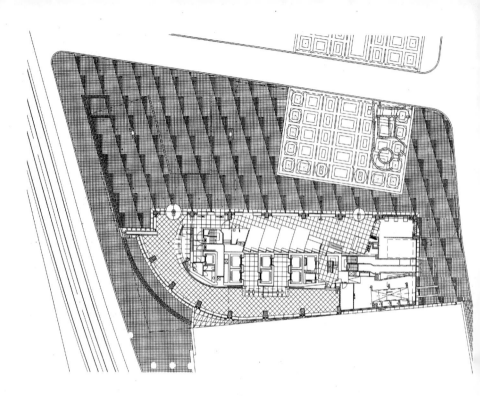

Looking at the building from different angles and positions, the images and perceptions we have of it are not the same.

Lorsque l'on regarde le bâtiment depuis des angles et des positions différents, les images et les perceptions que l'on reçoit de celui-ci changent.

Von verschiedenen Seiten aus betrachtet, ergibt sich jedesmal ein unterschiedlicher Eindruck.

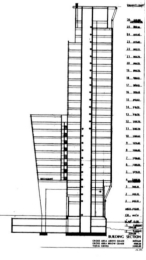

BUILDING SECTION

Above, the tower leaves part of the ground floor free, thus offering a view of the Maritime Museum as well as creating a square.

En haut, la tour dégage une partie du rez-de-chaussée, ce qui permet ainsi une vue sur le Musée Maritime et crée aussi une place.

Oben: der Turm läßt Teil des Erdgeschosses offen und schafft damit einen Platz, von dem man das Maritimmuseum erblicken kann.

GOLDEN CENTER

DENNIS LAU & N.G. CHUN MAN
ARCHITECTS & ENGINEERS (H.K) LTD

CLIENT / CLIENT / AUFTRAGGEBER: HANG LUNG DEVELOPMENT COMPANY LIMITED	**1991**
TOTAL AREA / SURFACE TOTALE / GESAMTOBERFLÄCHE: 14.535 m²	
FLOORS / PLANS / STOCKWERKE - HEIGHT / HAUTEUR / HÖHE: 31 fl / 112 m	

Commercial building constructed by a private agent over a metropolitan railway station, it is made up of a four-floor base which contains the most public usages – shops, restaurants- above which a 25 floor office tower rises. In spite of the form and the size of the siting – a triangle of only 800 m2 – which the base occupies totally, the tower is breeched from the most acute angle of the lot and obtains a fairly regular prismatic form. The façade is resolved with a reflective glass curtain wall of golden tones, which together with similar tones in the interior decoration, gives the building its name.

C'est un bâtiment commercial construit par une entreprise privée sur une station de métro, il est composé d'une base de quatre étages de haut qui dispose des usages publics –commerce, restaurants–, sur celle- ci s'élève une tour de bureaux de 25 étages. Malgré la forme et la grandeur de l'emplacement –un triangle de 800 m2 seulement– qui occupe toute la base, la tour se déplace de l'angle le plus aigu du terrain et adopte une forme prismatique assez régulière. La façade est résolue avec un mur rideau vitré réfléchissant au ton doré, ce qui, avec les tons similaires sur la décoration intérieure, apporte une identité au bâtiment.

Ein Privatunternehmen ließ dieses Geschäftsgebäude über die Station der Stadtbahn errichten. Über einem 4stöckigen Unterbau mit Läden und Restaurants ragt ein 25 stöckiger Turm. Trotz der Art und Ausmaße des Grundstücks – ein nur 800 m2 großes Dreieck – steht der Turm zurückgezogen auf dem im spitzen Winkel zur Straße verlaufenden Unterbau und erlangt eine relativ reguläre Prismenform. Die Außenhautverglasung in Goldtönen, die sich auch in der Inneneinrichtung widerspiegeln, gab diesem Gebäude seinen Namen.

The base is adapted to the lot, while the tower rises more freely, adopting irregular forms. The golden tone of the reflective glass dominates the building.

La base s'adapte au terrain, tandis que la tour s'élève avec plus de liberté adoptant des formes régulières. Le ton doré du verre réfléchissant domine sur le bâtiment.

Der Unterbau paßt sich der Eckform des Grundstücks an. Der darüber liegende Turm ist davon befreit und seine Formen sind regelmäßiger. Reflektierende Goldtöne beherrschen das Gebäude.

HONG KONG & SHANGHAI BANK HQTRS.

FOSTER & PARTNERS

1986

CLIENT / CLIENT / AUFTRAGGEBER: HONG KONG & SHANGHAI BANKING CORPORATION

TOTAL AREA / SURFACE TOTALE / GESAMTOBERFLÄCHE: 99.000 m²

FLOORS / PLANS / STOCKWERKE - HEIGHT / HAUTEUR / HÖHE: 44 fl / 180 m

This building was projected between 1979 and 1983, when Hong Kong was still under British government. Sited in a narrow plot, it was designed considering the local tradition of Feng Shui, which seeks cosmic equilibrium. It wanted to define the financial character of the city, seeking a new concept of the office building. The decision to move the structure and the vertical communications from the center of the plan breaks with the traditional diagram of skyscrapers with a central core. The exterior treatment is also different, foregrounding the structure instead of hiding it behind a curtain wall.

Ce bâtiment fut conçu entre 1979 et 1983, lorsque Hong Kong dépendait encore du gouvernement anglais. Il se trouve sur un terrain étroit, sa conception adopta la tradition locale du Feng Shui, qui recherche l'équilibre cosmique. Il désirait définir le caractère financier de la ville, recherchant une nouvelle conception de l'immeuble de bureaux. La décision de déplacer la structure et les communications verticales du centre du plan casse le schéma traditionnel du gratte-ciel à noyau central. Le traitement extérieur est aussi différent, la structure est placée au premier plan, au lieu d'être cachée derrière un mur rideau.

Zwischen 1979 und 1983 wurde dieses Gebäude entworfen als Hong Kong noch unter britischer Regierungsherrschaft stand. Es liegt auf einem schmalen Grundstück und entstand gemäß der traditionellen Lehre des Feng Shui, einer Lehre, die das kosmische Gleichgewicht sucht. Mit der Konzeption einer neuen Art von Bürogebäude sollte der Charakter als Finanzstadt hervorgehoben werden. Die Entscheidung, die vertikale Stahlstruktur sowie die Aufzugsanlagen von der Mitte auf die Gebäudeseiten zu verlagern, bedeuteten den Bruch mit dem traditonellen Wolkenkratzerschema, bei dem sich alles in einem Zentralkern befand. Auch gab es bei der Aussenflächenverarbeitung eine Änderung, indem die Gebäudestruktur sichtbar wird und nicht wie üblich hinter einer Aussenhaut verschwindet.

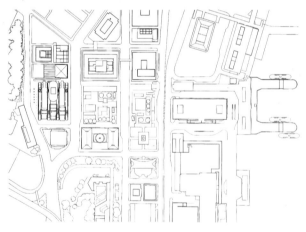

Different views of the building highlight the nocturnal view, where the transparency of the building is highlighted and the skeleton effect that the structure gives in the treatment of the façade.

Vues différentes du bâtiment, il faut souligner la vision nocturne qui met en valeur la transparence du bâtiment et l'effet de squelette produit par la structure sur le traitement de la façade.

Unterschiedliche Ausblicke auf das Gebäude. Die Nachtansicht macht die Transparenz sichtbar und läßt das Gebäudeskelett an der Außenseite hervortreten.

The plan is subdivided into
three rectangular bodies of 28,
45 and 41 floors respectively.
The interior of the building
is very luminous because
by moving the technical core
towards the perimeter,
it permits free floors.

*La vue en plan est divisée en
trois corps rectangulaires de
28, 45 et 41 étages
respectivement. L'intérieur du
bâtiment est très lumineux car
le déplacement du noyau
technique vers le périmètre
permet des étages libres.*

Der Komplex verteilt sich über
drei rechteckige Gebäudteile mit
jeweils 28, 45 und 41
Stockwerken. Lichtdurchflutetes
Innere, da durch seitliche
Verlagerung der
Versorgungstechnik erheblich
mehr offener Raum gewonnen
wurde.

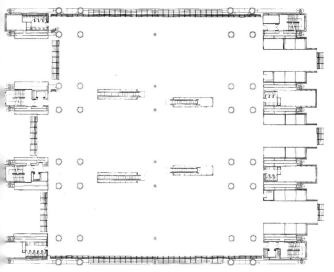

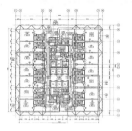

HOTEL ARTS

SKIDMORE OWINGS & MERRILL LLP (SOM)

TOTAL AREA / SURFACE TOTALE / GESAMTOBERFLÄCHE: 70.000 m²

FLOORS / PLANS / STOCKWERKE - HEIGHT / HAUTEUR / HÖHE: 47 fl / 152 m

1992

In 1985, Barcelona City Council began an ambitious project which would transform the maritime front and part of the gothic quarter. The Olympic Games 1992 nomination made them come true. The new residential neighborhood of the Olympic Village links the gothic city and the sea. Two towers will symbolize this urban transformation and signal the new Olympic Port and its surrounding area. Commercial areas, restaurants, cafés, offices and the Hotel de les Arts. It is characterized by the exterior view of its metallic structure, which is submerged in a pond where it reaches the ground. Thus, the whole building seems to emerge from the water.

La mairie de Barcelone commença, en 1985, un projet ambitieux qui transforma le front maritime et une partie du quartier gotique. La nomination des Jeux Olympiques en1992 l'a permis. Le nouveau quartier résidentiel de la Vila Olímpica unit la ville gotique et la mer. Deux tours symbolisent cette transformation urbaine et dessinent le nouveau Port Olímpic et son environnement. Des zones commerciales, des restaurants, des cafés, des bureaux et l'Hôtel de les Arts. Il est caractérisé par la vision extérieure de sa structure métallique blanche qui, lorsqu'elle arrive au sol, s'enfonce dans un étang. Ainsi, tout le bâtiment semble émerger de l'eau.

Die Stadtverwaltung Barcelonas startete 1985 ein ehrgeiziges Programm zur Umgestaltung des am Meer liegenden Stadtviertels sowie Teil des gotischen Viertels. Durch die Nominierung zur Ausrichtung der Olympischen Spiele in 1992 konnte dieses Projekt dann schließlich Realität werden. Das neue Wohnviertel "Vila Olímpica" verbindet den gotischen Teil der Stadt mit dem Meer. Zwei Türme symbolisieren diese Transfor-mation und stehen für den Port Olímpic und sein Umfeld. Einkaufscenter, Restaurants, Cafés, Büros und das Hotel de les Arts sind entstanden. Die alles überragende weiße Stahlstruktur des Hotels endet am Boden in einem Teich und man könnte vermuten, daß das Gebäude aus dem Wasser steigt.

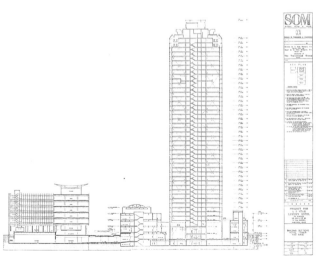

Aerial view from the summit of the tower, the sculpture of a fish with golden scales was designed by the American architect Frank Gehry.

Vue aérienne depuis le sommet de la tour, la sculpture d'un poisson avec des écailles dorées fut conçue par l'architecte américain Frank Gehry.

Luftaufnahme vom Turmdach aus auf die Skulptur des goldenen Fisches, der vom amerikanischen Architekten Frank Gehry entworfen wurde.

The hotel and the base of the tower are connected by means of terraces which offer intermediate spaces between the exterior and the public spaces of the interior.

L'hôtel et la base de la tour sont connectés avec des terrasses qui offrent des espaces intermédiaires entre l'extérieur et les espaces publiques de l'intérieur.

Terrassen verbinden das Hotel mit dem Turmsockel und ermöglichen den Zugang von außen in die Räumlichkeiten, die für das Publikum offen sind.

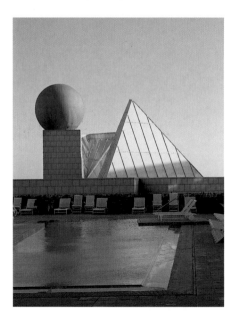

Both the Hotel Arts and the Mapfre Tower are currently
the tallest buildings in the city of Barcelona.

*Aussi bien l'Hôtel de les Arts, que la Torre Mapfre sont
aujourd'hui les plus grands bâtiments de la ville de
Barcelone.*

Sowohl das Hotel de les Arts als auch der Mapfre-Turm
sind gegenwärtig die höchsten Gebäude Barcelonas.

HOTEL ATTRACTION

ANTONI GAUDÍ

1908

CLIENT / CLIENT / AUFTRAGGEBER: UNKNOWN / INCONNU / UNBEKANNT	
TOTAL AREA / SURFACE TOTALE / GESAMTOBERFLÄCHE:	
FLOORS / PLANS / STOCKWERKE - HEIGHT / HAUTEUR / HÖHE: 120 fl - 360 m	

The Hotel Attraction began as five sketches drawn by Gaudí at the beginning of the 20th century as part of a project for a hotel in a skyscraper in New York. The sheer magnitude of the project was considerable for the time since there were no buildings of similar dimensions in the city. The design features a large central tower (like the Sagrada Família in Barcelona) flanked by smaller towers where the guestrooms were to be located. This project by Gaudí, whose promoter is unknown, was recuperated by one of his disciples, Joan Matamala. He analysed the original sketches in the late 1950s and tried to imagine what the cross section would be like. The Catalan artist Marc Mascort i Boix took up where Matamala left off, and his research into the final volumetric aspect of the building is shown in the digital mock-ups on these pages.

L'origine de l'Hotel Attraction, ce sont cinq schémas tracés par Gaudí au début du XXème siècle, un projet pour un gratte-ciel qui devait auberger un hôtel dans la ville de New York. La grandeur du projet était déjà importante à l'époque, car il n'y avait aucun bâtiment de ces dimensions dans la ville. La conception représente une grande tour centrale (comme celle de la Sagrada Família de Barcelone) qui est entourée par d'autres aux dimensions plus petites, où se trouvent les chambres. Ce projet de Gaudí, dont le promoteur n'est pas connu, fut récupéré par un de ses disciples, Joan Matamala, qui à la fin des années cinquante, après avoir les schémas originaux, imagina comment pourrait être la section du bâtiment. L'artiste catalan Marc Mascort i Boix reprit les recherches de Matamala et après plusieurs travaux quant à la volumétrie finale du bâtiment, il présenta les récréations numériques qui figurent sur ces pages.

Fünf Skizzen von Gaudí zu Beginn des XX. Jahrhunderts waren Grundlage des Entwurfes für das Hotel Attraction. Dieses Hotel sollte als Wolkenkratzer in New York entstehen. Die Gebäudeausmaße waren bereits seinerzeit revolutionär, denn noch gab es in der Stadt keinen Bau mit diesen Dimensionen. Der Entwurf sah einen hohen Zentralturm vor (wie die Sagrada Familia in Barcelona), der von mehreren kleineren Türmen, in denen die Hotelzimmer liegen sollten, umringt wurde. Dieses Gaudí-Projekt, dessen Auftraggeber unbekannt geblieben ist, wurde von einem seiner Anhänger, Joan Matamala, wiederentdeckt, der Ende der 50iger Jahre die Originalskizzen dieses Bau ausfindig machte und analysierte. Der katalanische Künstler Marc Mascort i Boix griff die Nachforschungen Matamalas erneut auf und nach anschließender Bearbeitung der endgültigen Volumetrie, entstanden die digitalen Nachbildungen des Projekts, die auf diesen Seiten zu sehen sind.

OAll the rooms are located in the perimeter of the façade, leaving the spacious central area free for an immense hall. There would be five in the entire building and each one would reflect the culture of each of the five continents.

Toutes les chambres sont disposées sur le périmètre de la façade, sur l'espace central ample se trouve un salon immense. Sur tout le bâtiment il devait en avoir cinq et chacun d'entre eux devait représenter la culture des cinq continents.

Alle Zimmer sind um einen enormen zentral gelegen Salon angeordnet. Im gesamten Bau sollte es fünf davon geben, die die Kultur der fünf Kontinente widerspiegeln sollten.

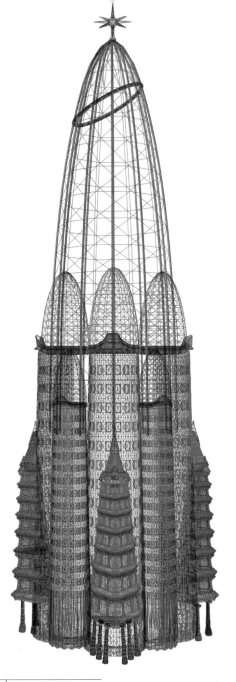

Besides accommodating the lobby, the ground floor could also be used for religious purposes such as a Catholic church or a Protestant or Buddhist temple.

Le rez-de-chaussée auberge le hall d'accès, mais pouvait aussi être réservée à plusieurs finalités religieuses, comme une église catholique, un temple protestant ou bouddhiste.

Das Erdgeschoss sollte neben seiner Funktion als Eingangshalle auch als Veranstaltungsraum für religiöse Feierlichkeiten, sei es katolischer, evangelischer oder budistischer Art, genutzt werden.

This project shows that the vision of the genius Catalan architect coincided at a specific, fleeting moment with the metropolitan energy of turn-of-the-century New York, a city which he himself never visited.

Ce projet démontre que la vision du génie catalan coïncida, à un moment concret et éphémère, avec l'énergie métropolitaine de la ville de New York au début du siècle, il ne la visita jamais.

Dieser Entwurf des katalanischen Genies vermittelt konkrete aber doch so flüchtige Visionen einer Metropole wie New York zu Beginn jenes Jahrhunderts, einer Stadt, die er allerdings nie besuchen konnte

gaudí 2o02

HOTEL DIAGONAL 1

OSCAR TUSQUETS BLANCA ARQUITECTURAS

CLIENT / CLIENT / AUFTRAGGEBER: ESPAIS, APEX & LANDSCAPE S.L.

TOTAL AREA / SURFACE TOTALE / GESAMTOBERFLÄCHE: 20.000 m²

FLOORS / PLANS / STOCKWERKE - HEIGHT / HAUTEUR / HÖHE: 26 fl - 92 m

2004

The Hotel Diagonal 1 is located in an exceptional spot of the city. This location will lend uniqueness to the building, which will be strengthened by municipal willingness to erect a tower and the geometry of the building site, a triangle with a sharp corner like the prow of a ship facing the immense square of the "Fòrum 2004". Initial response by architects was a double tower, but since the projection for the building was a hotel, it was not possible, so the original idea was maintained by projecting two towers linked by a glass walkway. The view of the hotel from Diagonal against the light will be the most frequent and characteristic, since the sunlight shining through the glass bridge will project a spectacular wake of light onto the pavement of l'Avinguda Diagonal.

L'Hotel Diagonal 1 se trouve sur un point exceptionnel de la ville. Cet emplacement donnera un caractère singulier au bâtiment qui sera renforcé grâce à la volonté municipale de bâtir une tour et à la géométrie du terrain. La forme triangulaire et le coin très prononcé, comme une proue qui vise la grande place du "Fòrum 2004". La réponse des architectes fut d'abord une tour double, mais le programme du bâtiment -un hôtel- l'empêchait, ainsi on conçut deux tours communiquées par un pont en verre, l'idée d'origine fut ainsi maintenue. De la Diagonal la vision du bâtiment à contre-jour sera très fréquente et elle sera, de même, caractéristique, car, grâce à l'incidence et au passage des rayons de soleil par la fissure vitrée (le pont), une frange spectaculaire de lumière sera projetée sur le sol de l'Avinguda Diagonal.

Das Hotel Diagonal 1 wird an einem außergewöhnlichen Punkt der Stadt gelegen sein, dort wo der "Eixample" und die Avenida Diagonal ihren Ursprung haben. Der Standort wird dem Gebäude einen einzigartigen Stempel verleihen. Hinzu kommt die verstärkte Absicht der Stadt, einen Turm zu errichten sowie ein Grundstück mit besonderem Ausmaß. Es handelt sich dabei um ein Dreieck mit einer lang herausragenden Grundstücksecke, die wie ein Schiffsbug in Richtung des Platzes "Forum 2004" zeigen wird. Der anfängliche Architektenentwurf sah die Entstehung eines Doppelturms vor, konnte aber nicht für das Bauprogramm – ein Hotel – verwendet werden, sodaß zwei nebeneinander liegende Türme geplant wurden, die durch eine Glasbrücke verbunden sein werden.

Access to the Hotel at ground level on the façade facing Diagonal via a downward extension of the glimmering walkway. In contrast with the south facing façade, this one is opaque and abstract, with a wide strip of polished granite running the length of the entire ground floor.

L'accès à l'Hôtel se produit par l'accroissement, au rez-de-chaussée, de la façade de la diagonale de la fissure lumineuse. Par opposition à la façade du sud, celle-ci est opaque et abstraite, un socle en granite poli s'étend tout au long du rez-de-chaussée.

Der Hoteleingang erfolgt im Erdgeschoss durch eine weitausladenden Aussenfassade, die zur Avenida Diagonal zeigt. Auf der Rückseite ist die südliche Aussenseite lichtdicht und abstrakt und wird von einem Gebäudesockel aus puliertem Granit im gesamten Untergeschoss umgeben sein.

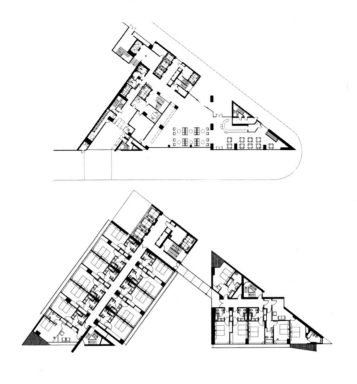

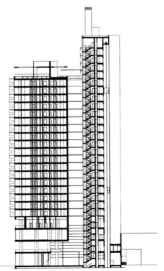

Guestrooms will be located on the large, south-facing clear glass façades, protected by an outer shell with panes of tinted or etched glass that weaken direct sunlight without impeding the view.

Les grandes façades vitrées où se trouvent les chambres s'ouvrent au sud, elles sont en verre transparent dupliqué par une peau extérieure avec des franges en verre fumé ou sérigraphique qui protège contre la radiation directe du soleil, sans interrompre les vues.

Riesige Glasfassaden, dort wo die Hotelzimmer liegen, öffnen sich in Südrichtung. Das transparente Doppelglas wird aus einer Aussenbeschichtung aus getöntem oder bedrucktem Glasblenden versehen sein, die zwar gegen die direkte Sonneneinstrahlung schützen, aber gleichzeitig eine freie Aussicht garantieren werden.

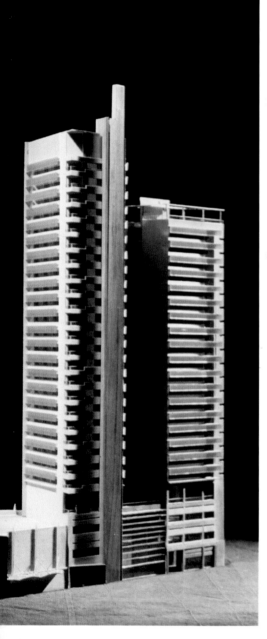

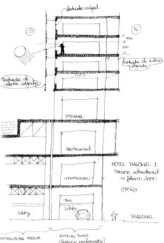

The idea of projecting a double tower stems from the desire to achieve a slim building. The building site is fractioned in two parts, increasing the sensation of height and visually strengthening the idea of a tower.

L'idée de concevoir une tour double est le fruit de la volonté d'obtenir un bâtiment svelte; le pâté est ainsi fractionné en deux volumes et la sensation de hauteur augmente, l'idée de tour est visuellement renforcée.

Die Idee eines Doppelturms entstand aus dem Wunsch, ein schlankes Gebäude zu errichten. Auf diese Art wird der Gebäudekomplex auf zwei Volumen verteilt, der Eindruck der Höhe wird verstärkt und bestärkt die visuelle Vorstellung des Turms.

HOTEL HESPERIA

RICHARD ROGERS PARTNERSHIP & ALONSO - BALAGUER ARQ. ASSOCIATS

CLIENT / CLIENT / AUFTRAGGEBER: HESPERIA

2002

TOTAL AREA / SURFACE TOTALE / GESAMTOBERFLÄCHE: 27.000 m²

FLOORS / PLANS / STOCKWERKE - HEIGHT / HAUTEUR / HÖHE: 32 fl / 105 m

Located in a new urban park of 2,5 hectares, the building is framed within a greater mixed-use operation and services package. Planned as an entrance gate to Barcelona on the edge of L'Hospitalet – the second highest populated city in Catalonia – it develops a hotel program of 304 rooms, a congress center with capacity for 4,500 people, an auditorium for 450 persons and a sports club. The building is crowned with a panoramic restaurant under a glass dome.

In the development of the program, sophisticated state of the art technology has been used for the structure and the electrical and water systems.

Situé sur un nouveau parc urbain de 2,5 hectares, le bâtiment appartient à une opération plus importante, usages mixtes, équipements et services. Conçu comme une porte d'entrée à Barcelone, sur les bords de L'Hospitalet –la seconde ville la plus peuplée de Catalogne– il développe un programme d'hôtel de 304 chambres, un centre de congrès pour 4.500 personnes, un auditorium pour 450 personnes et un club sportif. Le bâtiment est couronné d'un restaurant panoramique à coupole vitrée. Lors du développement du projet, on a employé une technologie de pointe sophistiquée sur la structure et les installations.

Gelegen in einem neuen 2,5 Hektar großen Stadtpark und als Multifunktionsgebäude geplant. Es soll zur Eingangstür Barcelonas am Stadtrand von L'Hospitalet werden, der zweitgrößten Stadt Kataloniens bezüglich der Einwohnerzahl. Ein Hotel mit 304 Zimmern, einem Kongresszentrum mit Platz für 4.500 Personen und einem Auditorium für 450 Personen sowie einem Sportclub. Das Gebäude wird von einem Panoramarestaurant in einer Glaskuppel gekrönt. Struktur und Einrichtungen wurden unter Anwendung außergewöhnlicher neuester Technologie geplant.

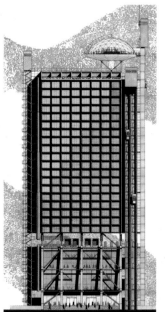

A rectangular prism is situated next to the cylindrical communication and electrical and water systems core, giving the whole a futuristic look.

Un prisme rectangulaire se trouve à côté du noyau cylindrique des communications et des installations, ce qui accorde à l'ensemble un aspect futuriste.

Ein rechteckiges Prisma daneben ein zylindrischer Bau, der die zentralen Versorgungsanlagen aufnimmt, vermitteln eine futuristische Ansicht.

HOTEL NOVA DIAGONAL

DOMINIQUE PERRAULT & VIRGÍNIA FIGUERAS

CLIENT / CLIENT / AUFTRAGGEBER: GRUP RIUSEC	**2004**

TOTAL AREA / SURFACE TOTALE / GESAMTOBERFLÄCHE: 28.000 m²

FLOORS / PLANS / STOCKWERKE - HEIGHT / HAUTEUR / HÖHE: 27 pl / 112,8 m

This building forms part of a series of skyscrapers that will be constructed during the next few years in Barcelona. The lack of a tradition of tall buildings means that the architects must find the means of relating the city (of constant height) and the skyscrapers which will automatically become an outstanding element from many points of the city. Dominique Perrault analyzes Barcelona as a horizontal city, that of the Eixample, and another vertical city, that of the towers of the Sagrada Família and the Olympic Village. The Hotel will respond to this reading with a building whose base is inserted in the horizontal city and whose body will be in the vertical city.

Ce bâtiment appartient à une série de gratte-ciel qui vont être construits prochainement à Barcelone. Le manque de tradition quant aux gratte-ciel oblige les architectes à trouver la façon de mettre en relation la ville (à hauteur constante) et le gratte-ciel qui sera automatiquement un élément remarquable depuis plusieurs points de la ville. Dominique Perrault analyse Barcelone comme une ville horizontale, celle de l'Eixample, et l'autre verticale, celle des tours de La Sagrada Família et de la Vila Olímpica. L'Hôtel correspondra à cette lecture avec un bâtiment dont la base s'inscrit dans la ville horizontale et le corps dans la verticale.

Dieses Gebäude wird das einer Serie von Wolkenkratzern sein, die in den kommenden Jahren in Barcelona errichtet werden. Da Hochhäuser in dieser Stadt bisher kaum üblich waren, müssen die Architekten nun einen Weg finden, diesen Wolkenkratzer in das Stadtbild (mit gleichmäßiger Bauhöhe) einzubinden, so daß er automatisch ein herausragendes Element sein wird, das von vielen Stellen in der Stadt aus zu erkennen sein wird. Dominique Perrault analysierte Barcelona mit seinem Eixample als Horizontale, die Türme der Sagrada Família und des olympischen Dorfes als Vertikale. Das Hotel entspricht dieser Erkenntnis und fügt seinen Unterbau in die Horizontalstadt und den Turm in die Vertikalstadt ein.

The morphology of the building creates a set of volumes, a cube (the base) which acts as a counterpoint to a parallelepiped (the body of the tower).

La morphologie du bâtiment crée un jeu de volumes, un cube (la base) qui est le contrepoint d'un parallélépipède (le corps de la tour).

Gebäude als Spiel der Volumen. Ein Kubus (Unterbau) mit Parallelepipedum (Turm).

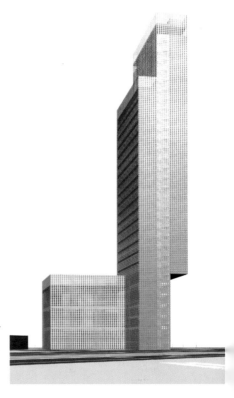

The building will house a five-star hotel and conference center, with gymnasium, restaurants, swimming pool and bar on the terrace of the cube-building.

Le bâtiment logera un hôtel à cinq étoiles et un centre de conférences, avec un gymnase, des restaurants, une piscine et un bar sur la terrasse du bâtiment-cube.

Ein 5 Sterne-Hotel und Konferenzzentrum mit Fitnessräumen, Restaurants, Schwimmbad und Bar auf der Terrasse des Kubusgebäudes werden entstehen.

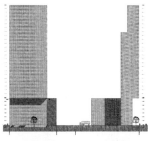

Each room will have exterior views as if the façade were a great screen made up of small apertures. These work like television sets constructing the wall of the façade through images.

Chaque chambre disposera de vues à l'extérieur, comme si la façade était un grand écran avec des petites ouvertures. Celles-ci jouent le rôle de télévisions, elles construisent le mur de la façade avec les images.

Jedes Zimmer wird durch Öffnungen in der Fassade Aussenansichten haben. Diese Öffnungen in der Außenhaut wirken wie eine Art Bildschirm.

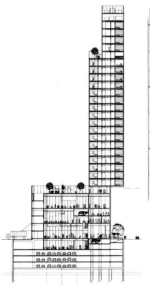

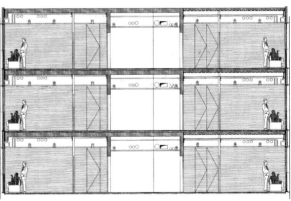

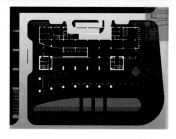

I&C BANK OF CHINA

FOX & FOWLE ARCHITECTS + FFGL PARTNERSHIP

CLIENT / CLIENT / AUFTRAGGEBER: THE INDUSTRIAL AND COMERCIAL BANK OF CHINA	**2000**
TOTAL AREA / SURFACE TOTALE / GESAMTOBERFLÄCHE: 58.000 m²	
FLOORS / PLANS / STOCKWERKE - HEIGHT / HAUTEUR / HÖHE: 28 fl / 114 m	

This is the first of five towers planned for the financial district of Pudong. To respond to the place, orientation and the program, the building is organized between three blocks (masses) which are interwoven parallel to the Pudong Avenue. Two frontal masses form the tower containing the private spaces and the third (not as tall) takes the traditional urban scale back up. It contains the public functions and shared private functions like rest areas and conference rooms. The access square to the building acts as an oasis in the middle of the urban boisterousness and the use of the traditional Chinese language, by means of bridges and artificial ponds, gives it a tempo that turns the transit towards the interior into an experience.

Elle est la première des cinq tours prévues pour le district financier de Pudong. Afin de répondre aux exigences du lieu, de l'orientation et du programme, le bâtiment est organisé sur trois blocs (masses) connectés parallèles à l'Avenue Pudong. Deux masses frontales établissent la tour, elles contiennent les espaces privés et la troisième (plus petite) reprend l'échelle urbaine traditionnelle. Elle inclut les fonctions publiques et les privées communes ainsi que des zones de repos et des salles de conférences. La place d'accès au bâtiment agit comme un oasis en plein mouvement urbain et l'utilisation du langage traditionnel chinois, avec les ponts et les étangs artificieux, la dote d'un tempo qui convertit le passage à l'intérieur en expérience.

Der erste von fünf geplanten Türmen im Finanzviertel von Pudong. Um sich dem Viertel, der Lage und dem Bauprogramm anzupassen, besteht das Gebäude aus drei parallel zur Pudong Ave verlaufenden Blöcken (Baumassen). Zwei der Gebäude ergeben den Turm, der Unternehmen beherbergt und das dritte, niedriger errichtet, hat die Höhe der umliegenden traditionellen Bebauung beibehalten. Hier befinden sich öffentliche Bereiche wie aber auch Erholungszonen und Konferenzräume. Der vor dem Komplex liegende Platz ist eine Oase im quirligen Stadtbild, der mit Brücken, künstlichen Teichen sowie Tempel die chinesische Tradition verkörpert, sodaß der Eintritt in das Gebäude zum Erlebnis wird.

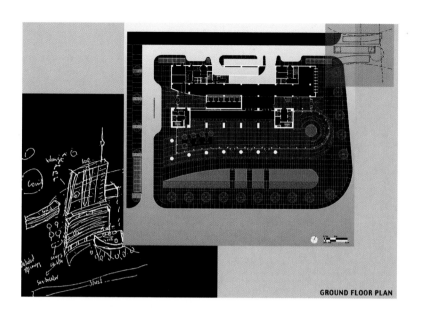

GROUND FLOOR PLAN

LONGITUDINAL SECTION

Rationality in the design of areas destined to work space contrasts with the gestural flexibility of public spaces.

La rationalité de la conception des espaces consacrés au travail contraste avec la flexibilité gestuelle des espaces publiques.

Das rationale Design der Arbeitsumgebungen kontrastiert mit der großzügigen Gestik der öffentlich genutzten Räumlichkeiten.

The approach of the building is perceptible in the composition of its façades; the opaque north contrasts with the south, which is completely open to the exterior. Protected by a "brise-soleil" and crowned by a sunshade, glass combines with stainless steel and granite.

L'orientation du bâtiment est percevable sur la composition des façades, celle du nord, opaque, comparée à celle du sud qui s'ouvre complètement vers l'extérieur. Protégée par un "brise-soleil" et couronnée d'un parasol, le verre est combiné avec l'acier inoxydable et le granite.

Die Ausrichtung des Gebäudes ist an der Zusammensetzung der Außenseiten zu erkennen. Die Nordseite ist lichtundurchlässig, die Südseite öffnet sich nach außen. Sie wird von einer sogenannten "bris-solei" und einer Gebäudebedachung in Form eines Sonnenschirms geschützt. Das Glas der Aussenseite wurde mit Edelstahl und Granit kombiniert.

The base of the tower is a volume which is characterised by the curved, inclined forms of the north side that swirl around the corner behind the pillars on the ground floor on the south-facing façade, which provides access to the large foyer that connects the public and the private areas.

La base de la tour est un volume qui est caractérisé par les formes courbes et inclinées du côté nord qui tourne sur le coin et passe derrière les piliers au rez-de-chaussée de la façade sud où l'on accède au grand hall qui connecte le public et le privé.

Der Turmsockel charakterisiert sich durch seine geschwungenen Formen, die sich zur Nordseite neigen und sich hinter den Säulen über die südliche Erdgeschoßaußenseite an der großen Eingangshalle ziehen, dort wo sich der öffentliche Bereich mit dem privaten verbinden.

TRANSVERSE SECTION

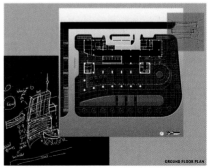

GROUND FLOOR PLAN

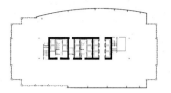

IDX TOWER

ZIMMER GUNSUL FRASCA PARTNERSHIP (ZGF)

CLIENT / CLIENT / AUFTRAGGEBER: HINES INTERESTS LIMITED PARTNERSHIP

TOTAL AREA / SURFACE TOTALE / GESAMTOBERFLÄCHE: 97.800 m²

FLOORS / PLANS / STOCKWERKE - HEIGHT / HAUTEUR / HÖHE: 38 fl / 134 m

2002

Conceived by private promoters as the biggest building constructed in Seattle in the last decade, its program includes an underground car park with 637 spaces, a three-floor base which includes shopping and public areas and two juxtaposed towers of offices of 38 and 32 floors. The architectural expression of the building seeks to distinguish itself from other nearby financial districts through the creation of a slender tower covered in lightly colored metal and a glass-covered curtain wall. The building incorporates high level technological features, ready to enter the 21st Century.

Conçu par un promoteur privé comme le bâtiment le plus grand construit à Seattle pendant les dix dernières années, son programme inclut un parking souterrain à 637 places, une base de trois étages qui disposent des surfaces commerciales et de relations et de deux tours juxtaposées de bureaux de 38 et de 32 étages. L'expression architectonique du bâtiment recherche une distinction face aux autres districts financiers proches grâce à la création d'une tour svelte recouverte de métal légèrement coloré et un mur rideau vitré. Le bâtiment incorpore performances technologiques à haut niveau, il est préparé pour le XXIème siècle.

Als jemals größtes Privatgebäude der vergangenen Jahrzehnts in Seattle entworfen. Es wird über 637 unterirdische Parkplätze, einem 3 stöckigen Unterbau mit Geschäftsbereichen und zwei nebeneinander aufragenden Bürotürmen mit 38 und 32 Stockwerken verfügen. Die Architektur dieses eleganten Gebäudes möchte sich von anderen im Finanzviertel der Stadt gelegenen Bauten durch seine leicht kolorierte Metallaußenhaut und Verglasung unterscheiden. Das Gebäude wird den höchsten technologischen Anforderungen gerecht, um in das 21. Jahrhundert zu starten.

The project, on a site occupying three corners of a block at a different levels, takes advantage of this to generate a base with multiple entrances.

Le projet, dont l'emplacement occupe trois coins d'un pâté à un niveau différent, il engendre ainsi une base à accès multiples.

Der Bau liegt an drei Straßenecken mit unterschiedlichem Gefälle, so daß sich mehrfache Zugangsmöglichkeiten zum Gebäude ergeben.

The façade will be formed by a curtain wall which has the particular feature of being sustained by structural glass and lightly colored metal.

La façade est constituée d'un mur rideau particulier, elle se maintient sur du verre structurel et du métal légèrement coloré.

Die Besonderheit der Fassade besteht in einer Außenhaut, die von der Glasstruktur und leicht koloriertem Metall gehalten wird.

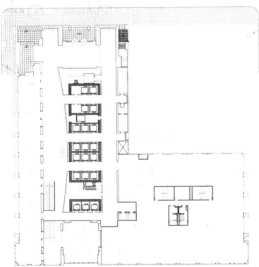

The entrance floor allows crossed traffic and distribution, avoiding communication cores in the relation areas in the lower body.

L'étage d'accès permet des circulations en croix et une distribution, évitant les noyaux de communications des surfaces de relations sur le corps du bas.

Die Eingangsetage ermöglicht den freien Durchgang in alle Richtungen ohne dabei auf die Aufzugsbereiche zu treffen, die sich im unterem Gebäudebereich befinden.

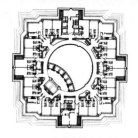

JIN MAO TOWER

SKIDMORE, OWINGS & MERRILL LLP SOM

CLIENT / CLIENT / AUFTRAGGEBER: CHINA SHANGHAI FOREIGN TRADE CO. LTD.

1988

TOTAL AREA / SURFACE TOTALE / GESAMTOBERFLÄCHE: 279.000 m²

FLOORS / PLANS / STOCKWERKE - HEIGHT / HAUTEUR / HÖHE: 88 fl / 420,6 m

This building, which is currently the tallest in China, is sited in the commercial and financial district of Pudong. It is a multi-use complex (offices, hotel, shopping center, conference halls, exhibitions and cinema) distributed between the tower and a six-floor podium building. The base of the tower is surrounded by a garden courtyard with a pond. The entrance lobby is a glass shopping atrium with wavy forms which give the visitor a lively spatial experience. The architecture of Jin Mao is reminiscent of the forms of Chinese pagodas, based on multiples of eight (traditonally a lucky number in China). Its metallic profile takes on different color ranges as the sun slides over its articulated surfaces, to become a lighthouse of the Shanghai sky when night falls.

Ce bâtiment qui est actuellement le plus haut de Chine se trouve dans le district commercial et financier de Pudong. Il s'agit d'un complexe à usages multiples (bureaux, hôtel, centre commercial, salles de conférences, expositions et cinéma) distribués entre la tour et un bâtiment-podium d'une hauteur de six étages. La base de la tour est entourée d'une cour avec des jardins et un étang. Le hall d'accès, un parvis commercial vitré aux formes ondulantes qui apporte une vive expérience spatiale au visiteur. L'architecture du Jin Mao nous fait penser aux formes de las pagodes chinoises, il a pour base les multiples de huit (le chiffre porte bonheur dans la tradition Chinoise), son profil métallique acquiert des gammes chromatiques différentes selon le déplacement du soleil sur les surfaces articulées et devient un phare du ciel de Shanghai lorsque la nuit tombe.

Gegenwärtig China's höchstes Gebäude im Handels- und Finanzviertel von Pudong gelegen. Diese Multifunktionsanlage (mit Büros, Hotel, Einkaufszentrum, Konferenzsälen, Ausstellungsräume und Kino) verteilt sich auf einem Tower und einem podiumförmigen 6stöckigen Gebäude. Die Turm ist von einer Grünanlage mit Teich umgeben. Der Eingangshalle ist ein verglastes wellenförmig angelegtes Atrium und vermittelt dem Besucher das Gefühl, sich im Weltraum zu befinden. Die Architektur des Jin Mao erinnert an chinesischen Pagoden, die in der geschwungenen Form der Zahl 8 (in der chinesischen Tradition eine Glückszahl) errichtet wurden. Die Metallkontur der gegliederten Aussenflächen schillert je nach Stand der Sonne in verschiedenen Farbstufen und vermittelt bei Anbruch der Nacht den Eindruck eines Leuchtturms am Himmel von Shanghai.

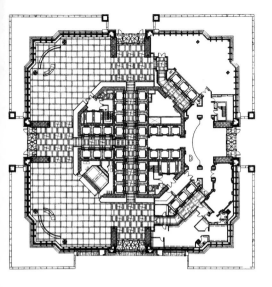

The base of the tower holds a shopping area, an auditorium and spaces connected with the five-star Grand Hyatt Hotel. Offices take up the next 47 floors and the following 38 floors contain the hotel, with spectacular view from its more than 500 rooms.

La base de la tour auberge une zone commerciale, un auditorium et des espaces relatifs au Grand Hotel Hyatt à cinq étoiles. Les bureaux se trouvent sur les 47 étages suivants et sur les 38 autres s'étend l'hôtel, avec des vues spectaculaires depuis plus de 500 chambres.

Im unteren Geschoß des Turms befindet sich eine Shoppingmeile, ein Auditorium und Räumlichkeiten, die mit dem 5-Sterne Gran Hotel Hyatt verbinden. Büroräume belegen die nächsten 47 Etagen und in den 38 nachfolgenden befindet sich das Hotel mit seinen spektakulären Aussichten aus mehr als 500 Zimmern.

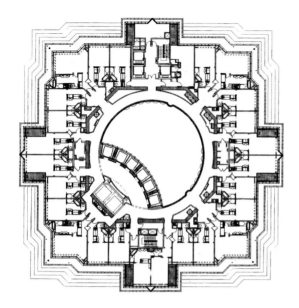

Beneath the ground floor there are three underground parking levels, hotel facilities, a shopping area, a courtyard, a foyer and areas set aside for electrical, water and waste treatment installations, as well as central heating and airconditioning units.

Sous le niveau du sol se trouvent trois niveaux de parking, des installations de l'hôtel, un espace commercial, une cour, un hall et des dépendances pour les installations électriques, l'eau, le traitement des résidus et des équipements en chauffage et climatisation.

3 unterirdische Etagen beherbergen Parkplätze, Hoteleinrichtungen, einen Einkaufsbereich, einen Innenhof, ein Vestibül und Versorgungsanlagen wie Strom, Wasser, Müllaufbereitung, Heizung und Klimatisierung.

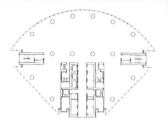

JIUSHI CORP. HQTRS.

FOSTER & PARTNERS

CLIENT / CLIENT / AUFTRAGGEBER: JIUSHI CORPORATION	**2000**
TOTAL AREA / SURFACE TOTALE / GESAMTOBERFLÄCHE: 62.000 m²	
FLOORS / PLANS / STOCKWERKE - HEIGHT / HAUTEUR / HÖHE: 40 fl / 168 m	

The Chinese city of Shanghai has experienced a drastic transformation caused by the emergence of tall office buildings. The location of this building, half way between the river and the traditional neighborhoods, conditions its structure (form and layout). Thus, a semi-circular glass-covered façade opens towards the river and two sloping planes towards the city. The building tries to propose a respectful architecture to the city and people, proposing novel mechanisms like the triple ventilated façade system which allows natural light to enter without altering the energetic behavior of the interior of the building, or the incorporation of gardens in the interior of the building.

La ville chinoise de Shanghai a constaté une transformation drastique provoquée par l'émergence de grands immeubles de bureaux. L'emplacement de ce bâtiment, à cheval entre la rivière et deux quartiers traditionels, détermine sa structure (forme et distribution). Ainsi, une façade vitrée en demi-cercle s'ouvre sur la rivière et deux plans inclinés sur la ville. Le bâtiment propose une architecture respectueuse face à la ville et aux personnes, il propose de mécanismes nouveaux comme le système de triple façade ventilée qui laisse pénétrer la lumière naturelle sans altérer le comportement énergétique de l'intérieur du bâtiment ou l'incorporation de jardins à l'intérieur du bâtiment.

Die chinesische Stadt Shanghai erfuhr durch die Entstehung von hohen Bürotürmen eine drastische Veränderung.
Die Lage zwischen dem Fluß und zwei traditionellen Stadtvierteln bestimmen die Baustruktur in ihrem Umriß und Verteilung. Eine halbkreisförmige Glasfassade öffnet sich zur Flußseite und zur Stadtseite liegen zwei zueinander strebende Seitenteile. Die Architektur dieses Gebäudes möchte der Stadt und seinen Menschen respektvoll gegenübertreten und bietet Vorteile wie z.B. natürliche Ventilation der dreiseitigen Fassade, rundherum Tageslichteinfall ohne den Energieverbrauch im Gebäude oder die Innengärten zu beeinträchtigen.

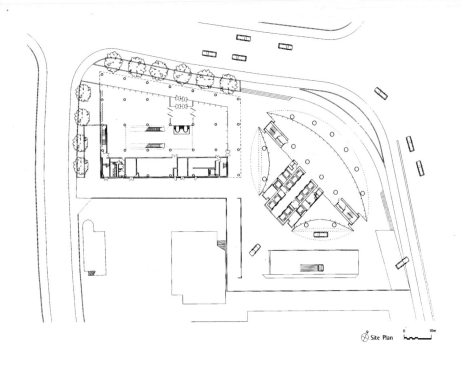

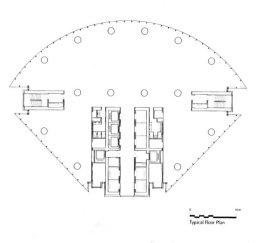

Typical Floor Plan

The tower is located on the corner of a lot with a gentle gesture, next to the base, a six-floor building with shops, restaurants and bars follows the line of the street, a porch with arcades is situated on the ground floor, reminiscent of the city's traditional shops.

La tour est placée sur un coin du terrain avec un geste suave; près de la base, un bâtiment à six étages avec des boutiques, des restaurants et des bars suit l'alignement de la rue, un porche avec des arcades se trouve au rez-de-chaussée, il a l'aspect des boutiques traditionnelles de la ville.

Der Turm liegt auf einem Eckgrundstück mit sanfter Kurvengestik.. Der Unterbau, in dem über 6 Stockwerke Läden, Restaurants und Bars verteilt liegen, sowie der darüber errichtete Turm folgen der Linie des Straßenverlaufs. Arkadendurchgänge in der unteren Etage erinnern an die typischen Läden der Stadt.

Site Plan

The tower occupies a very significant neighborhood in the city which has been turned into a new financial area. Jiushi Corporation's investments have helped in the development of the South Bund and its building wishes to be a positive symbol of the new economic and town planning development of the city.

La tour se trouve dans un quartier très significatif de la ville qui est devenu une nouvelle aire financière. Les investissements de la Jiushi Corporation ont permis le développement du South Bund et son bâtiment désire être un symbole positif du nouveau développement économique et urbanistique de la ville.

Der Turm entstand in einem Stadtteil, der sich mittlerweile zu einem neuen Finanzviertel entwickelt hat. Die Investitionen der Jiushi Corporation in den South Bund tragen mit diesem Gebäude als positives Symbol zum wirtschaftlichen und städtebaulichen Fortschritt der Stadt bei.

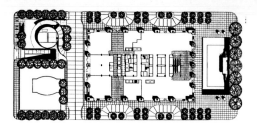

JOHN HANCOCK CENTER

SKIDMORE, OWINGS & MERILL LLP (SOM)

CLIENT / CLIENT / AUFTRAGGEBER: JOHN HANCOCK MUTUAL LIFE INSURANCE CO.

1969

TOTAL AREA / SURFACE TOTALE / GESAMTOBERFLÄCHE: 260.000 m²

FLOORS / PLANS / STOCKWERKE - HEIGHT / HAUTEUR / HÖHE: 100 fl / 344 m

Popularly known as Big John, it occupies a dominant place in the city's skyline. The complexity of the program (offices, shopping areas, leisure and residential zones) reflects the multiple activities of the luxurious district where it is located. The tower, whose surface area shrinks from the ground floor to the top floor, contains a chunk of the city. The base contains the shopping and leisure areas together with the lobbies of the office floors immediately above. Half way up are the 711 apartments of different typologies which have their own lobbies and parking spaces. The metallic structural system is the material of the façade, which acts as a corset, strengthening the building along with the structural floors.

Il est populairement connu comme Big John et il se trouve à un endroit élevé sur la ligne de l'horizon de la ville. La complexité du programme (bureaux, zones commerciales, loisirs et parc immobilier) représente la multiplicité des activités du luxueux district où il se trouve. La tour dont la surface diminue du rez-de-chaussée jusqu'au dernier étage, contient un morceau de ville. Sur la base se trouvent les zones commerciales et de loisirs, avec les halls des étages de bureaux qui sont juste au dessus, sur une hauteur moyenne sont disposés les 711 appartements de différents types qui disposent de halls propres et de parkings. Le système de structure métallique est le matériau de la façade, il agit comme un corset, il rend le bâtiment rigide et aussi les étages structurels.

Populär auch bekannt als Big John, ragt dieses Gebäude am Horizont der Stadt heraus. Die Angebotsfülle (Büros, Shopping- und Freizeitbereiche sowie Wohnungen) spiegelt die Lebhaftigkeit dieses vornehmen Stadtviertels wieder. Der Tower, der sich vom Erdgeschoss bis in das oberste Stockwerk verjüngt, ist eine eigene Stadt. Im Erdgeschoss befinden sich Shopping- und Freizeitbereiche neben der Eingangshallen für die darüber gelegenen Büroetagen. Auf halber Höhe befinden sich 711 Appartments unterschiedlichster Art, die über eigene Eingangshallen und Parkmöglichkeiten verfügen. Die Fassade besteht aus einer korsettähnlichen Metallstruktur.

Due to the considerable functional approach required by the John Hancock Center, a 70-storey office block and a 45-storey apartment block, the building site was too small. The problem was resolved by building a sole, 100-storey tower that freed a large portion of the ground floor.

À cause du programme fonctionnel importante requis par le Centre John Hancock, une tour de bureaux de 70 étages et une autre de 45 étages à appartements, représentait une surface qui dépassait du terrain permis. Pour résoudre cela, on construisit une seule tour de 100 étages, ce qui libéra une grande partie du rez-de-chaussée.

Aufgrund eines bedeutenden funktionellen Programms, sollte das John Hancock Center mit einem 70stöckigem Büroturm sowie einem weiteren von 45 Stockwerken mit Apartments entstehen. Allerdings überschritt dieses Ausmaß die Kapazität des Grundstücks, sodaß man sich für den Bau eines einzigen Turmes mit 100 Stockwerken entschieden hat.

The core of the tapered tower lends structural stability to the whole and resolves the functional requirements at the same time. The tower gradually tapers from the ground floor to the top, with offices on the lower floors and apartments on the upper floors.

Le tronc de la tour étranglé apporte une stabilité structurelle à l'ensemble et résout aussi les besoins fonctionnels, de façon à ce que la tour rétrécit sa surface du rez-de-chaussée au dernier étage, elle auberge des bureaux sur les étages du bas et des appartements sur celles de haut.

Der Turmstumpf in spindelförmiger Ausführung verleiht der Baustruktur Stabilität und ermöglicht andererseits eine funktionelle Verteilung der Flächen. So verringert der Turm bei wachsender Höhe seine Oberfläche. In den unteren Etagen befinden sich Büroräume und in den oberen Apartments.

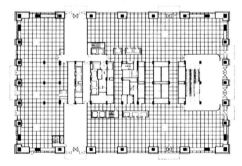

The tower's rigidity is achieved through diagonal elements on the façade together with the structural floors, which are determined by the intersection of diagonal elements and corner pillars. In its time, this great tubular structure was both innovative and economical.

La rigidité de la tour est obtenue grâce aux éléments diagonaux sur la façade près des étages structurels qui sont déterminés par les intersections des éléments diagonaux et des piliers sur les coins. Cette grande structure tubulaire fut à cette époque innovatrice et économique.

Die Turmsteifigkeit wird durch diagonal verlaufende Bauelemente an der Aussenseite, gemeinsam mit den Strukturetagen erreicht, welche durch die Schnittstellen der Diagonalelemente und den Eckpfeilern des Turms bestimmt werden. Diese großartige Schlauchstruktur galt zum gegebenen Moment als innovativ und kostengünstig.

The steel structure that makes up the façade is covered with black aluminium and anti-dazzle glass with bronze coloured window frames. Both the base of the building and its several foyers are walled with travertine marble.

La façade, la structure en acier, est recouverte d'aluminium noir et de vitres anti-réfléchissantes avec des cadres en aluminium d'une couleur bronze sur les fenêtres. Aussi bien la base du bâtiment que les différents halls disposent d'un placage en marbre travertin.

Die Fassade besteht aus einer Stahlstruktur überzogen mit schwarzem Aluminium und nichtreflektierender Fensterverglasung, die von bronzefarbenen Aluminiumrahmen eingefaßt ist. Sowohl der Gebäudesockel wie auch die verschiedenen Eingangshallen sind mit Travertinomarmor ausgestattet.

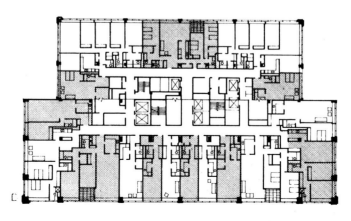

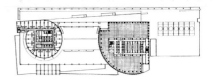

JR CENTRAL TOWER & STATION

KOHN PEDERSEN FOX ASSOCIATES PC (KPF)

CLIENT / CLIENT / AUFTRAGGEBER: JR TOKAI

2000

TOTAL AREA / SURFACE TOTALE / GESAMTOBERFLÄCHE: 409.000 m²

FLOORS / PLANS / STOCKWERKE - HEIGHT / HAUTEUR / HÖHE: 59 fl / 250 m

The JR Central is a complex for different uses like shops, hotel, cultural center, offices, car park and a train station. It is a complex work of architecture and engineering because apart from the metro, there are other trains circulating and it is ready to welcome the magnetic train in the future (which is in the development phase). The structural solution plays a very important role in the design of the building because it conditions it, allowing a large and complex mixed-use building with the great flows of people an intermodal station implies. The JR Central works as a door to the 21st Century.

Le JR Central est un complexe à usages différents: des boutiques, un hôtel, un centre culturel, des bureaux, un parking et une gare. Il s'agit d'une oeuvre architectonique complexe et de génie car le métro et d'autres trains y passent, elle est prête pour recevoir, dans le futur, le train magnétique (qui se trouve en développement). La solution structurelle joue un rôle très important sur la conception du bâtiment car il le conditionne, permettant un bâtiment grand et complexe à usages mixtes, son affluence importante de personnes correspond à celui d'une gare intermodale. Le JR Central représente une porte sur le XXIème siècle.

JR Central als Multifunktionskomplex mit Läden, Hotel, Kulturzentrum, Büros, Parking und Bahnstation. Eine architektonische sowie ingenieurtechnische Hochleistung, die neben der Metro und anderer Züge, in Zukunft auch die Magnetschwebebahn (in Entwicklung) aufnehmen wird. Die strukturelle Lösung spielte eine besondere herausragende Rolle beim Design des Baues, denn der Bau muß zur Aufnahme von großen Menschenmengen fähig sein, die sich üblicherweise in einem Gebäude mit Mehrfachfunktionen bewegen. Das JR Central gilt als Tor in das 21. Jahrhundert.

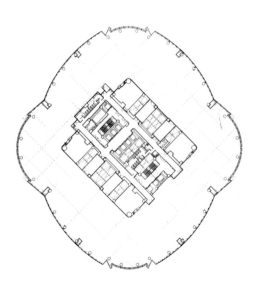

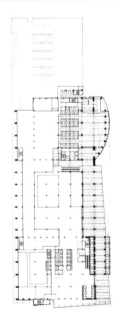

The layout of the towers corresponds to the offices and hotel program, in both cases, the communications are concentrated in the center, leaving the rest of the space free.

La distribution des tours correspond au programme de bureaux et hôtel, elle concentre dans les deux cas les communications au centre, ce qui libère l'espace restant.

Im Büro- sowie im Hotelturm liegen die Lift- und andere Versorgungsanlagen in der Mitte der Gebäude und schaffen so eine größeres Platzangebot.

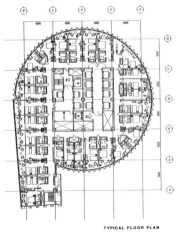

TYPICAL FLOOR PLAN

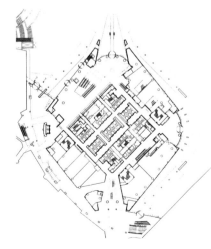

The vertical elements intersect with horizontal volume. The composition of all the façades is based on the rhythm of stripes.

Les éléments verticaux s'intersectionnent avec le volume horizontal. La composition de toutes les façades a pour base le rythme des franges.

Vertikale Elemente überschneiden sich mit horizontalen Volumen. Sämtliche Fassaden bestehen aus sich gleichmäßig abwechselnder Längst- und Querstrukturen.

North-South Sectional View

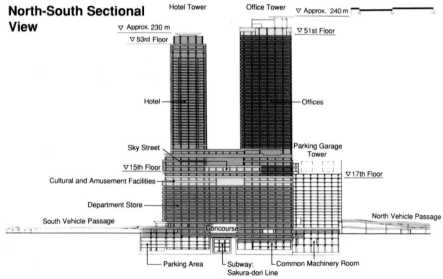

Hotel Tower
Office Tower
▽ Approx. 240 m
▽ Approx. 230 m
▽ 51st Floor
▽ 53rd Floor
Hotel
Offices
Sky Street
Parking Garage Tower
▽ 15th Floor
▽ 17th Floor
Cultural and Amusement Facilities
Department Store
North Vehicle Passage
South Vehicle Passage
Concourse
Parking Area
Subway: Sakura-dori Line
Common Machinery Room

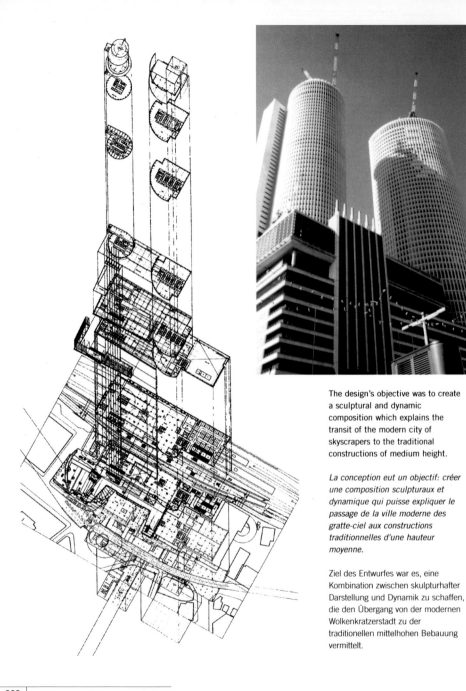

The design's objective was to create a sculptural and dynamic composition which explains the transit of the modern city of skyscrapers to the traditional constructions of medium height.

La conception eut un objectif: créer une composition sculpturaux et dynamique qui puisse expliquer le passage de la ville moderne des gratte-ciel aux constructions traditionnelles d'une hauteur moyenne.

Ziel des Entwurfes war es, eine Kombination zwischen skulpturhafter Darstellung und Dynamik zu schaffen, die den Übergang von der modernen Wolkenkratzerstadt zu der traditionellen mittelhohen Bebauung vermittelt.

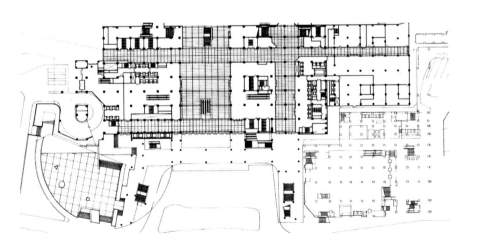

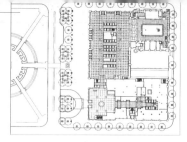

KEY TOWER

CESAR PELLI & ASSOCIATES INC.

1991

CLIENT / CLIENT / AUFTRAGGEBER: RICHARD & DAVID JACOBS GROUP	
TOTAL AREA / SURFACE TOTALE / GESAMTOBERFLÄCHE: 116.200 m²	
FLOORS / PLANS / STOCKWERKE - HEIGHT / HAUTEUR / HÖHE: 57 fl / 289,6 m	

This office tower, also known as Society Center, is found between the two main public spaces of the city center, the Mall and the Public Square. It is situated next to the Society for Savings Bank (1890, Burnham y Root). The base follows the basic lines of the Society from the stone cladding, the changes of material and the treatment of the façade plan which moves towards the interior for the tower to rise gently without absorbing the building, which is much less tall. Both buildings form part of the same financial entity, which is why they are connected internally, although this is not reflected in the exterior treatment.

Cette tour de bureaux, connue aussi comme le Society Center, se trouve entre deux des principaux espaces publiques principales du centre de la ville, le Mall et la Public Square. Il se trouve à côté de Society for Savings Bank (1890, Burnham y Root). La base suit les lignes principales du Society à partir du revêtement en pierre, les changements de matériau et le traitement de la surface de la façade qui se déplace vers l'intérieur pour ainsi élever la tour doucement sans absorber le bâtiment, plus petit. Les deux bâtiments appartiennent à la même société financière, ce qui explique pourquoi ils sont connectés à l'intérieur même si le traitement extérieur ne permet pas de le distinguer.

Büroturm, auch als Society Centre bekannt, zwischen den Plätzen bekannt als "Mall" und "Public Square"– direkt neben dem Gebäude der Society for Savings Bank (1890, Burnham und Root) gelegen. Der Unterbau paßt sich den Grundlinien der Steinfassade des Societygebäudes an. Nach einem Materialwechsel und anschließendem stufenähnlichem Zurücksetzen zur Fassadenmitte erhebt sich der Turm sanft und absorbiert somit nicht das wesentlich niedrigere Nebengebäude. Beide Bauten gehören zur selben Bank und sind im Innern miteinander verbunden, was allerdings an der Außenfassade nicht zu erkennen ist.

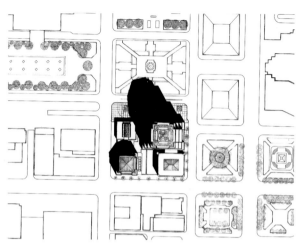

Siting plan of the tower which is situated in the northern corner of the Public Square, where the BP America Tower and the Terminal Towers are also located.

Plan de l'emplacement de la tour qui se trouve sur le coin nord de la Public Square, où l'on trouve aussi la BP America Tower et les tours Terminal.

Lageplan des Turms. Er liegt an der Nordseite des Public Square, wo sich außerdem der BP America Tower und die Terminal Towers befinden.

The tower gradually loses mass as it rises, starting out from the base which is at the same height as the Society, an example of the classical American skyscraper of the end of the 19th Century.

La tour perd de la masse selon elle s'élève, en partant de la base qui est à la hauteur du Society, un exemple du gratte-ciel classique américain de la fin du XIXème siècle.

In dem Moment, in dem der Turm über die Höhe des Societygebäudes (klassisches Beispiel amerikanischer Wolkenkratzer des 19. Jahrhunderts) hinausgeht, verliert er an Umfang.

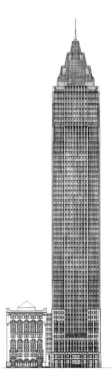

LEE THEATRE PLAZA

DENNIS LAU & NG CHUN MAN
ARCHITECTS & ENGINEERS (H.K) LTD

CLIENT / CLIENT / AUFTRAGGEBER: HYSAN DEVELOPMENT COMPANY LIMITED

1994

TOTAL AREA / SURFACE TOTALE / GESAMTOBERFLÄCHE: 29.300 m²

FLOORS / PLANS / STOCKWERKE - HEIGHT / HAUTEUR / HÖHE: 24 fl / 99 m

The building is a high-rise shopping center, its classical style is a reference to the large department stores of the past. The project has 22 commercial floors in a tower, which contain shops, stores, restaurants and a cinema, which rise above two more floors, defined by the base of the building, where the projects are developed for access, relationship with the city and the most public activities of the complex. Formally, the tower is a series of prisms which combine with a glass-covered cylinder topped with a dome which contains viewing platform spaces related to the patio.

Le bâtiment est un centre commercial en hauteur, le style classique fait référence aux grandes surfaces commerciales du passé. Le projet dispose de 22 étages commerciaux sur une tour, qui englobe des boutiques, des magasins, des restaurants et une salle de cinéma, qui s'élèvent sur deux autres étages, définies par la base du bâtiment, où se développent les espaces d'accès, de relation avec la ville et les activité publiques du complexe. Du point de vue formel, la tour est une série de prismes combinés par un cylindre vitré dont le sommet est une coupole qui contient des espaces de mirador en relation avec la cour.

Hier handelt es sich um ein Einkaufszentrum, das den klassischen Stil der früheren großen Kaufhäuser übernommen hat. 22 Geschäftsetagen mit Boutiquen, Warenhäusern, Restaurants und einem Cinema über einem Unterbau, in dem sich Eingangs- und Durchgangspassage befindet. Die Außenflächen des Gebäudes entsprechen einer Reihe von Prismen, krönender Dachabschluß ist eine gläserne Aussichtskuppel in zylindrischer Form über dem offenen Innenhof.

The design of the main staircase aims for continuity from the lobby to the dome by means of an interior patio.

La conception de l'escalier principal recherche la continuité du hall à la coupole avec une cour intérieure.

Die Gestaltung des Treppenhauses erlangt eine durchgehende Linie vom Vestibül bis in die Dachkuppel durch die Schaffung eines offenen Innenhofes.

The public areas of the building aim to express their social vocation by means of the use of triple spaces and viewing platforms.

Les espaces des relations du bâtiment recherchent l'expression de leur vocation sociale avec les triples espaces et les miradors.

Gesellschaftlicher Treffpunkt verteilt über drei Etagen mit Aussichtspunkten.

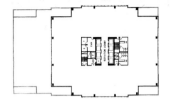

LIBERTY PLACE

MURPHY / JAHN INC. ARCHITECTS + ZEIDER ROBERTS

CLIENT / CLIENT / AUFTRAGGEBER: ROUSE & ASSOCIATES

1990

TOTAL AREA / SURFACE TOTALE / GESAMTOBERFLÄCHE: 112.000 m² (I) + 111.600 m² (II)

FLOORS / PLANS / STOCKWERK : 61 fl / 58 fl
HEIGHT / HAUTEUR / HÖME: 288 m (I) / 258,5 m (II)

The Liberty Place complex was the first to rise above the height limit of 150 meters, defined by the upper part of the William Penn (the founder of the city) statute in the City Hall. In 1983, a promoter presented a plan to build two office buildings, the Liberty Place towers, several blocks from City Hall, in Market Street. Following its approval, the plan radically altered the city's silhouette, because the municipal council established a special corridor of high-rise buildings along this street. With the construction of Two Liberty Place, a shopping complex and a hotel were incorporated into the program.

Le complexe Liberty Place fut le premier qui s'éleva au-dessus de la limite en hauteur de 150 mètres, défini sur la partie supérieure par la statue de William Penn (le fondateur de la ville) au City Hall. En 1983, un promoteur présenta un plan pour construire deux immeubles de bureaux, les tours Liberty Place à plusieurs pâtés du City Hall, à Market Street. Après l'accord, le plan modifia radicalement la silhouette de la ville, car le conseil municipal établit un couloir spécial de grands bâtiments au long de cette rue. Lors de la construction de la Two Liberty Place un complexe commercial et un hôtel s'incorporèrent au programme.

Der Liberty Place war der erste Gebäudekomplex, der über die Höhe von 150 Meter der William Penn-Statue (dem Gründer der Stadt) in der City Hall hinaus errichtet wurde. 1983 präsentierte ein Promoter einen Entwurf zweier Bürotürme einige Ecken von der City Hall entfernt, in der Market Street und zwar die Liberty Place–Türme. Nachdem das Projekt genehmigt wurde, veränderte sich der Bauplan drastisch, denn der Stadtrat beschloß, in dieser Straße einen ganze Hochhauszeile zu errichten. Mit dem Bau des Two Liberty Place fügten sich ein weiterer Geschäftskomplex sowie ein Hotel in das Bebauungsprogramm.

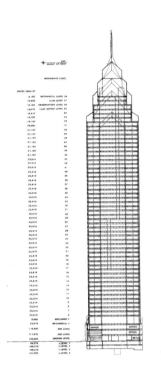

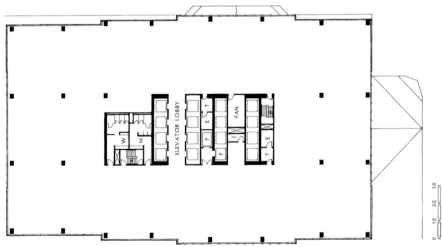

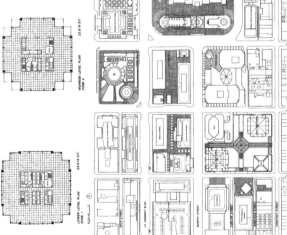

One Liberty Place is a square-plan tower, while Two is rectangular to obtain greater office space.

La One Liberty Place est une tour au plan carré, tandis que la Two est rectangulaire afin de gagner en surface de bureaux.

One Liberty Place ist ein Hochhaus mit quadratischem Grundriß, dagegen ist das Two rechteckig, um so über mehr Bürofläche zur verfügen.

Above, panoramic view of
Philadelphia before the construction
of Two Liberty Place. On the right,
interiors of the elegant split-level
lobby of One Liberty Place.

*En haut, panorama de Philadelphia
avant la construction de la Two
Liberty Place. À droite, intérieurs du
hall élégant à plusieurs hauteurs du
One Liberty Place.*

Oben: Panoramablick über
Philadelphia vor dem Bau des Two
Liberty Place. Rechts, elegantes
Interieur der Eingangshalle des One
Liberty Place in unterschiedlichen
Höhen zu sehen.

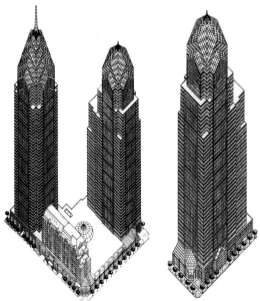

The two towers hold a formal dialog. Thus the use of materials and the form of the coverings serve to link them both together.

Les deux tours établissent un dialogue formel. Ainsi, l'emploi des matériaux et la forme des recouvrements servent de lien entre les deux.

Harmonischer Formdialog zwischen beiden Türme. Die Verwendung der selben Materialien und des selben Dachbaues verbinden beide Hochhäuser.

LVMH TOWER

CHRISTIAN DE PORTZAMPARC

CLIENT / CLIENT / AUFTRAGGEBER: LVMH	**1999**

TOTAL AREA / SURFACE TOTALE / GESAMTOBERFLÄCHE: 8.683 m²

FLOORS / PLANS / STOCKWERKE - HEIGHT / HAUTEUR / HÖHE: 24 fl -100 m

The building, headquarters of the French firm of luxury goods Louis Vuitton Moët Hennessy, is located on a narrow site with very little façade, flanked by the grey granite Chanel building and the brick Chemical Bank and facing the green granite IBM prism at the landmark corner of Madison Avenue with 57th street. With all these premises, the architect was faced with the dilemma of how to resolve a façade that was supposed to be representative without getting absorbed by the surroundings and without reflecting it as a mirror by using a conventional curtain wall. Christian de Portzamparc skilfully resolved the problem by designing a translucent curtain wall that folds back at several levels creating a stepped effect as it gains height.

Le bâtiment est situé sur un terrain étroit avec très peu de façade, c'est le siège corporatif d'une firme française d'articles de luxe (Louis Vuitton et Moët Hennessy), il se trouve entouré par le bâtiment en granite gris de Chanel et celui qui est en brique du Chemical Bank; il est confronté au prisme en granite vert de IBM, sur la confluence de la Madison Avenue avec la rue 57, un endroit emblématique. Avec toutes ces prémisses, l'architecte a affronté le problème de résoudre une façade qui devait être représentative sans être absorbée par tout cet environnement et sans le reflet d'un miroir, avec un mur rideau conventionnel. Christian de Portzamparc a résolu formidablement cet exercice, il a conçu un mur rideau translucide aux franges horizontales qui se replie sur des plans différents et se déplace selon l'augmentation de la hauteur.

Das Gebäude befindet sich auf einem schmalen Grundstück mit kleiner Frontseite. Es ist der Hauptsitz französischer Luxusartikelhersteller wie Louis Vuitton und Moët Hennessy an der Ecke Madision Avenue und 57. Straße. Benachbarte Gebäude sind das Chanel-Gebäude aus grauem Granit, der Backsteinbau der Chemical Bank sowie das gegenüberliegende IBM-Haus aus grünem Granit. Aufgrund all dieser Vorbedingungen war der Architekt gefordert, für dieses Gebäude eine repräsentative Aussenseite zu schaffen, die nicht durch solch ein Umfeld absorbiert werden würde und ohne die Entstehung einer Spiegelfassade als konventionelle Außenhaut. Christian de Portzamparc hat diese Aufgabe meisterlich gelöst, indem er eine durchscheinende Außenhaut mit querverlaufenden, unterschiedlich versetzten Blenden schuf, die sich bei wachsender Höhe immer mehr zurückzieht.

Christian Dior

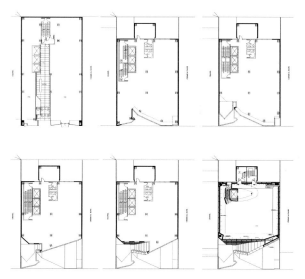

Floors of different levels of the tower where the lower floors have a greater surface area since an adjoining, narrow, four-storey building was bought by the owners.

Étages des différents niveaux de la tour, où les premiers étages disposent de plus de surface sur le plan, car il est adossé au terrain de la tour et il y avait un bâtiment avec peu de galeries et d'une hauteur de quatre étages qui fut acquis par le propriétaire.

Entwürfe unterschiedlicher Turmbereiche. Die ersten Stockwerke verfügen über größere Oberflächen, da das Gebäude hier in das angrenzende Grundstück reinreicht, auf dem ein 4stöckiges Gebäude mit geringer Geschoßbreite stand, das durch den Auftraggeber des Turms aufgekauft wurde.

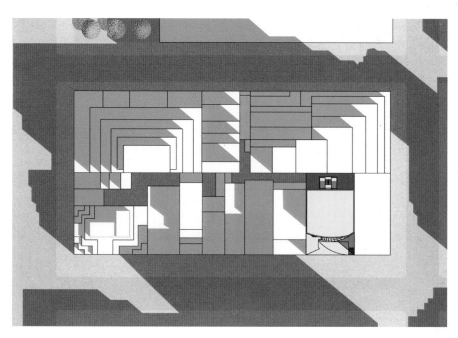

The wall curtain on the façade is the result of a well-thought design that creates a quality atmosphere in which to work and through which the city can be observed through a screen with different degrees of transparency.

Le mur rideau de la façade est le fruit d'une conception étudiée qui crée un environnement de qualité pour les postes de travail, d'où la ville es perçue à travers de un tamis avec des degrés de transparence différents.

Bei der Außenhaut der Fassade handelt es sich um ein ausgereiftes Design, das ein qualitativ hochwertiges Arbeitsumfeld geschaffen hat. Mittels unterschiedlicher Transparenzen ergeben sich Stadtansichten von sämtlichen Arbeitsplätzen.

Christian Dior

FRANKFURT

MAX BUILDING

MURPHY / JAHN INC. ARCHITECTS

CLIENT / CLIENT / AUFTRAGGEBER: DEUTSCHE GRUNDBESITZ
MANAGEMENT GMBH

1999

TOTAL AREA / SURFACE TOTALE / GESAMTOBERFLÄCHE: 111.334 m²

FLOORS / PLANS / STOCKWERKE - HEIGHT / HAUTEUR / HÖHE: 63 fl / 228 m

This office tower seeks its space among the forest of buildings which surround it, its own merits shining forth like a torch which finally melts with the sky. How did this idea come about? By means of the use of a few strategies; for example, treating the volume of the building as an ascending figure. At the same time, the design of the plan and the choice of materials create a sense of lightness. The building gradually loses mass as it ascends, the floor surface gradually diminishes and the façade gradually gains more glass and leaves steel behind in the race to the summit of the city.

Cette tour de bureaux recherche son espace dans la forêt de bâtiments qui l'entourent, elle brille comme une torche, et se confond finalement avec le ciel. ¿Comment est matérialisée cette idée? Avec l'emploi de quelques stratégies; par exemple, le volume du bâtiment est traité comme une figure ascendante. La conception du plan et le choix des matériaux créent, eux aussi, une sensation de légèreté. Le bâtiment perd de la masse au fur et à mesure que l'on monte, la surface du plan diminue graduellement et la façade gagne en verre et perd en acier, sur la course au sommet de la ville.

Dieser Büroturm hat sich seinen eigenen Platz in einem Meer von Hochhäusern gesucht. Er leuchtet mit seinem eigenen Licht wie eine Fackel, um sich dann schließlich im Himmel zu verlieren. Wie konnte diese Idee zur Realität werden? Indem man unterschiedliche Strategien verfolgte, wie z.B. das Gebäude als hochwachsende Figur zu betrachten. Gleichzeitig vermitteln das Design und ausgewählte Baumaterialien ein Gefühl von Leichtigkeit. Mit wachsender Höhe verliert das Gebäude allmählich an Umfang, die Verglasung der Aussenfassade nimmt ständig zu, um sich dann schließlich über der Stadt von der Stahlstruktur abzuheben.

The Max Building is found in the financial center of Frankfurt, where the majority of the skyscrapers rise, very close to the Commerzbank by N. Foster and the new Rhein-Main Tower.

Le Max Building se trouve dans le centre financier de Frankfort, où s'élèvent la plupart des gratte-ciels, très près du Commerzbank de N. Foster et de la nouvelle Rhein-Main Tower.

Das Max Building liegt im Frankfurter Finanzzentrum - dem Wolkenkratzerviertel -ganz in der Nähe der Commerzbank vom Architekten N. Foster entworfen und dem neuen Rhein-Main Tower.

OK Dach +228,00
63. OG
62. OG

28.000

Abschnitt 7
56.OG Büro + 200,00

28.000

Abschnitt 6
48.OG Büro + 172,00

28.000

Abschnitt 5
40.OG Büro + 144,00

28.000

Abschnitt 4
32.OG Büro + 116,00

28.000

Abschnitt 3
24.OG Büro + 88,00

28.000

Abschnitt 2
16.OG Büro + 60,00

42.000

Abschnitt 1

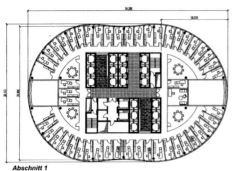

Abschnitt 1

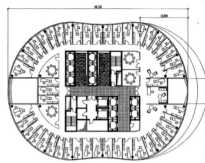

Abschnitt 3

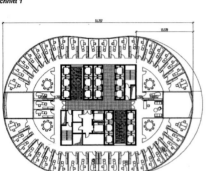

Abschnitt 2

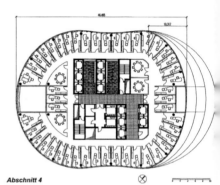

Abschnitt 4

The project was the winner of a competition to build on a block with existing mixed-use buildings.

Le projet fut le vainqueur d'un concours pour bâtir sur un pâté avec des bâtiments existants à usages mixtes.

Das Projekt war Gewinner einer Ausschreibung zur Bebauung eines Eckgrundstücks mit bereits bestehenden Multifunktionsgebäuden.

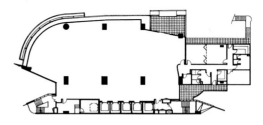

MENARA-UMNO

T.R. HAMZAH & YEANG SDN BHD

CLIENT / CLIENT / AUFTRAGGEBER: SOUTH EAST ASIA DEVELOPMENT CORPORATION BREAD KOMPLEK KEWANGAN, JALAN RAJA CHULAN, KUALA LUMPOUR	**1998**

TOTAL AREA / SURFACE TOTALE / GESAMTOBERFLÄCHE: 19.091 m²

FLOORS / PLANS / STOCKWERKE - HEIGHT / HAUTEUR / HÖHE: 21 fl / 94 m

This office building incorporates an auditorium with its own entrance from the exterior, as well as locating on the ground floor the different lobby spaces of a bank. The design of the office floors responds to the following requirements: To use as far as possible natural ventilation (although the building has an air conditioning system as a reinforcement) and that no work space is more than 6·5 m from a window to receive illumination and renew the natural air. This was the first high-rise building in Malaysia to use the wind as a ventilation system to create interior conditions of comfort instead of using mechanical systems.

Cet immeuble de bureaux incorpore un auditorium à accès propre de l'extérieur, il situe aussi, au rez-de-chaussée, les différents espaces du hall d'une banque. La conception des étages de bureaux répond aux exigences suivantes: utiliser au maximum la ventilation naturelle (même si le bâtiment dispose de climatisation de renfort), et aucun espace de travail ne doit se trouver à plus de 6,5 m. d'une fenêtre afin de recevoir de la lumière et afin de rénover l'air naturel. Il fut le premier bâtiment en hauteur de Malaisie qui utilisa le vent en tant que système de ventilation afin de créer de conditions intérieures de confort au lieu d'utiliser de systèmes mécaniques.

In diesem Bürogebäude liegt ein Auditorium mit eigenem Zugang und beherbergt außerdem im Erdgeschoss Räumlichkeiten des Vestibuls einer Bank. Der Entwurf der Büroetagen entspricht folgenden Anforderungen: maximale Nutzung der natürlichen Belüftung (auch wenn im Gebäude ersatzweise eine Klimaanlage installiert wurde) und kein Arbeitsplatz darf nicht mehr als 6,5 Meter von einem Fenster entfernt liegen, um natürliches Licht und Belüftung zu nützen. Dies ist das erste Hochhaus Malaysien´s welches Wind als Innenbelüftungssystem, anstatt mechanischer Systeme nützt.

Air walls, an experimental element designed by the architects, besides forming part of the energy system, also serve the purpose of a powerful aesthetic element. The building rises as an urban sculpture, trimmed off by the sky over the city.

Les murs à chambre à air, un élément expérimental conçu par les architectes, outre leur appartenance au système d'énergie, ils représentent un élément esthétique puissant. Le bâtiment s'élève comme une sculpture urbaine qui est coupée contre le ciel de la ville.

Die Luftmauern sind experimentelle Elemente von den Archtekten entworfen. Neben ihrer Funktion als Energieelemente dienen sie insbesonders der Ästhetik. Das Gebäude erhebt sich ähnlich einer urbanen Skulptur, die sich gegen den Himmel abzeichnet.

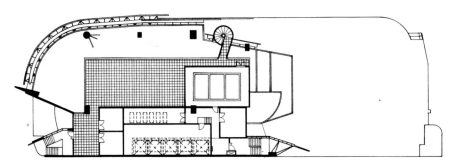

The relationship between the building and the exterior is constant, incorporating terraces and balconies, which is unusual in a traditional office block, usually characterised by a closed space which is isolated from the exterior.

Le rapport du bâtiment avec l'extérieur est constant, il incorpore des terrasses et des balcons inusités sur un immeuble de bureaux traditionnel, il est lui-même un réceptacle fermé et isolé face à l'extérieur.

Konstant öffnet sich das Gebäude nach außen über Terrassen und Balkons, was eigentlich bei traditionellen Bürohäusern nicht üblich ist. Diese verschließen sich normalerweise in ihrem Umfeld und wirken abschottend.

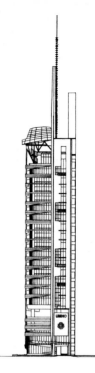

The tower is full of elements that
serve both functional and aesthetic
purposes, where looks is not the at
the centre of its architectural
planning. The end result is a
personal, innovative and revolutionary
language.

La tour est pleine d'éléments
satisfaisant aussi bien les besoins
fonctionnels que les esthétiques;
cette dernière prémisse n'est pas le
point de départ de l'architecture,
néanmoins le résultat final est un
langage personnel, innovateur et ...
révolutionnaire.

Der Turm ist voll von Elementen, die
funktionelle wie ästhetische Aufgaben
erfüllen. Das Endresultat spricht
allerdings eine ganz persönliche,
innovative und revolutionäre Sprache.

MESSETURM

MURPHY / JAHN INC. ARCHITECTS

CLIENT / CLIENT / AUFTRAGGEBER: MESSE FRANKFURT GMBH	**1990**
TOTAL AREA / SURFACE TOTALE / GESAMTOBERFLÄCHE: 85.200 m²	
FLOORS / PLANS / STOCKWERKE - HEIGHT / HAUTEUR / HÖHE: 63 fl / 251 m	

The Messe Tower or Messeturm is located in the Messe Frankfurt complex, a large exhibition center where the historical buildings, the Festhalle of 1909 and the Kongresshalle, from after the Second World War, are found. The tower is like a bell tower functioning as the main gate to the site and was at one time the tallest building in Europe. Its design should symbolize the commercial power of Frankfurt. The architects were inspired by those American skyscrapers of the twenties and thirties. The result is a classical building which aims to stand out from the anonymous container buildings of the contemporary city.

La Messe Tower ou Messeturm est situé dans le complexe Messe Frankfurt, un grand centre d'expositions où se trouvent deux édifices historiques, le Festhalle de 1909 et le Kongresshalle, postérieur à la 2ème Guerre Mondiale. La tour ressemble à un campanile, elle a la fonction de porte principale de l'enceinte et fut jadis le bâtiment le plus haut d'Europe. Sa conception devait symboliser le pouvoir commercial de Frankfort, les architectes s'inspirèrent sur les gratte-ciel américains des années vingt et trente. Le résultat est un bâtiment classique qui désire se distinguer des bâtiments anonymes contenus dans la ville contemporaine.

Der Messeturm befindet sich auf dem großen Messegelände in Frankfurt, auf dem auch zwei historische Gebäude stehen, wie die Festhalle von 1909 und die Kongreßhalle, die nach dem 2. Weltkrieg entstand. Ein Turmbau wie ein Kampanile, gilt er gleichzeitig als Haupteingangstor zum Messegelände und war seinerzeit Europas höchstes Gebäude. Er verkörperte die kommerzielle Macht Frankfurts. Die Architekten inspirierten sich dabei in amerikanischen Wolkenkratzern der zwanziger und dreißiger Jahre. Das Ergebnis ist ein klassischer Bau, der sich von den anonymen Baublocks der kontemporären Stadt unter- scheidet.

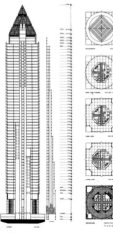

The building has a square base from which the tower emerges. The tower is also square, and a glass cylinder emerges from the tower and is finally crowned with a pyramid.

Le bâtiment a une base carrée d'où surgit la tour, carrée aussi, de celle-ci jaillit aussi un cylindre en verre qui est, enfin, dominée par une pyramide.

Bau mit quadratischem Unterbau. Darüber erhebt sich der Turm, ebenfalls quadratisch, der dann im oberen Teil die Zylinderform annimmt und schließlich mit einer Pyramide als Dachaufsatz endet.

The materials used are glass and red granite. The way they combine makes the changes of volume of its tripartite design stand out.

Les matériaux employés sont le verre et le granite rouge. Le mode des combinaisons souligne les changements de volume de sa conception tripartite.

Angewandte Materialien sind Glas und roter Granit. Ihre Kombinationsweise hebt die Wechsel von einer Gestaltung zur nächsten hervor.

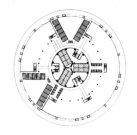

TOKYO

MILLENNIUM TOWER
FOSTER & PARTNERS

CLIENT / CLIENT / AUFTRAGGEBER: OBAYASHI CORPORATION	**1989**
TOTAL AREA / SURFACE TOTALE / GESAMTOBERFLÄCHE: 1.040.000 m²	
FLOORS / PLANS / STOCKWERKE - HEIGHT / HAUTEUR / HÖHE: 170 fl / 840 m	

Growth predictions for Tokyo predict that it will outstrip fifteen million inhabitants in 2020. The Millennium Tower approaches the growth of the city of the future proposing solutions to the social challenges that urban expansion generates and particularly, in the case of Tokyo, where the lack of land will impede continued construction in the city. The project was commissioned by a Japanese corporation to promote housing, offices and shopping areas on land reclaimed from the sea A conical tower was proposed, the tallest in the world, where a community of 60,000 people could be self-sufficient, generating their own resources.

Les prédictions de croissance de Tokyo de 2020 dépassent les quinze millions d'habitants. La Millenium Tower pense à la croissance de la ville du future, elle propose des solutions aux défis sociaux engendrés par la croissance urbaine et, en particulier, dans le cas de Tokyo où le manque de sol ne permettra plus la construction sur la ville. Le projet fut conçu par une corporation japonaise afin de construire des appartements, des bureaux et des surfaces commerciales sur des terrepleins gagnés sur la mer. L'on proposa une tour en cône, la plus haute du monde, dans laquelle une communauté de 60.000 personnes puisse être autosuffisante et générer ses propres ressources.

Die Voraussagen für das Bevölkerungswachstum Tokios in 2020 belaufen sich auf eine Einwohnerzahl von mehr als 15 Millionen. Der Millenium Tower stellt sich der Frage nach dem Wachstum der Stadt sowie der sozialen Herausforderung, da wie im Falle von Tokio, die Errichtung von weiterem Wohnraum aufgrund fehlendem Baugrund in der Stadt unmoglich ist. Das Projekt wurde von einer japanische Gesellschaft in Auftrag gegeben, die sich mit der Promotion von Wohn–, Büro– und Geschäftsräumen auf Grundstücken befaßt, die auf dem vom Meer gewonnenem Land entstehen. Man entwarf einen konischen Turm, den höchsten der Welt, in dem 60.000 Menschen unabhängig von Fremdressourcen leben könnten.

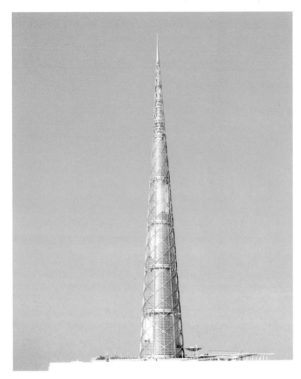

Reminiscent of Frank Lloyd Wright's one mile tower, the Millennium Tower is a vertical city where a high velocity train travels both horizontally and vertically.

La Millenium Tower qui présente des réminiscences de la tour d'une mille de F.LL. Wright, est une ville verticale où circule un train à grande vitesse, aussi bien en horizontal qu'en vertical.

In Anlehnung an den Meilenturm von F.LL. Wright, ist der Millenium Tower eine senkrechte Stadt, in dem ein Hochgeschwindigkeitszug sowohl senkrecht als auch horizontal zirkuliert.

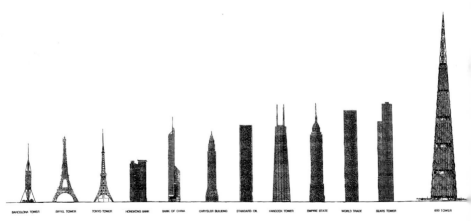

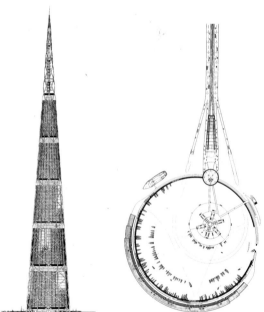

The tower groups its flats in vertical neighborhoods. Built on an artificial island and surrounded by a marina, it is connected to the coast by a bridge.

La tour dispose ses appartements en quartiers verticaux. Élevée sur une île artificielle, entourée d'un port sportif, elle est connectée à la côte par un pont.

Der Turm gruppiert seine Stockwerke in Senkrechtvierteln. Er steht auf einer künstlichen Insel umgeben von einem Sporthafen und ist mit dem Festland über eine Brücke verbunden.

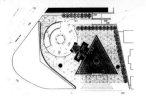

NATIONAL COMMERCIAL BANK

SKIDMORE, OWING & MERRILL LLP (SOM)

CLIENT / CLIENT / AUFTRAGGEBER: NATIONAL REAL ESTATE COMPANY OF JEDDAH	**1984**
TOTAL AREA / SURFACE TOTALE / GESAMTOBERFLÄCHE: 71.160 m²	
FLOORS / PLANS / STOCKWERKE - HEIGHT / HAUTEUR / HÖHE: 27 fl / 126 m	

Located on a square at the shore of the Red Sea, the project's geometry, conceived from its location and the climatology, consists of a 27-floor triangular prism of offices next to a 6-floor circular garage. The verticality of the tower is drastically interrupted by three large gaps, two of seven floors towards the city and one of nine floors towards the northwest and the sea. The windows of the offices open directly onto these courtyards, leaving the exterior volumetry of the building absolutely smooth and white, as a reference to the typical introverted orientation of the design of inner courtyards of Islamic architecture.

Située sur une place sur le bord de la Mer Rouge, la géométrie du projet, conçue à partir de l'emplacement et du climat, est composée par un prisme triangulaire de bureaux de 27 étages près d'un garage circulaire de 6 étages. La verticalité de la tour est interrompue drastiquement par trois grands ajourages, deux à sept étages au sud vers la ville et un à neuf étages au nord-ouest, vers la mer. Les bureaux ouvrent leurs fenêtres directement sur ces cours, ils laissent la volumétrie extérieure du bâtiment tout à fait lisse et blanche, en référence à l'orientation introvertie typique de la conception de cours intérieures de l'architecture islamique. Située sur une place sur le bord de la Mer Rouge, la géométrie du projet, conçue à partir de l'emplacement et du climat, est composée par un prisme triangulaire de bureaux de 27 étages près d'un garage circulaire de 6 étages.

Auf einem Platz am Roten Meer gelegen, wurden für die Geometrie dieses Gebäudes der Standort sowie die klimatischen Bedingungen beachtet. In einem dreieckigen Prisma sind in 27 Stockwerken Büros untergebracht. Daneben liegt ein 6stöckiger Rundbau, der als Parkhaus fungiert. Die senkrechten Außenwände werden von drei riesigen Durchbrüchen beherrscht. Zwei auf der Südseite zur Stadt gelegen über eine Höhe von jeweils 7 Stockwerken und ein 9 Stockwerke hoher Durchbruch auf der Nordwestseite in Richtung Meer. Die Fenster der Büros zeigen in die so geschaffenen Innenhöfe, so daß sich die weiße Außenhaut des Gebäudes als absolut eben darstellt. Bei der Gestaltung der Innenhöfe hat man die islamische Architektur genutzt, die Abschottung nach außen vorsieht, das Leben aber im Inneren stattfinden läßt..

The interior decoration presents exquisite finishes and materials, including black granite and marble.

La décoration intérieure présente des finissions et des matériaux exquis, y compris du granite noir et du marbre.

Exquisite Verarbeitung und Materialien wie schwarzer Granit und Marmor bei der Innenausstattung.

The program develops meeting spaces of a high level, a luxurious restaurant floor with mobile partitions for executives and a cafeteria full of color for employees.

Le programme développe des espaces de relations à haut niveau; un luxueux étage restaurant aux murs amovibles pour les hommes d'affaires et une cafétéria pleine de couleurs pour employés.

Der Bau weist Gesellschaftsräume höchsten Niveaus vor. Eine Etage mit einem Luxusrestaurant für das Führungspersonal mit beweglichen Trennwänden und eine bunt gestaltete Cafeteria für die Angestellten.

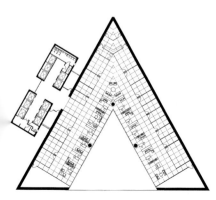

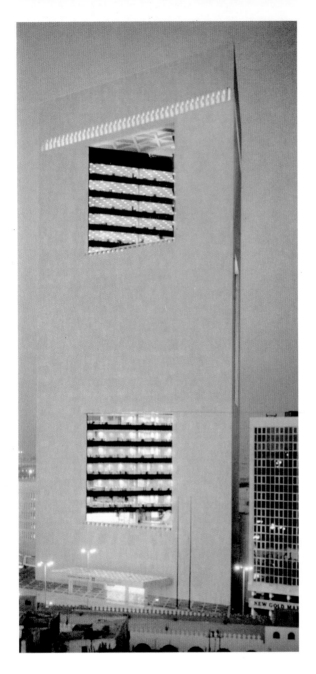

The building offers an introverted image towards the city, showing part of the interior through three large windows.

Le bâtiment offre une image introvertie vers la ville et expose une partie de l'intérieur à travers trois grandes fenêtres.

Das Gebäude zeigt sich zur Stadt hin verschlossen und erlaubt nur einen Teileinblick in das Innere durch drei Öffnungen in den Außenseiten.

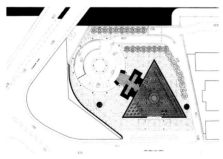

NOVA BOCANA

RICARD BOFILL TALLER D'ARQUITECTURA

CLIENT / CLIENT / AUFTRAGGEBER: PORT DE BARCELONA

2004

FLOORS / PLANS / STOCKWERKE - HEIGHT / HAUTEUR / HÖHE: 56 fl / 168 m

The port of Barcelona is going to be transformed over the next few years into the great port facility which symbolizes the definitive opening of the city to the sea. With the construction of the Nova Bocana, Barcelona acquires the triple vocation of capital of Catalonia, the western Mediterranean and intermodal city of the southern Mediterranean. The port enlargement project will be carried out over 15 hectares of land reclaimed from the sea, on which a new fishing port, a luxury hotel at the edge of the sea in the shape of a sail and a multimedia center for leisure and interactive activities will be built.

Le port de Barcelone va se transformer dans les prochaines années, il sera le grand équipement portuaire qui symbolise l'ouverture définitive de la ville sur la mer. Grâce à la construction de la Nova Bocana, Barcelone obtient sa triple vocation d'être la capitale de Catalogne, de laMéditerranée occidentale et la ville intermodale du sud de la Méditerranée. Le projet de développement du port seront réalisées sur 15 hectares de terre-pleins gagnés sur la mer, l'on y construira un nouveau port de pêche, un hôtel de luxe au bord de la mer d'une forme en voile et un centre multimédia pour les activités ludiques et interactives.

Der Umbau des Hafens von Barcelona in den nächsten Jahren symbolisiert die endgültige Öffnung der Stadt zum Meer. Mit dem Bau der Nova Bocana wird Barcelona dann zur dreifachen Hauptstadt: die Hauptstadt Kataloniens, des westlichen Mittelmeers und als südliches Tor zum Mittelmeer. Die Hafenerweiterung sieht den Ausbau auf einem 15 Hektar großem –dem Meer abgerungenem Land – vor. Dort werden der neue Fischerhafen sowie ein am Wasser gelegenes Luxushotel mit der Form eines Segels und ein Freizeit– und Multimediazentrum entstehen.

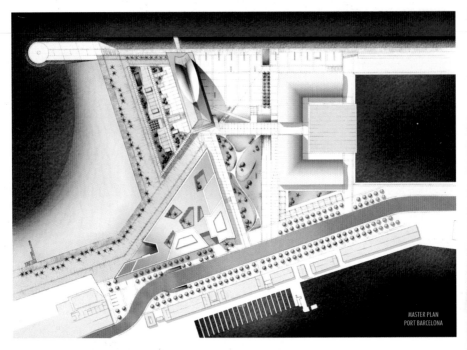

MASTER PLAN
PORT BARCELONA

The seashore hotel is conceived of as a signal, a sail billowing in the wind.

L'hôtel sur le bord de la mer est conçu en tant que signal, une voile hissée au vent.

Das Hotel am Meer ist als geöffnetes Segel entworfen.

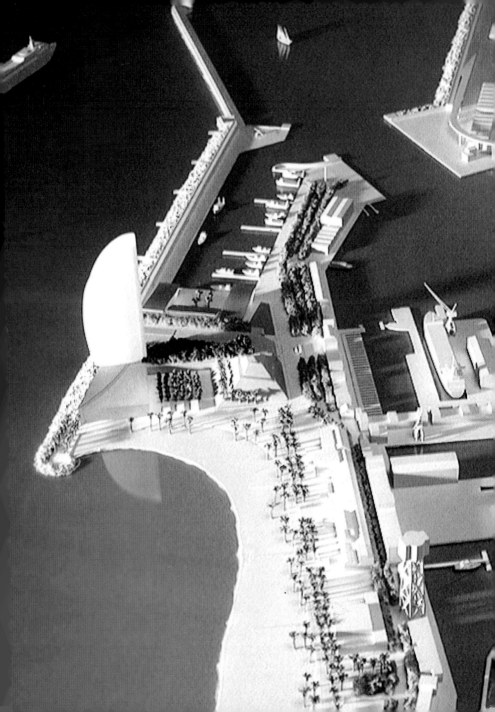

NTT HQTRS.

CESAR PELLI & ASSOCIATES INC.

CLIENT / CLIENT / AUFTRAGGEBER: NTT CORPORATION

1995

FLOORS / PLANS / STOCKWERKE - HEIGHT / HAUTEUR / HÖHE: 30 fl / 127 m

The NTT was conceived as an integrated model of one of the most important commercial, corporate and cultural centers in Japan. The rectangular form of the lot is conditioned by the passage of two important streets, one of which is a transited dual carriageway raised above street level. This factor conditions the volumetric ordering of the block: a low body acts as a protective screen, closing the space devoted to a public garden and the entrance to the office tower. It also has a telecommunications center, conference hall and a bar-restaurant hall for all the staff.

Le NTT fut conçu comme un modèle intégré dans un des centres commerciaux, corporatifs et culturels les plus importants au Japon. La forme rectangulaire du terrain est conditionnée par le passage de deux rues importantes, une de celles-ci est une voie rapide de transit, élevée par rapport à la rue. Ce facteur conditionne l'ordre volumétrique du pâté: un corps bas adopte le rôle d'un écran, il protège et ferme l'espace destiné au jardin public et l'accès à la tour de bureaux. De plus, il dispose d'un centre de télécommunications, d'une salle de conférences et d'un salon-bar-restaurant pour tout le staff.

Das NTT als Integralmodel entworfen, ist Japans größtes Einkaufs–Geschäfts und Kulturzentrum. Das rechteckige Grundstück wird von zwei wichtigen Verkehrswegen begrenzt, einer davon ist eine höher liegende verkehrsreiche Stadtautobahn. Dieser Faktor be-stimmt die volumetrische Anordnung auf dem Eckgrundstück. Der Unterbau dient als Schutzwall für die dahinter liegenden Grünanlagen und ist gleichzeitig Eingangsbereich zum Büroturm.
Im Gebäude befindet sich neben einem Telekommunikationszentrum auch Konferenzräume und ein Restaurant mit Bar für die Angestellten.

Superimposition of the tower and the base building. The chosen materials are steel, glass and Minnesota stone.

Superposition de la tour et du bâtiment socle. Les matériaux choisis sont l'acier, le verre et la pierre de Minnesota.

Turmaufsatz auf dem Unterbau. Ausgewählte Materialien sind Stahl, Glas und Minnesota-Stein.

Corner of the tower with the low building, point where one of the entrances to the garden is.

Coin de la tour et du bâtiment bas, point où se produit un des accès au jardin.

Ansicht einer Gebäudeecke mit dem Unterbau – hier befindet sich einer der Eingänge zu den Gartenanlagen.

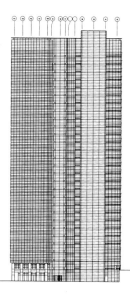

The garden is a public space where leisure and cultural acts can be held.The aim is to boost the leisure and corporate character of the building.

Le jardin est un espace publique où l'on peut effectuer des activités ludiques et culturelles.
L'on désire souligner le caractère ludique et corporatif du bâtiment.

Ein öffentlicher Garten für Freizeit- und Kulturaktivitäten.

The connection between the two buildings is made via the square and the bridge. Interiors: lobbies of both buildings.

La connexion entre les deux bâtiments se produit à travers de la place et du pont. Intérieurs: hall des deux bâtiments.

Beide Gebäude sind über einen Platz mit einer Brücke verbunden. Innenansicht: Eingangshallen in beiden Gebäuden.

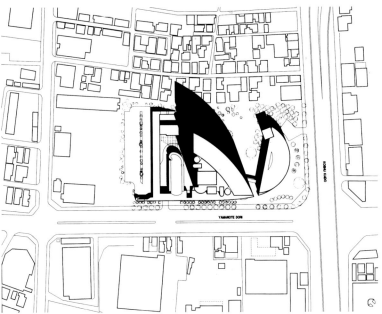

ONE CHASE MANHATTAN PLAZA

SKIDMORE, OWINGS & MERRILL LLP (SOM)

CLIENT / CLIENT / AUFTRAGGEBER: CHASE MANHATTAN BANK	**1961**
TOTAL AREA / SURFACE TOTALE / GESAMTOBERFLÄCHE: 214.000 m²	
FLOORS / PLANS / STOCKWERKE - HEIGHT / HAUTEUR / HÖHE: 60 fl / 247,8 m	

This was the first great corporate skyscraper which moved from the financial center of Manhattan to be located in the area south of the Brooklyn Bridge. Its interesting design, a rectangular body of glass and aluminum with no more ornamentation than the structure, contrasts with the stone building which surround it. From the town planning point of view, it marked a new concept in 1961 by changing the zonification of the district by replacing the breeches of the first skyscrapers with the tower form, understood to mean a rectangular body, in exchange for ceding part of its surface area for a 8,300 m² public square.

Il fut le premier grand gratte-ciel corporatif qui s'éloigna du centre financier de Manhattan afin de s'installer sur la zone sud du pont de Brooklyn. Sa conception intéressante, un corps rectangulaire en verre et aluminium, la seule décoration est la structure, contraste avec les bâtiments en pierre qui l'entourent. Du point de vue urbanistique il représenta un nouveau concept car il favorisa, en 1961, un changement de la zonification du district, puisqu'il remplaça les déplacements des premiers gratte-ciel par la forme de tour, comprise comme un corps rectangulaire; par contre cela représenta une perte de surface favorisant une place publique de 8.300 m².

Erster bedeutender Wolkenkratzer eines Unternehmens, der nicht wie üblich im Finanzviertel Manhattan errichtet wurde, sondern im Südteil der Stadt an der Brooklynbrücke. Interessante rechteckige Konstruktion aus Glas und Aluminium ohne weitere Verzierung als nur seine eigene Metallstruktur, die sich von den umliegenden Backsteingebäuden abhebt. Vom urbanistischen Punkt aus gesehen, stellte diese Konstruktion 1961 ein neues Bebauungskonzept des Stadtviertels dar. Ein gradliniger Turmkörper ersetzte Gebäudeeinzüge, so wie man sie bei den ersten Wolkenkratzer anwandte, dafür wurde Teil seiner Oberfläche für einen öffentlichen Platz von 8.300 m² freigegeben.

Rising up from a glass structure below the level of the square, a sculptural fountain known as "the water garden" lies in an 18 meter diameter orientally inspired pond.

Sur une structure en verre sous le niveau de la place, s'élève une fontaine sculpturale connue comme «Le jardin de l'eau» sur un étang dont l'aspect est oriental, de 19 mètres de diamètre.

Unterirdisch erhebt sich über einer Glasstruktur eine orientalische inspirierte Brunnenanlage mit einem Teich von 18 m2 Durchmesser, auch bekannt als „Wassergarten".

Above, ground floor of the building showing part of the metallic structure. The plan, long and narrow, is fortified with three stretches of columns, a central one defining the service area, and two more defining the diaphanous office areas.

En haut, rez-de-chaussée du bâtiment où l'on aperçoit une partie de la structure métallique vue. La vue en plan, longue et étroite, est armée par trois trames de colonnes, une centrale qui définit la zone des services et les deux autres, la zone réservée aux surfaces de bureaux sont diaphanes.

Oben: Die Gebäudeparterre zeigt Teil der freiliegenden Metallstruktur. Das langgezogene und schmale Geschoß verteilt sich über drei Säulenabschnitte. Im mittleren Bereich befinden sich die Betriebsanlagen, links und rechts davon helle Bürozeilen.

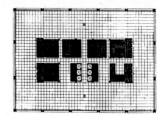

ONE LIBERTY PLAZA

SKIDOMORE, OWINGS & MERRILL LLP (SOM)

CLIENT / CLIENT / AUFTRAGGEBER: GALBREATH-RUFFIN CORP. & U.S. STEEL CORP	**1973**

TOTAL AREA / SURFACE TOTALE / GESAMTOBERFLÄCHE: 200.000 m²

FLOORS / PLANS / STOCKWERKE - HEIGHT / HAUTEUR / HÖHE: 54 fl / 226,5 m

Found in the heart of Wall Street, in Manhattan. The lot is divided into two different-sized blocks. And a proposal was made to use the full amount of building land in the biggest block to create a public green area in the other. The square covers the 3 meter disparity with regard to street level and concentrates part of the surface of the building in two levels below ground. When it was built, the latest structural technology advances in illumination and design were used, integrating the air conditioning systems and the vertical transport elements, thus obtaining diaphanous office floors.

Il se trouve au coeur de Wall Street, à Manhattan. Le terrain était divisé en deux pâtés d'une grandeur différente. Et l'on proposa ajouter la totalité du sol à bâtir sur la plus grande afin de créer une zone verte publique sur l'autre. La place résout la dénivellation de 3 mètres par rapport à la rue et concentre une partie de la surface du bâtiment sur deux niveaux sous le sol. Lors de la construction, on employa les dernières techniques technologiques structurelles en illumination et conception, on y intégra les installations de climatisation et les éléments de transport vertical; on obtint ainsi des étages diaphanes de bureaux.

Im Herzen der Wall Street in Manhattan. Unterschiedlich hohe Gebäudeblocks teilten sich zuvor den Baugrund. Der größere freigebliebene Teil wurde zur Bebauung, der kleiner Teil als öffentlicher Platz genutzt. Zur Straße hin weist dieser Platz ein Gefälle von 3 Metern auf, so daß ein Teil der Gebäudeoberfläche auf zwei unterirdischen Etagen steht. Als das Gebäude konstruiert wurde, wandte man die neuesten strukturellen Beleuchtungs und Formgebungstechnologien als auch Klimaanlagen und vertikale Beförderungseinrichtungen an und erreichte damit helle und klare Büroetagen.

The design selected in the structure of the building uses the intumescent flanges to protect the struts of the façade beams, thus notably reducing the cost of the building as well as giving character to its exterior image.

La conception choisie sur la structure du bâtiment emploie des ailes ignifuges afin de protéger l'âme des supports de la façade; grâce à ce fait, le coût du bâtiment baissa assez et cela caractérisa aussi son image extérieure.

Der Entwurf sah für die Seitenwände des Gebäudes die Nutzung einer feuerfesten Struktur vor, um auf diese Weise die Stahlprofile der Frontfassade zu schützen. Damit wurden die Gebäudekosten erheblich gesenkt, der Charakter seines äußeren Anblicks aber aufgewertet.

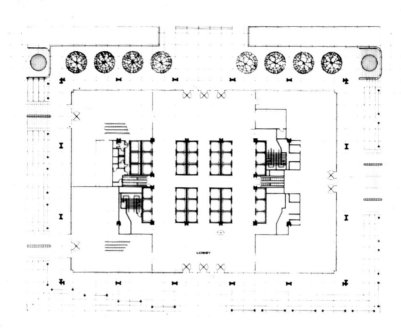

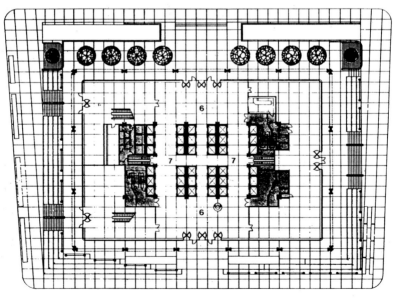

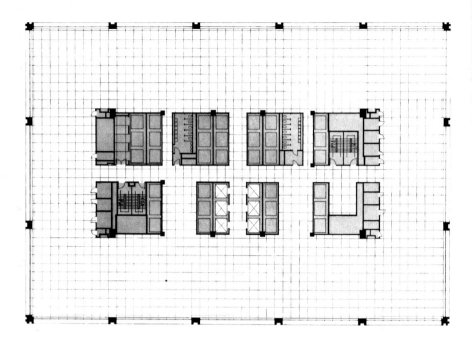

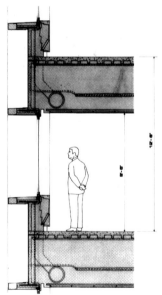

After the collapse of the Twin Towers (the result of the brutal attacks of September 11th 2001), this building has been affected in the structure and foundations.

Après la chute des Twin Towers (à cause du terrible attentat du onze septembre 2001), ce bâtiment a été affecté quant à la structure et cimentation.

Durch den Einsturz der Twin Towers (als Folge des brutalen Attentats vom 11. September 2001) wurden Fundament und Struktur derartig beschädigt, daß bei Schließung dieser Ausgabe eine ernsthafte Einsturzgefahr für dieses Gebäude besteht.

OSAKA
WORLD TRADE CENTER

NIKKEN SEKKEI

1995

TOTAL AREA / SURFACE TOTALE / GESAMTOBERFLÄCHE: 150,000 m²

FLOORS / PLANS / STOCKWERKE - HEIGHT / HAUTEUR / HÖHE: 55 fl / 256 m

The WTCO is an office building which incorporates a series of public spaces such as shops, restaurants, bars, banquet and convention halls, the WTCO club, an auditorium and an observation platform in the form of a pyramid from which the whole bay can be seen.

The building incorporates a highly sophisticated technology which, by means of an IT system, regulates all the electricity and water systems. It is currently the tallest building on the west coast of Japan and has become a visual landmark of the coastal silhouette and the region of Kansai.

Le WTCO est un immeuble de bureaux qui incorpore une série d'espaces publiques tel que des boutiques, des restaurants, des bars, des salons de banquets et de conventions, le WTCO club, un auditorium et un mirador en forme pyramidale depuis lequel on divise toute la baie.

Le bâtiment incorpore une technologie très sophistiquée qui, avec un système informatique, régule toutes les installations. Il est actuellement le bâtiment le plus haut sur la côte ouest japonaise et il est devenu une marque visuelle de la silhouette de la côte et de la région de Kansai.

Das WTCO ist ein Bürogebäude, daß eine Reihe öffentlicher Bereiche beinhaltet wie Läden, Restaurants, Bars, Fest- und Versammlungsräumlichkeiten, den WTCO – Club, ein Auditorium sowie ein pyramidenförmiger Aussichtspunkt mit Ausblick über die gesamt Bucht. Das Gebäude wurde unter Anwendung raffiniertester neuester Technologien errichtet. So kontrolliert und reguliert beispielsweise ein Computersystem sämtliche Anlagen. Derzeitig ist dies das höchste Gebäude an der Westküste Japans und es wird bereits als absoluter Blickpunkt an der Küstensilhouette und der Region Kansai betrachtet.

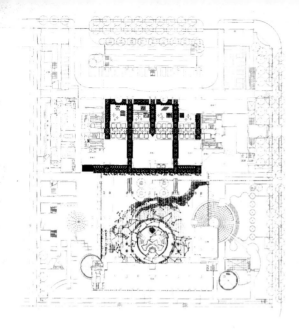

Shot of entrance to the building, ground floor. On the right, a view of an interior corridor where the choice of materials produces multiple reflections.

Surface d'accès au bâtiment, rez-de-chaussée. À droite une vue d'un couloir intérieur où le choix des matériaux produit des reflets multiples.

Zeichnung des Zugangsbereichs im Erdgeschoß. Rechts, Blick in einen der Flure, in denen angewandte Materialien absolute Transparenz schaffen,

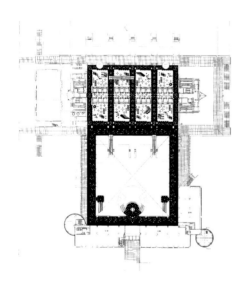

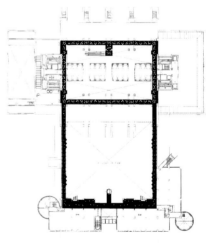

The ample 3000 m2 hall also performs
the function of relating the building to
the floor, both from the functional and
volumetric point of view.

*Le grand hall de 3.000 m2 a aussi la
fonction de mettre en relation le
bâtiment et le sol, aussi bien du
point de vue fonctionnel que
volumétrique.*

Das 3.000 m2 große Hallengebäude
dient dem Gebäude als Verbindung
zum Boden.

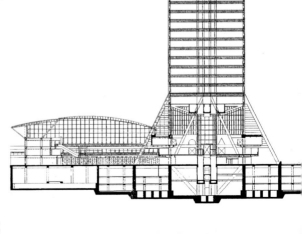

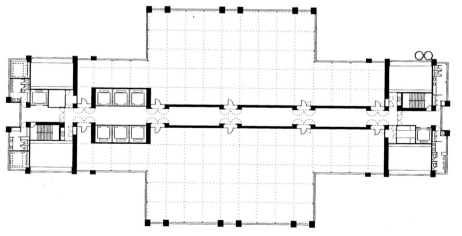

Different interior spaces, above WTCO club, the hall which is an atrium, the observation platform on the top floor and on the right, another detail of the hall.

Plusieurs espaces intérieurs, en haut le WTCO club, le hall qui est un parvis, le mirador du dernier étage et à droite un autre détail du hall.

Verschiedene Innenansichten, oben der WTCO-Club, ein Atrium als Eingangshalle, die Aussichtsetage und rechts weitere Details der Halle.

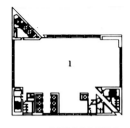

OUB CENTER

KENZO TANGE ASSOCIATES

CLIENT / CLIENT / AUFTRAGGEBER: OVERSEAS UNION BANK

1986

TOTAL AREA / SURFACE TOTALE / GESAMTOBERFLÄCHE: 68.000 m²

FLOORS / PLANS / STOCKWERKE - HEIGHT / HAUTEUR / HÖHE: 62 fl / 280 m

The Overseas Union Bank is one of the big Singapore banks. Its office headquarters is currently the tallest corporate building in Asia, although its battle with height hegemony is not solitary. This can be seen in the photographs taken on the banks of the Singapore River where building and financial area are perceived with all their strength.
The OUB Center is found in Raffles Place where it relates to the pedestrian by means of a six-floor high base. The tower offers a double vision, rectangular from the river, triangular from the avenue.

Le Overseas Union Bank est une des grandes banques de Singapour. Le siège de ses bureaux est actuellement le bâtiment corporatif le plus haut en Asie, même si sa lutte pour l'hégémonie des hauteurs n'est pas solitaire. Cela peut être apprécié sur les photographies prises sur les bords du fleuve Singapour, où bâtiment et aire financière sont perçues avec toute leur force.
Le Oub Center se trouve à Raffles Place où il rencontre le piéton avec un socle d'une hauteur de six étages. La tour offre une vision double et rectangulaire depuis la rivière, triangulaire depuis l'avenue.

Die Overseas Union Bank ist eine der Großbanken Singapurs. Der Firmensitz ist derzeit das höchste Gebäude eines Unternehmens in Asien. Allerdings kämpft es nicht allein um die Vorherrschaft am Stadthimmel. Dies ist an den Aufnahmen zu erkennen, die vom Ufer des Flusses Singapur aus gemacht wurden. Von hier aus gesehen stellen sich dieses Gebäudes wie auch das gesamte Finanzviertel mit voller Kraft dar.
Das Oub Center steht am Raffles Place, von wo aus der Fußgänger über einen 6stöckigen seitlichen Unterbau Zugang in den Wolkenkratzer hat. Zur Flußseite ist das Gebäude rechteckig, auf der Rückseite zur Avenida dreieckig.

View of the main entrance to the
tower where the base withdraws seen
from different angles, also from the
avenue.

*Vue de l'accès principal de la tour où
le socle se déplace, depuis des
angles différents, et aussi depuis
l'avenue.*

Ansichten auf den zurückgesetzten
Haupteingang im Gebäudesockel,
auch von der Avenida aus.

This broken view which the building produces from the exterior is obtained with the passage from rectangle to triangle and a subtle dodge in the design of the plan.

Cet aspect de virement que produit le bâtiment de l'extérieur est obtenue grâce au passage du rectangle au triangle et un virement subtile sur la conception de l'étage.

Unterschiedliche sich verändernde Außenansichten beim Übergang der Rechteckform zur Dreieckform des Gebäudes.

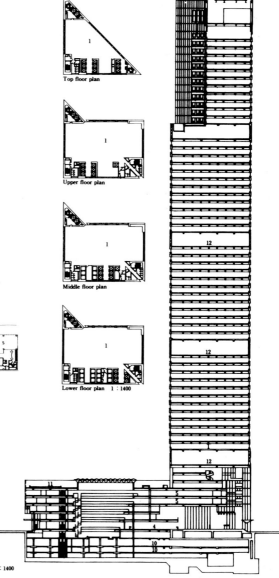

Top floor plan

Upper floor plan

Middle floor plan

Lower floor plan   1 : 1400

First floor plan   1 : 1400

Section   1 : 1400

PETRONAS TOWERS

CESAR PELLI & ASSOCIATES INC.

CLIENT / CLIENT / AUFTRAGGEBER: KUALA LUMPUR CITY CENTER	**1998**
TOTAL AREA / SURFACE TOTALE / GESAMTOBERFLÄCHE: 884.000 m²	
FLOORS / PLANS / STOCKWERKE - HEIGHT / HAUTEUR / HÖHE: 88 fl / 452 m	

The Petronas Towers, apart from being the tallest in the world at the moment, are an example of good architecture. In the rules of the competition for two towers for the city center it was requested that they have a Malaysian identity. The architects worked to define this architecture which had to reflect and resolve the physical and cultural conditions of the country: tropical climate and Islamic culture. The juxtaposition of the two squares (the most characteristic shape of Islam) gave rise to the type of plan. Meanwhile, the silhouette of the towers throws shadows reminiscent of those thrown by the traditional buildings of Malaysia.

Les Tours Petronas ne sont pas seulement les plus hautes du monde, elle sont, aujourd'hui, un exemple d'une bonne architecture. Sur les bases du concours de deux tours pour le centre de la ville l'on demandait une identité malaienne. Les architectes travaillèrent afin de définir cette architecture qui devait représenter et résoudre les conditions physiques et culturelles du pays: climat tropical et culture islamique. La juxtaposition de deux carrés (la forme géométrique la plus caractéristique de l'islam) engendrera le plan type. À son tour, la silhouette des tours projette des hombres semblables à celles des bâtiments traditionnels de Malaisie.

Die Petronas Türme sind derzeitig die höchsten der Welt und gelten auch als Beispiel einer gelungenen Architektur. Die Bedingungen der Ausschreibung verlangten für das Stadtzentrum zwei Turmgebäude, die gleichzeitig Malaysias Identität repräsentieren sollten. Die Architekten entwickelten einen Entwurf, bei dem sowohl die physischen wie auch kulturellen Bedingungen wie Tropenklima und islamistische Kultur in Betracht gezogen wurden. Zwei nebeneinander liegende Quadrate (typische islamische Charakteristik) ergeben den Grundriß. Die Schatten der Turmsilhouette erinnern an die typische Form malaiischer Gebäude.

The façade is made of aluminum, glass and stainless steel. The structure is mixed: steel and concrete.

La façade est en aluminium, en verre et en acier inoxydable. La structure est mixte: acier et béton.

Außenfassaden aus Aluminium, Glas und Edelstahl. Die Mischstruktur besteht aus Stahl und Beton.

At a height of 170 meters, floors 41 and 42 of the building, a panoramic bridge unites the two towers.

À 170 m. de haut, niveau 41-42 du bâtiment, un pont panoramique unit les deux tours.

170 m über der Erde auf Höhe der 41. und 42. Etage verbindet eine Panoramabrücke beide Türme.

This bridge, aside from being a structural element, is symbolic at the same time, describing a gate open to the sky.

Ce pont est un élément structurel et il est aussi symbolique, il décrit une porte ouverte sur le ciel.

Neben ihrer Funktion als Teil der Baustruktur, ist die Brücke das Symbol einer offenen Tür am Himmel.

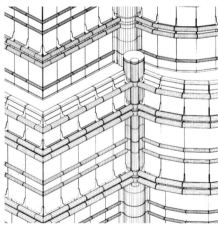

Detail of the crowning of the towers and a stretch of the facade with the solar protection elements.

Détail du couronnement des tours et d'une trame de la façade avec les éléments de protection solaire.

Detailansichten des krönenden Turmabschluß und Ausschnitt der Außenfassade mit Sonnenschutzblenden.

PLAZA 66
NANJING XI LU

KOHN PEDERSEN FOX ASSOCIATES PC

CLIENT / CLIENT / AUFTRAGGEBER: HANG LUNG DEVELOPEMENTB CO.LTD.

2001

TOTAL AREA / SURFACE TOTALE / GESAMTOBERFLÄCHE: 298.000 m²

FLOORS / PLANS / STOCKWERKE - HEIGHT / HAUTEUR / HÖHE: 60 fl / 288 m

This building is currently being built. It responds to a new typology of high-rise buildings. It consists of two towers connected by means of a structural bridge. The building rises along the most commercial street in the center of Shanghai. The program is a mixture of offices and shops. At street level a base of five floors with large interior public spaces houses the shops.
This atrium maintains the height of the traditional Chinese city, while the office towers maintain themselves at another level of the city.

Ce bâtiment qui est actuellement phase de construction, répond à une nouvelle typologie du gratte-ciel. Il s'agit de deux tours connectées entre elles par un pont structurel. Le bâtiment s'élève tout au long de la rue la plus commerciale du centre de Shanghai. Le programme est mixte, bureaux et boutiques. Au niveau de la rue un socle à cinq étages de haut aux grands espaces publiques intérieurs loge les boutiques.
Ce parvis conserve la hauteur de la ville chinoise traditionnelle, tandis que les tours de bureaux sont disposées sur un autre niveau de la ville.

Dieses Gebäude befindet sich derzeitig in der Bauphase und stellt einen neuen Hochhaustyp dar- zwei Türme durch eine Brücke verbunden – . Der Bau steht an der Hauptgeschäftsstraße mitten im Zentrum von Shanghai und sieht die Nutzung als Büro- wie auch Einkaufscenter vor. Auf Straßenhöhe beherbergt ein 5 stöckiger Unterbau große öffentliche Bereiche wie z.B. Boutiquen. Dieser Unterbau als Atrium ausgerichtet, behält die Bauhöhe der traditionellen chinesischen Stadt bei, wobei sich die Bürotürme in andere Sphären begeben.

While at street level one perceives a group of buildings with different uses, the unitary use of granite in the treatment of the building gives an idea of the mass which unifies the group.

Tandis qu'au niveau de la rue l'on perçoit un ensemble de bâtiments à plusieurs usages, l'usage unitaire du granite quant au traitement du bâtiment donne une idée de masse qui unit l'ensemble.

Während man auf Straßenhöhe ein Multifunktionsgebäude erblickt, vermittelt die einheitliche Verarbeitung von Granitsteinen eine Idee über die Ausmasse des gesamten Komplexes.

Above, the covered catwalk which
unites the two towers. On the right,
interior view of the shopping building
with ample public spaces and
different levels.

*En haut, la passerelle couverte qui
unit les deux tours. À droite,
perspective intérieure du bâtiment
commercial aux espaces publiques
amples et à plusieurs niveaux.*

Oben, überdachter Durchgang
zwischen den Türmen. Rechts:
Perspektiven unterschiedlicher Höhen
im Innern des Geschäftsgebäudes.

REPUBLIC NATIONAL BANK OF NEW YORK

ELI ATTIA ARCHITECTS

CLIENT / CLIENT / AUFTRAGGEBER: EDMOND SAFRA AND REPUBLIC NATIONAL BANK OF NEW YORK.	**1984**

TOTAL AREA / SURFACE TOTALE / GESAMTOBERFLÄCHE: 75.000 m²

FLOORS / PLANS / STOCKWERKE - HEIGHT / HAUTEUR / HÖHE: 29 fl / 122 m

Building projected to become the headquarters of the bank, incorporates a new building to three pre-existing buildings. Two of the previous buildings have considerable surface areas which the new diagram of the project incorporate as banking operation zones. The third, a beautiful stylish building which occupies the most significant corner of the project and which was the banks original headquarters, will become the centerpiece of the final design. The new building is the nexus linking all the others, contributing all the necessary technological infrastructures and the connections between the buildings.

Bâtiment destiné à devenir le siège central de la banque, il ajoute un nouveau bâtiment aux trois bâtiments déjà présents. Deux des bâtiments antérieurs présentaient des surfaces considérables que le nouveau schéma du projet incorpora en tant que zones d'opérations bancaires, le troisième, un joli bâtiment de style qui se trouve sur le coin le plus remarquable du projet et qui représentait à l'origine le siège de la banque, devint la pièce centrale de la conception finale. Le nouveau bâtiment représente le nexe d'union entre tous les autres, apportant toutes les infrastructures technologiques nécessaires et les connexions entre les bâtiments.

Dieses Gebäude wurde als neuer Hauptsitz dieser Bank entworfen und zieht drei bereits bestehende Gebäude in die Bebauung mit ein. Zwei dieser vorhandenen Gebäude verfügen über großzügige Oberflächen, die jetzt zur Abwicklung der täglichen Bankgeschäfte genutzt werden und das dritte Gebäude, ein stilvolles und besonders auffallendes Eckgebäude, war anfänglich der Sitz der Bank. Sie alle runden den nun gemeinsam mit dem Hochhaus den Gesamtanblick ab. Das neu erbaute Gebäude entstand unter Anwendung aller notwendigen infrastrukturellen Technologien und gilt als Bindeglied.

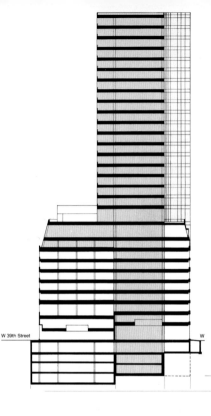

The main façade of the new tower combines bronze-toned glass, aluminum and granite, and is the formal result of the interaction of a positive faceted prism with a negative elliptical cylinder.

La façade principale de la nouvelle tour combine le verre aux tonalités en bronze, aluminium et granite, elle est le résultat formel de l'interaction d'un prisme à facettes positif et d'un cylindre elliptique négatif.

Die Hauptfassade des neuen Gebäudes kombiniert bronzefarbenes Glas mit Aluminium und Granit und ist das förmliche Ergebnis des Zusammenspiels zwischen einem geschliffenen Prisma und einem elliptischen Zylinder.

W 39th Street

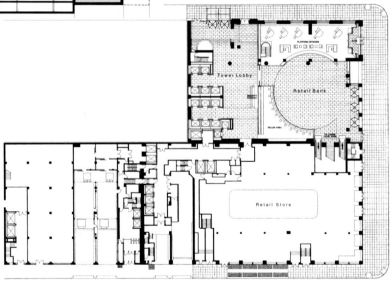

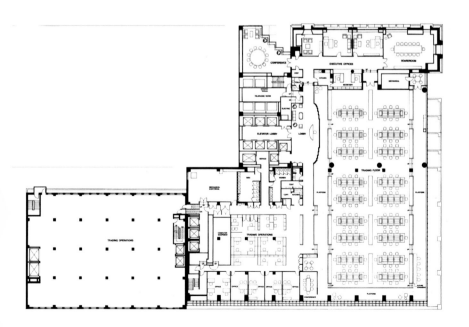

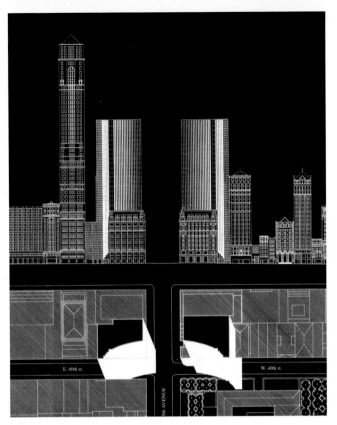

The fragmented curve embraces the representative building simply and dynamically, proposing complementary textures in shape and color.

La courbe fragmentée embrasse le bâtiment représentatif simplement et dynamiquement,
Il propose des textures complémentaires quant à la forme et à la couleur.

Die fragmentierte Gebäudekurve legt sich um den davor liegenden Stilbau und ergänzt durch seine unterschiedliche Textur das phantastische Spiel zwischen Form und Farben.

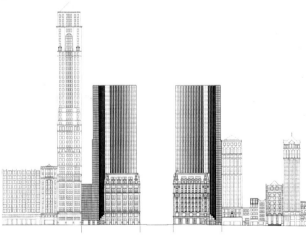

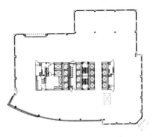

REUTERS BUILDING

FOX & FOWLE ARCHITECTS

2001

CLIENT / CLIENT / AUFTRAGGEBER: 3 TIMES SQUARE ASSOCIATES,LLC	
TOTAL AREA / SURFACE TOTALE / GESAMTOBERFLÄCHE: 855.000 m²	
FLOORS / PLANS / STOCKWERKE - HEIGHT / HAUTEUR / HÖHE: 30 fl -201 m	

The new Reuters Building, also known as 3 Times Square, is situated at a strategic point, the most dynamic junction in the city, the heart of Manhattan, that of the commercial Seventh Avenue and the boisterous 42nd Street (in addition, it so happens that it is opposite a building by the same architect). At urban scale, the building is a pivot where all the energy of these two arteries converges, thus the south corner of the ground floor is cylinder-shaped. Formally, it responds to the heterogeneity of the siting, orthogonal ground plan, curved and irregular, it assembles plans and counterpoints textures, colors and languages, fighting to abandon the purity of the prism left by the Modern Movement.

Le nouveau Reuters Building, connu aussi comme le 3 Times Square, se trouve sur un point stratégique, le croisement le plus dynamique de la ville, le coeur de Manhattan, celui de la Septième Avenue commerciale et la bruyante Rue 42 (circonstentiellement, il est en face d'un bâtiment du même architecte). Sur l'échelle urbaine, le bâtiment est un pivot où conflue toute l'énergie de ces deux artères, ainsi le coin sud du rez-de-chaussée adopte la forme d'un cylindre. Quant à la forme, il répond à l'hétérogénéité de l'emplacement, la vue en plan est octogonale, courbée et irrégulière, il assemble des plans et contrepose des textures, de la couleur et des langages, il lutte pour abandonner la pureté du prisme du Mouvement Moderne.

Das neue Reuters Building, auch als 3 Times Square bekannt, liegt strategisch im Herzen von Manhattan ausgerichtet an der dynamischsten Kreuzung, der Einkaufsmeile 7th Avenue mit der belebten 42. Straße (außerdem liegt es gegenüber eines Gebäudes des selben Architekten). Aus urbaner Sicht ist das Gebäude ein Treffpunkt sämtlicher Energien dieser beiden Arterien, was sich durch die zylindrische Formgebung der Südecke des Erdgeschosses ausdrückt. Gestalterisch entspricht das Gebäude dem heterogenen Umfeld. Mit achteckigem, unregelmäßig geschwungenem Grundriss, vereinigt es Ebenen und hält Texturen, Farben und Ausdruck dagegen und kämpft gegen die Gleichförmigkeit der Moderne.

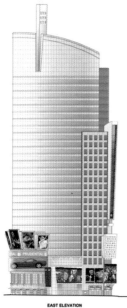

EAST ELEVATION

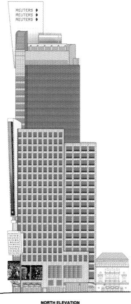

NORTH ELEVATION

WEST ELEVATION

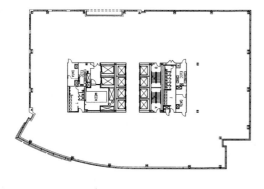

The architects confronted the unusual site of this building with the idea of designing a building that required the elegance of a 7th Avenue office block combined with the popular, commercial and theatrical charisma of New York's 42nd street.

Les architectes abordèrent l'emplacement exceptionnel de ce bâtiment avec le désire de concevoir un bâtiment qui puisse répondre à l'élégance obligée sur un immeuble de bureaux Septième Avenue avec le charisme populaire, commercial et théâtral de la Rue 42 de New York.

Der außergewöhnliche Standort dieses Gebäudes war für die Architekten die Herausforderung für den Entwurf eines Gebäudes mit der notwendigen Eleganz, die ein Bürohaus an der 7th Avenue Ecke 42. Straße, der populären Einkaufs- und Theaterstraße New Yorks, aufzuweisen hatte.

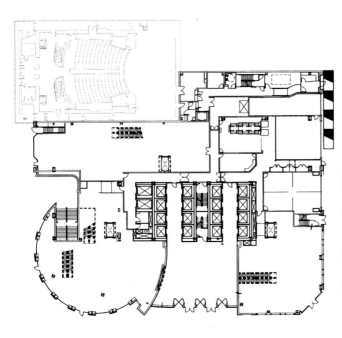

The floor plan is organised around a central communications core, leaving the rest of the space towards the perimeter of the building bare. The formal evenness of the lower, more public floors contrasts with the rest of the building, which seeks a more functional shape.

Le plan est organisé à partir d'un noyau de communications intérieur, l'espace restant est libre jusqu'au périmètre du bâtiment. Il contraste l'hétérogénéité formelle des étages inférieurs, les plus publics, par rapport au reste du bâtiment qui recherche une forme plus fonctionnelle.

Der Grundriß sieht die Anordnung der Versorgungsanlagen als Kern des Gebäudes vor, wobei die umliegenden Flächen freibleiben. Die Heterogenität der unteren Etagen bilden einen Kontrast zu den restlichen, öffentlichen Teilen des Gebäudes, die wesentlich funktioneller gestaltet wurden.

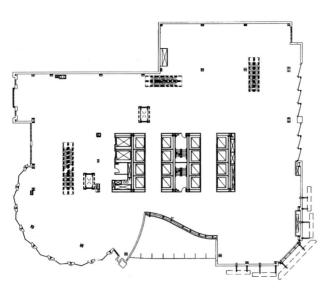

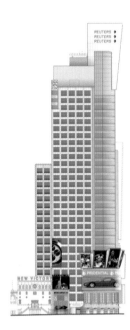

The façades of the building, Cubist in their plasticity, offer several views at each 45 degree turn. The building itself is clothed in different outfits that represent the diversity of its urban surroundings.

Les façades du bâtiment, plastiquement cubistes, offrent plusieurs visions qui s'ouvrent tous les 45 degrés. Le bâtiment, lui même, est revêtu de plusieurs costumes, ce qui représente la diversité de son environnement urbain.

Die Aussenfassaden des Gebäudes bestehend aus plastischen kubistischen Formen, die sich jeweils bei einer Drehung um 45 Grad unterschiedlich entfalten. Das Gebäude selbst zeigt sich in verschiedenen Gewändern und repräsentiert die Verschiedenartigkeit seiner Stadtumgebung.

RITZ-CARLTON HOTEL

ZEIDLER GRINNELL PARTNERSHIP

CLIENT / CLIENT / AUFTRAGGEBER: THE BOWMORE GROUP OF COMPANIES	**2004**
TOTAL AREA / SURFACE TOTALE / GESAMTOBERFLÄCHE: 79.000 m²	
FLOORS / PLANS / STOCKWERKE - HEIGHT / HAUTEUR / HÖHE: 65 fl / 300 m	

The program of the building includes a 219 room hotel, 112 company rooms, 300 apartments –including a luxurious duplex on the deck -, gymnasium with spa on two floors, hotel reception and all kinds of habitual services, conference halls and two dancehalls. Formally, the building is a square prism which loses section as it gains height, highlighting the corner between Adelaide and Bay streets, its main focus of attention. On a stone entrance base, the building starts with an exterior structure of limestone to give way to glass and aluminum on the final floors.

Le programme du bâtiment inclut un hôtel de 219 chambres, 112 chambres d'entreprise, 300 appartements –y compris un luxueux duplex sur le sommet–, un gymnase avec un établissement balnéaire sur deux étages, la réception de l'hôtel et tous types de services habituels, des salles de conférences et deux salles de danse. Formellement, le bâtiment est un prisme carré qui perd la section selon la hauteur, le coin entre les rues Adelaide et Bay se distingue, il est le point de repère principal. Sur une base à accès en pierre, le bâtiment commence par une structure extérieure en pierre calcaire et adopte le verre et l'aluminium sur les derniers étages.

Der Bau wird ein Hotel mit 219 Zimmern, 112 Firmenräume und 300 Apartments – einschließlich einem Luxus-Duplex auf dem Dach – Fitnessraum mit Bädern auf zwei Etagen, Hotelrezeption und allen möglichen Serviceangeboten sowie Konferenzsäle und zwei Tanzsäle beherbergen. Das Gebäude wird als aufsteigendes Quadrat, das mit wachsender Höhe an Umfang abnimmt, als Blickpunkt an der Ecke Adelaide/Bay-Street errichtet werden. Über einen auf Säulen stehenden Unterbau gelangt man in das Gebäude mit Kalksteinfassade, die dann in den letzten Etagen zu Glas und Aluminium überwechselt.

The building, built from reinforced concrete, has a façade covered in limestone, glass and aluminum.

Le bâtiment, construit avec du béton armé, recouvre sa façade de pierre calcaire, de verre et d'aluminium.

Gebäude aus Stahlbeton mit Kalkstein-, Glas- und Aluminiumfassade.

SEA HAWK
HOTEL & RESORT

CESAR PELLI & ASSOCIATES INC.

CLIENT / CLIENT / AUFTRAGGEBER: FUKOKA DAIEI REAL ESTATE INC	**1995**
TOTAL AREA / SURFACE TOTALE / GESAMTOBERFLÄCHE: 140.000 m²	
FLOORS / PLANS / STOCKWERKE - HEIGHT / HAUTEUR / HÖHE: 34 fl / 143,2 m	

The building is found on the bay of Hakata, an old fishing village which now forms part of the city of Fukoka. Its design responds to the place, the program and the role as a social center that hotels play in Japan. It was necessary for the property to play the role of hotel as holiday place in an urban environment. The diversity of forms that make up the parts of the building respond to a design which reinterprets traditional concepts of the imagery of holiday places offering an escape from the routine of the city.

Le bâtiment se trouve sur la baie de Hakata, un ancien village de pêcheurs qui appartient aujourd'hui à la ville de Fukoka. Sa conception répond au site, au programme et au rôle du centre social, c'est la fonction des hôtels au Japon. Le propriétaire désirait absolument réinterpréter le rôle de l'hôtel comme un lieu de vacances dans une ambiance urbaine. La variété des formes qui composent les parties du bâtiment répondent à une conception qui réinterprète les concepts traditionnels de l'imagerie du lieu de vacances, offrant un échappement face à la routine quotidienne de la ville.

Liegt in der Bucht von Hakata, einem ehemaligen Fischerdorf , das heute bereits Teil der Stadt Fukoka geworden ist. Sein Design entspricht seinem Umfeld sowie dem aktuellen Stil der japanischen Hotels, die auch gleichzeitig als gesellschaftliches Zentrum fungieren. Dem Auftraggeber war es besonders wichtig, mit diesem Hotel die Funktion eines Urlaubszentrums mitten in einem urbanen Bereich hervorzuheben. Die unterschiedliche Gestaltung von Gebäudeteilen entwickeln eine Ferienlandschaft, die zur Flucht aus der täglichen Stadtroutine einlädt.

The complex has 1044 bedrooms
and different leisure areas like the
Atrium, the terraces and the gardens.

*Le complexe dispose de 1044
chambres et de plusieurs zones
ludiques telles que le Parvis, les
terrasses et les jardins.*

Der Komplex verfügt über 1044
Zimmer und Erholungszonen wie dem
Atrium, Terrassen und Gärten.

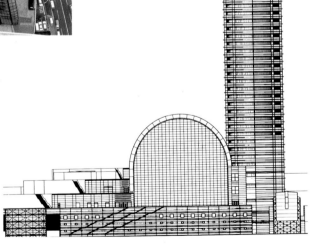

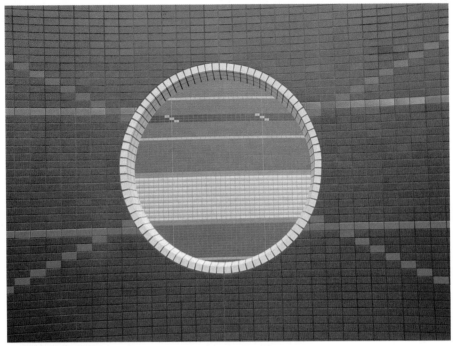

The façades are covered with ceramics of different colors and designs. At night the building throws out reflections of warm tonalities.

Les façades sont recouvertes de céramique de plusieurs couleurs et aspects. Le soir le bâtiment projete des reflets aux tonalités chaudes.

Fassaden mit Keramikfließen unterschiedlicher Formen und Farben. Nachts hüllt sich das Gebäude in warme Farbtöne.

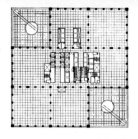

SEARS TOWER

SKIDMORE, OWING & MERRILL LLP (SOM)

CLIENT / CLIENT / AUFTRAGGEBER: SEARS ROEBUCK & CO.

1974

TOTAL AREA / SURFACE TOTALE / GESAMTOBERFLÄCHE: 410.000 m²

FLOORS / PLANS / STOCKWERKE - HEIGHT / HAUTEUR / HÖHE: 110 fl - 450 m

The Sears Tower is close to the Chicago Loop and is currently the second-tallest private office building in the world. It is the property of a department store company, and contains 109 floors of offices, ground floor entrance and three basement floors which house shopping areas, cafeterias and restaurants, a gymnasium, service areas and a large loading and unloading dock for trucks. It was designed attending to the needs of the property which required the combination of ample office floors with other smaller ones to be rented out. Starting out from a ground plan type comprising a reticle of 9 squares, it arrives at different combinations of full and empty spaces which disintegrate the solid mass of the building.

La tour Sears se trouve près du Loop de Chicago, actuellement, elle est le deuxième immeuble privé de bureaux le plus haut du monde. Elle appartient à une société de grands magasins, elle dispose de 109 étages de bureaux, d'un rez-de-chaussée d'accès et de trois étages souterrains où l'on trouve des zones commerciales, cafétérias et des restaurants, un gymnase, des aires de service et une grande plate-forme de chargement-déchargement pour camions. Elle a été conçue selon les besoins du propriétaire qui demandait la combinaison d'étages amples de bureaux et d'autres plus petits à louer. Le point de départ est un étage type composé d'un réticule de 9 carrés, l'on arrive à des combinaisons différentes d'espaces pleins et vides qui désintègrent la masse solide du bâtiment.

Der Sears–Turm befindet sich in der Nähe vom Loop de Chicago und ist gegenwärtig das zweithöchste private Bürogebäude der Welt. Als Eigentum eines Kaufhauskonzerns, besteht das Gebäude aus 109 Büroetagen mit Zugang im Erdgeschoss und 3 Kellergeschossen, die Shoppingcenter, Cafeterias und Restaurants, einen Fitnessraum, Servicebereiche und eine große Be– und Entladezone für LKWs beherbergen. Der Entwurf des Gebäudes berücksichtigte den Bedarf des Eigentümers an einer Kombination von weitläufigen Büroetagen mit kleineren Mieteinheiten. Ausgehend von einer aus 9 Quadraten gegliederten Grundfläche, erreichte man unterschiedliche Kombinationen bebauter und offenen Flächen, die die solide Gebäudemasse auflockern.

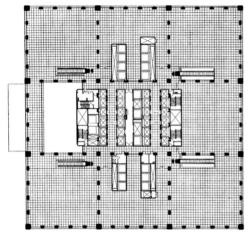

The basic floor plan is a grid of 9 blocks measuring 22.8 metres on each side, with pillars on the perimeter. The first 49 floors form a compact block made up of 9 squares, and from there on it is layered at intervals, removing two corner squares at every 16 and 23 storeys alternately. At the 109th floor there are only two squares.

Le plan type surgit d'un réticule de 9 carrés de 22,80 m de long, les piliers se trouvent sur les périmètres. Les 49 premiers étages établissent un bloc compact constitué par 9 carrés, et à partir de ce point là, la tour s'échelonne, supprimant deux carrés des coins tous les 16 et 23 étages, alternativement, de façon à ce qu'il ne reste plus que deux carrés à l'étage 109.

Der Grundriß besteht aus einem Netz von 9 Quadraten mit einer Seitenlänge von 22,80 m. Die Stützpfeiler stehen jeweils an den äußeren Seiten. Die ersten 49 Stockwerke ergeben einen kompakten Block aus 9 Quadraten. Ab diesem Punkt verläuft der Turm stufenartig, wobei dann abwechselnd alle 16 und 23 Stockwerke zwei Quadrate an den Gebäudeecken entfallen. Im 109. Stockwerk angekommen, besteht das Ganze nur noch aus zwei Quadraten.

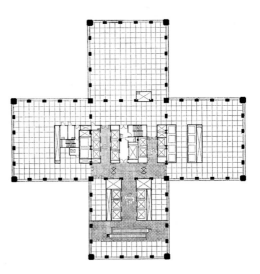

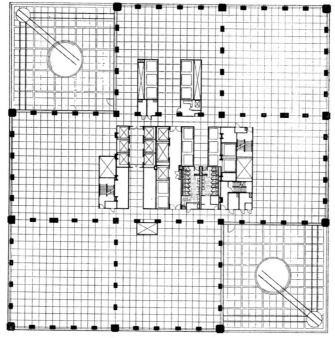

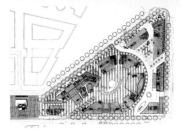

SONY CENTER-BERLIN

MURPHY / JAHN INC. ARCHITECTS

	2000
CLIENT / CLIENT / AUFTRAGGEBER: CLIENTE: SONY	
TOTAL AREA / SURFACE TOTALE / GESAMTOBERFLÄCHE: 159.000 m²	
FLOORS / PLANS / STOCKWERKE - HEIGHT / HAUTEUR / HÖHE: 26 fl / 103 m	

In the reconstruction of the Berlin of the 21st Century, the Sony-Center was proposed as a complex of buildings for the "new millennium". It is a cultural forum, a place for meetings and social interchanges, activity center, residential area and business center where the most advanced technology has been used in both its construction and its fitting out. It aims to be a virtual city within the city, where light (natural and artificial) is one of the essences of the design. Façades and roof work as tissues: transparent, permeable, reflective and sophisticated tissues which allow a constant succession of images, both night and day.

Lors de la reconstruction du Berlín XXIème siècle, le Sony Center fut conçu comme un complexe de bâtiments pour le «nouveau millénaire». Il s'agit d'un forum culturel, un lieu de rencontres et échanges sociaux, un centre d'activités, une zone résidentielle et un centre d'affaires où l'on a employé la technologie la plus sophistiquée, aussi bien quant à la construction que sur ses équipements. Elle prétend être une ville virtuelle dans la ville, où la lumière (naturelle et artificielle) est une des essences de la conception. Les façades et les toits fonctionnent comme des tissus: transparents, perméables, réfléchissants et sophistiqués, ils permettent une succession constante d'images, aussi bien de jour, que de nuit.

Das Sony-Center liegt als "Millenium-Komplex" im wiederaufgebauten Berlin des 21 Jahrhunderts. Es handelt sich um ein Kulturforum, das als gesellschaftlicher Treff– und Austauschpunkt, Zentrum unterschiedlicher Aktivitäten sowie als Wohn– und Arbeitsort entstand. Beim Bau wie auch in der Ausstattung wurden neueste Technologien angewandt. Der Bau beabsichtigt eine virtuelle Stadt in der Stadt zu sein, wo Licht (ob künstlich oder natürlich) eine der Essenzen des Design ist. Fassaden und Dächer wirken wie eine transparente, durchlässige, raffiniert spiegelnde Hülle, die ständig Tages– und Nachtbilder aufnimmt und wiedergibt.

Ground floor, ground plan and interior of the lobby of one of the four towers of offices. They are positioned at the corners of the lot, locating the medium and low buildings between them.

Rez-de-chaussée, plan type et intérieur du hall d'une des quatre tours de bureaux. Elles sont disposées sur les coins du terrain, les bâtiments dont la hauteur est moyenne et petite sont placés entre celles-ci.

Erdgeschoß, Zeichnung einer Etage und Innenansicht einer der Empfangshallen der vier Türme. Sie liegen links und rechts an den Ecken des Grundstücks; dazwischen liegen die Gebäude der mittleren und niedrigen Höhe.

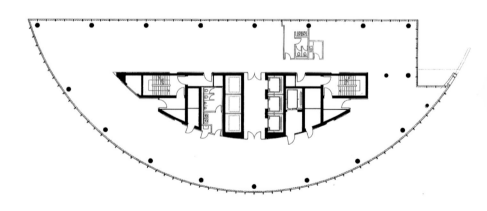

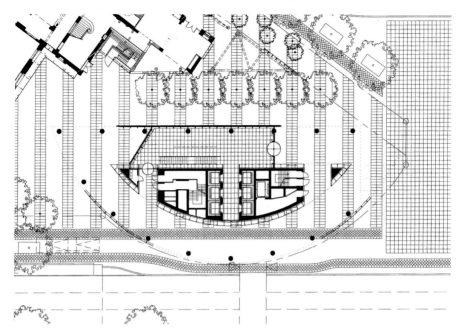

The complex consists of different buildings and various uses: homes, offices, shops, cultural activities (music, cinema, exhibitions), leisure centers and restaurants.

Le complexe comprend plusieurs bâtiments et usages: appartements, bureaux, boutiques, activités culturelles (musique, cinéma, expositions), centres de loisirs et restauration.

Der Komplex besteht aus verschiedenen Gebäuden mit unterschiedlicher Nutzung: Wohnungen, Büros, kulturelle Aktivitäten (Musik, Cinema, Ausstellungen), Vergnügungszentren und Gastronomie.

Both the glass (which is the predominant material in the façades of the towers) and the steel elements (mullions) are the most advanced available technology.

Aussi bien le verre (qui est le matériau principal de la façade des tours) que les éléments en acier (montants) répondent à la technologie la plus récente.

Sowohl Glas (hervorstechendes Material der Turmfassaden) als auch Stahl (Träger), entsprechen der neuesten Technologie.

SUYOUNG BAY TOWER 88

KOHN PEDERSEN FOX ASSOCIATES PC (KPF)

CLIENT / CLIENT / AUFTRAGGEBER: DAEWOO CORPORATION	**1988**
TOTAL AREA / SURFACE TOTALE / GESAMTOBERFLÄCHE: 256.000 m²	
FLOORS / PLANS / STOCKWERKE - HEIGHT / HAUTEUR / HÖHE: 102 fl / 462,1 m	

This tower project would be located in the coastal area of Pusan. It forms part of an urban plan to transform the bay of Suyong and the Landfill area. The plan will bring about an image of modernity by converting this part of the Korean coast into tourist and leisure areas. The program is complex and varied because it includes offices, hotel, apartment hotel, shops, museum, center for contemporary art, dancehalls and a convention center. The juxtaposition of these uses in a building responds to a vertiginous and artificial form of growth which businessmen, politicians and technicians think is a symbol of the growing economic development of the Asian continent.

Ce projet d'une tour devrait avoir son emplacement sur la zone de la côte de Pusan. Il appartient à un plan urbanistique pour transformer la baie de Suyong et la zone de Landfill. Le plan supposera une image de modernité, car il convertit cette partie de la côte coréenne en zones touristiques et de loisir. Le programme est complexe et varié, car il dispose de bureaux, d'un hôtel, d'un aparthôtel, de boutiques, de musée, d'un centre d'art contemporain, de salles de danse et d'un centre de conventions. La juxtaposition de ces usages dans un bâtiment répond à une forme vertigineuse et artificielle de croissance, les chefs d'entreprise, les hommes politiques et les techniciens pensent qu'il est le symbole de la croissance du développement économique du continent asiatique.

Dieses Hochhausprojekt ist für die Küstenzone von Pusan vorgesehen. Es ist Teil eines Bebauungsplans zur Neugestaltung der Bucht von Suyong und des Bereiches Landfill. Der Plan bedeutet die Verwandlung dieses Teil der koreanischen Küste in einen modernen Touristen- und Freizeitbereich. Es handelt sich um einen komplexen Bau mit Büros, Hotel, Aparthotel, Läden, Museum, Zentrum für zeitgenössische Kunst, Diskotheken und Konferenzzentrum. Das Vereinigen unterschiedlicher Bestimmungen in einem Gebäude entspricht den Vorstellungen von Unternehmern, Politikern und Technikern, die meinen, daß dies das Symbol wirtschaftlichen Wachstums auf dem asiatischen Kontinent versinnbildlichen würde.

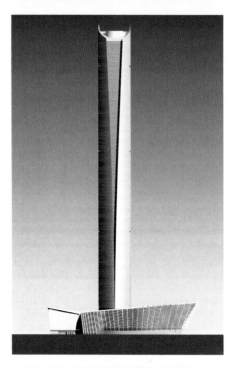

The extruding form of the tower and the curvature when reaching the ends (thus deleting two lateral façades) aim to lighten the volume of the building.

La forme extrudeuse de la tour et sa courbature sur les extrémités (deux façades latérales sont ainsi supprimées) désirent alléger le volume du bâtiment.

Die langgezogene Form des Turms und seine Drehung in sich selbst (so entfallen die Seitenfassaden), sollen dem Volumen Leichtigkeit verleihen.

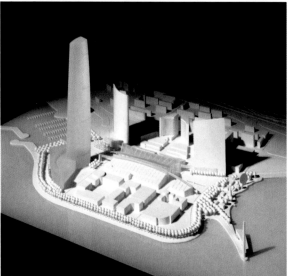

In addition to the idea of lightness, the design of the tower aims to emulate the wavy lines which are produced by its reflection in the water. This is what happens with the wavy forms of the base.

Outre l'idée de légèreté, la conception de la tour désire émuler les lignes ondulées que leur reflet produit sur l'eau. Il en est de même sur les formes ondulées du socle.

Neben der Idee der Leichtigkeit soll die Gestaltung auch die wellenförmigen Linien des Wassers darstellen. Dementsprechend ist der Unterbau wellenartig ausgerichtet.

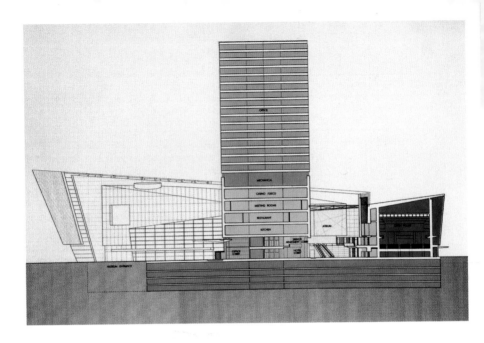

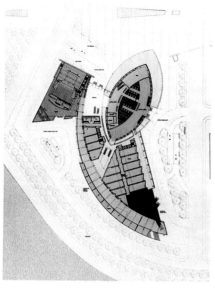

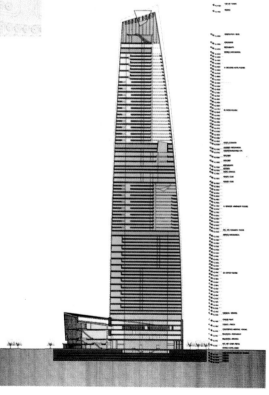

Location plans of the urban
development complex of the bay.
Sections of the base and the tower,
on whose top floor there is a
panoramic observation platform.

*Plans de l'emplacement du complexe
urbanistique de la baie. Sections du
socle et de la tour, sur le dernier
étage sur lequel se trouve un mirador
panoramique.*

Zeichnungen des urbanen Lageplans
des Komplexes in der Bucht.
Querschnitt des Unterbaus und des
Gebäudeturms ou in dessen obersten
Stock eine Panoramaterrasse liegt.

SWISS RE HQTRS.

FOSTER & PARTNERS

1997

CLIENT / CLIENT / AUFTRAGGEBER: SWISS REINSURANCE COMPANY

TOTAL AREA / SURFACE TOTALE / GESAMTOBERFLÄCHE: 76.400 m²

FLOORS / PLANS / STOCKWERKE - HEIGHT / HAUTEUR / HÖHE: 42 fl / 179,8 m

The building, which will house offices and a shopping area, will be located in a special place in the City, where the IRA demolished the Baltic Exchange. Conceptually, the project returns to the ideas of the "Climatroffice" projected together with B. Fuller in the 70s. Back then they proposed the harmonious relationship between nature and place of work. The scaly skin which protects the building settles from the façade to the roof. This membrane and the interior gardens of the building would create macroclimates which would render practically unnecessary the use of mechanical means to condition the interior temperature of the building during most of the year.

Le bâtiment qui disposera de bureaux et d'une surface commerciale, se trouve sur un endroit spécial de la City, où l'IRA a détruit le Baltic Exchange. Conceptuellement, le projet reprend les idées du «Climatroffice» conçu avec le B. Fuller pendant les années 70. Ils proposaient déjà la relation harmonique entre nature et lieu de travail. La peau écaillée qui protège le bâtiment est présente de la façade au toit. Cette membrane et les jardins intérieurs du bâtiment doivent créer des microclimats qui ne rendront presque pas nécessaire l'usage de moyens mécaniques pour conditionner la température intérieure du bâtiment pendant la plupart de l'année.

Das Gebäude wird Büros und Geschäftsräume beherbergen und liegt an einem besonderen Ort in der City, nämlich dort wo die IRA den Baltic Exchange zerstörte. Das Projekt greift das in den 70igern gemeinsam mit B. Fuller entworfene Konzept des „Climatroffice" wieder auf. Seinerzeit wurde bereits die Idee geboren, die Natur und den Arbeitsplatz harmonisch miteinander zu verbinden. Eine Schuppenhaut umhüllt das Gebäude von unten bis oben. Diese Haut und die Gärten im Inneren des Gebäudes schaffen ein Mikroklima, wobei man praktisch den größten Teils des Jahres auf künstliche Anlagen zur Innenklimaregulierung verzichten könnte.

The shape of the tower responds to the constraints of the city, making it more slender than a rectangular building of equivalent surface area.

La forme de la tour répond au resserrement de la ville, résultant plus svelte qu'un bâtiment rectangulaire d'une surface équivalente.

Die Gestalt des Turms paßt in das Bild der eng zusammenliegenden Stadt. Diese abgerundete konische Struktur ist wesentlich formschöner als die eines rechteckigen Gebäudes mit gleicher Oberfläche.

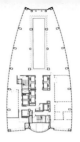

TAICHUNG TOWER II

KOHN PEDERSEN FOX ASSOCIATES PC (KPF)

CLIENT / CLIENT / AUFTRAGGEBER: TZUNG TANG DEVELOPMENT GROUP CO. LTD.	**2000**

TOTAL AREA / SURFACE TOTALE / GESAMTOBERFLÄCHE: 55.000 m²

FLOORS / PLANS / STOCKWERKE - HEIGHT / HAUTEUR / HÖHE: 47 fl / 176 m

The design of this hotel is inspired by the symbolism of Chinese culture. The ground plan reproduces the form of a fish oriented towards the east, a figure believed to be a good omen. The levels of the tower become reduced as they rise, curving towards the inside of the glass curtain wall and giving the building great poetic simplicity. The communication and service cores are situated to the west of the ground plan, freeing the rest for views of the park and minimizing the action of the setting sun. On September 21st 1999 this building, almost finished, faultlessly overcame an earthquake of 7·3 on the Richter scale, a situation which is by no means unusual in Taiwan.

La conception de cet hôtel s'inspire sur le symbolisme de la culture chinoise, elle reproduit sur le plan la forme d'un poisson orienté vers l'est, figure considérée comme un bon auspice. Les niveaux de la tour se réduisent selon ils s'élèvent, ils courbent le mur rideau vitré vers l'intérieur et dotent le bâtiment d'une grande simplicité poétique. Les noyaux de communication et de services se trouvent à l'ouest de l'étage, ce qui libère le reste aux vues sur le parc et minimise l'action du soleil de ponent. Le 21 septembre 1999 ce bâtiment, presque achevé, surmonta sans erreurs un tremblement de terre de 7,3 degrés sur l'échelle Richter, circonstance qui n'est pas si étrange à Taiwan.

Das Design dieses Hotels inspiriert sich im Symbolismus der chinesischen Kultur. Der Grundriß ist hat die Form eines zum Osten ausgerichteten Fisches. Der Fisch bedeutet ein gutes Omen. Mit wachsender Höhe werden die Planebenen des Gebäudes schmaler. Die gläserne, leichte gebogene Außenhaut beider Gebäudeseiten läuft aufeinander zu und verleihen dem Bau eine poetische Schlichtheit. Die Kommunikations– und Servicebereiche liegen auf der Westseite des Gebäudes und bieten den restlichen Einrichtungen freie Aussicht auf den Park und minimieren die Einstrahlung des Lichtes der untergehenden Sonne. Am 21. September 1999 konnte dieses fast fertiggestellte Gebäude einem Erdbeben der Stärke 7,3 auf der Richterskala standhalten; eine Situation, die in Taiwan nicht außergewöhnlich ist.

The tower consists of two glass-covered ground plans, slightly curved towards the sides and the summit raised on big pillars.

La tour est composée de deux plans vitrés légèrement courbés sur les côtés et le sommet repose sur des grands piliers.

Der Turm besteht aus zwei Glasfassaden, die sich auf hohen Pfeilern über dem Boden leicht an den Seiten in den Himmel zueinander biegen.

The building is calculated to
withstand earthquakes of great
intensity and last 475 years.
In 1999 it had the opportunity to
demonstrate the first point.

*Le bâtiment est conçu pour supporter
des tremblements de terre très
intenses et pour durer 475 ans. En
1999 elle put démontrer le premier
point.*

Das Gebäude ist so ausgerichtet, daß
es heftigen Erdbeben widersteht und
soll 475 Jahre halten. 1999 hatte es
bereits die zuerst erwähnte Situation
überstanden.

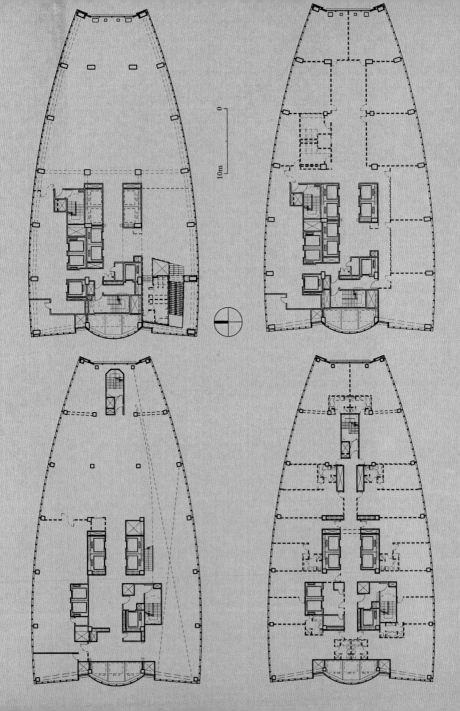

0

10m

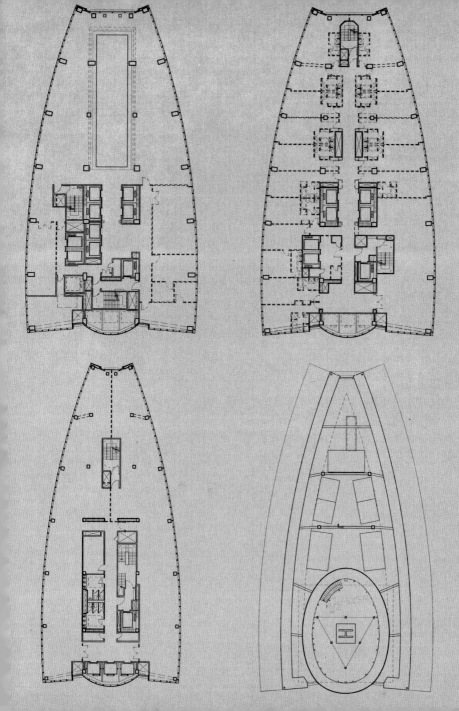

The beautiful and pure form of the building makes it recognizable from anywhere in the city, making it a landmark building.

La forme, belle et pure, du bâtiment permet de le reconnaître dans toute la ville, il est devenu en un signe du bâtiment.

Die schöne und puristische Form läßt das Gebäude von allen Stadtseiten aus erkennen und ist bereits zu einem Baudenkmal geworden.

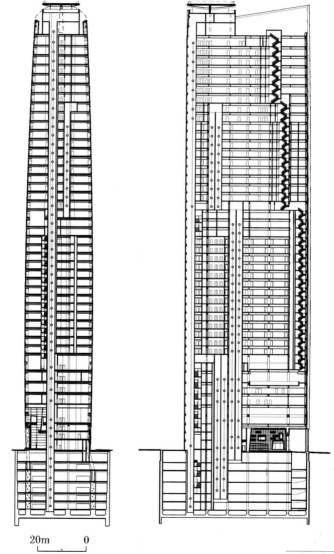

20m   0

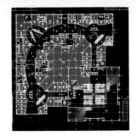

TAIPEI FINANCIAL CENTER

C.Y. LEE & PARTNERS

2003

CLIENT / CLIENT / AUFTRAGGEBER: TAIPEI FINANCIAL CENTER CORPORATIC	
TOTAL AREA / SURFACE TOTALE / GESAMTOBERFLÄCHE: 350.000 m²	
FLOORS / PLANS / STOCKWERKE - HEIGHT / HAUTEUR / HÖHE: 101 fl / 488 m	

In Taipei, the government has donated a large area where a director plan has been proposed which contains the Taipei Financial Center as a launching point. Formally, the tower places groups of eight floors on top of each other as a unit, assimilating the Chinese aesthetic with economic prosperity. Developed from the concepts of high technology and energy saving, it incorporates novel vitreous materials in the curtain walls of the façades of the tower, which confer on it transparency during the day and the appearance of a lighthouse - a new metaphor - at night.

À Taipei, le gouvernement a donné une grande zone où l'on a proposé un plan directeur qui inclut le Taipei Financial Center comme le sommet. Formellement, la tour superpose des groupes à huit étages en tant qu'unité, elle assimile l'esthétique chinoise et la prospérité économique. Développé sous les concepts de la grande technologie et l'économie de l'énergie, il incorpore des nouveaux matériaux en verre sur les murs rideau des façades de la tour qui lui confèrent une transparence le jour et l'aspect d'un phare –une nouvelle métaphore– le soir.

In Taipeh hat die Regierung einen weitläufigen Bebauungsbereich zur Verfügung gestellt und der Generalplan sieht bereits vor, das Taipeh Financial Center als eine Art Speerspitze zu präsentieren. Förmlich gesehen ist das Gebäude eine Aufstapelung von Baugruppen von jeweils acht Etagen als Nachempfindung des traditionellen chinesischen Pagodenturms und versinnbildlicht wirtschaftliche Prosperität. Neueste Technologie- und Energieeinsparungskonzepte wurden in die Entwicklung eingebracht. Glasartige Materialien als Außenhaut der Fassaden vermitteln tagsüber Transparenz und– ähnlich einer Metapher - wirkt es als Fackel in der Nacht.

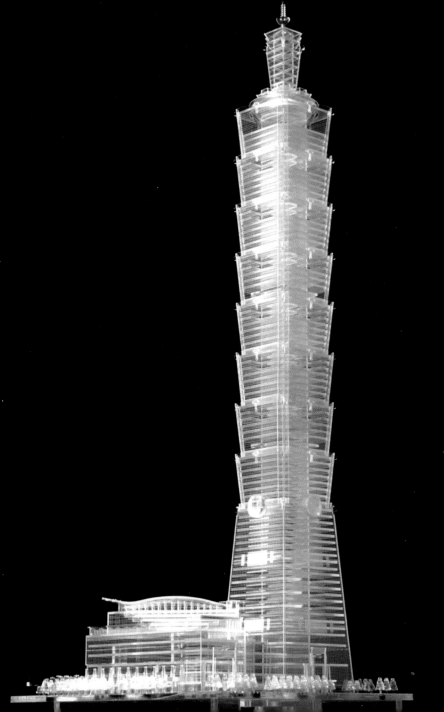

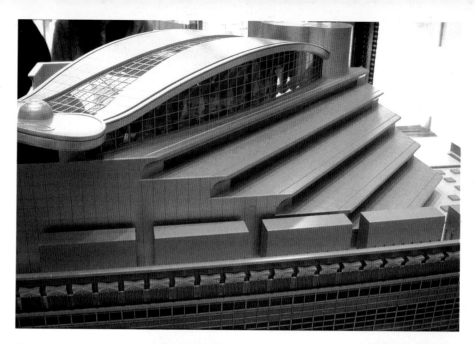

The tower will be complemented at ground level by a building which contains the most public uses; shopping center, leisure areas, conference hall, etc...

La tour est complétée, au niveau du sol, par un bâtiment qui dispose des usages publics le plus communs; centre commercial, surfaces de loisir, salle de conférences, etc...

Auf Bodenhöhe ergänzt sich der Turm durch ein Gebäude mit öffentlichen Bereichen wie Einkaufscenter, Freizeitbereiche, Konferenzsaal usw.

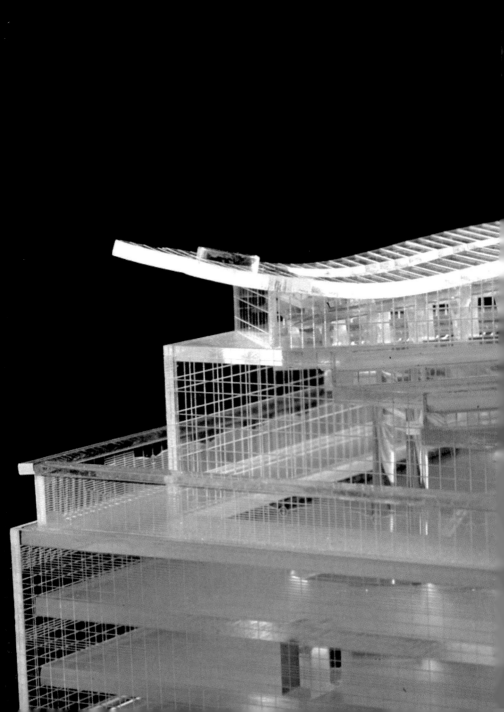

This building reproduces the constants of the firm of architects; the importance of the landmark, the formal Chinese language and being the tallest building in the world in 2003.

Ce bâtiment reproduit les constantes de la firme des architectes; l'importance du signe, le langage formel chinois et être le bâtiment le plus haut du monde en 2003.

Dieses Gebäude stellt die Zielvorstellungen der Architekten dar: die Errichtung eines architektonischen Meilensteins, den Ausdruck der chinesischen Art und 2003 das höchste Gebäude der Welt zu werden.

THE CENTER

DENNIS LAU & N.G. CHUN MAN
ARCHITECTS & ENGINEERS (H.K.) LTD.

CLIENT / CLIENT / AUFTRAGGEBER: URBAN RENEWAL AUTHORITY AND CHEUNG KONG LTD.	**1998**

TOTAL AREA / SURFACE TOTALE / GESAMTOBERFLÄCHE: 130.000 m²

FLOORS / PLANS / STOCKWERKE - HEIGHT / HAUTEUR / HÖHE: 78 fl / 346 m

This is currently the third highest building in Hong Kong. Characterized as an "intelligent building", it incorporates several service systems, including raised floors and technical paving, the first automatic gondola (hanging basket for façade maintenance) in Hong Kong and computer-controlled façade illumination. Formally, the building presents very pure volumes which accentuate their regularity with the totally glass-covered treatment of the curtain wall, with the sole exceptions of the meeting with the ground to allow access and the culmination.

Il est actuellement le troisième bâtiment, quant à la hauteur, de Hong Kong. Qualifié «bâtiment intelligent», il incorpore plusieurs systèmes de services et inclut le sol élevé et le revêtement technique, ainsi que la première gondole (panier suspendu de maintenance de la façade) automatique à Hong Kong et l'illumination de la façade contrôlée par ordinateur. Formellement, le bâtiment présente des volumes très pures qui accentuent sa régularité quant au traitement du mur rideau totalement vitré, sauf le contact au sol afin de permettre l'accès et le couronnement*.

Gegenwärtig das dritthöchste Gebäude in Hong Kong. Es wird als intelligentes Gebäude bezeichnet, welches verschiedene System nützt, wie z.B. Schwebeböden, die erste automatische Fassaden wartungsbühne in Hong Kong und eine computergesteuerte Aussenbeleuchtung. Der puristische Gebäudeumriß wird durch die gleichmäßige, durchgehende Außenhautverglasung betont, nur am Boden durch den Gebäudeeingang und oben von der Dachkrone unterbrochen wird.

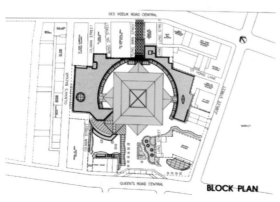

BLOCK PLAN

The form of the base of the building corresponds to two equal squares positioned at 45°, forming a star-shaped polygon.

La forme de la base du bâtiment correspond à deux carrés égaux installés à 45°, ils décrivent un polygone en étoile.

Zwei gleiche übereinandergelegte um 45 Grad Winkel gedrehte sternförmig angeordnete Quadrate ergeben den Gebäudegrundriß.

In its contact with the ground, the basic prism of the building dispenses with enclosure, allowing access through the trunk of a cylinder.

Sur son contact au sol, le prisme de base du bâtiment n'adopte pas de bardage, ce qui permet l'accès par un tronc de cylindre.

Dort wo der Turm Kontakt mit der Erde aufnimmt, verzichtet die Gebäudestruktur auf Mauereinfriedung Der Zugang erfolgt durch einen zylinderförmigen Bau, der das Gebäude umgibt.

The totally glass-covered treatment of the façade and the height of the building give it a great capacity for domination over its surroundings.

Le traitement de la façade totalement vitrée et la hauteur du bâtiment lui confèrent une grande capacité pour dominer son environnement.

Totale Fassadenverglasung und die Höhe verleihen dem Gebäude eine dominierende Position in seiner Umgebung.

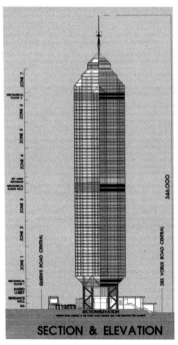

SECTION & ELEVATION

THE SHALOM CENTER

ELI ATTIA ARCHITECTS

CLIENT / CLIENT / AUFTRAGGEBER: CITY OF TEL AVIV AND CANIT	**2002**
TOTAL AREA / SURFACE TOTALE / GESAMTOBERFLÄCHE: 255.000 m²	
FLOORS / PLANS / STOCKWERKE: 38, 42, 46 fl HEIGHT / HAUTEUR / HÖHE: 153, 168, 184 m	

This regionally, nationally and internationally important project develops a very wide program, shopping center, theatres and community spaces in a low Y-shaped volume which contains all the public activities (plus a garage for 3500 cars in three basement floors) and three tall towers which contain the most private activities, such as office spaces and residential areas on the top floors. This complex is situated in an important communications hub, which makes it extremely accessible at the same time as isolating it from the rest of the city.

Projet d'une importance régionale, nationale et internationale, il développe un programme très ample, un centre commercial, des théâtres et des espaces communitaires sur un volume bas en «Y», qui contient toutes les activités publiques (et un garage pour 3.500 voitures sur trois étages souterrains) et trois gratte-ciel qui disposent des activités les plus privées comme par exemple les espaces de bureaux et les zones résidentielles sur les derniers étages. Ce complexe se trouve sur un noyau de communications important, qui le rend très accessible et, aussi, l'isole du reste de la ville.

Ein Projekt von regionaler, nationaler und internationaler Bedeutung. Es wird Einkaufszentrum, Theater und Gesellschaftsräumlichkeiten in einer "Y"-förmigen Flachbauanlage unterbringen (darunter eine dreistöckige unterirdische Garage für 3.500 Fahrzeuge). Dazu kommen drei Gebäudetürme, die Büros sowie Wohneinheiten in den oberen Stockwerken beherbergen werden. Dieser Komplex wird an einem absolut erreichbaren Kommunikationsknotenpunkt liegen, isoliert sich aber gleichzeitig vom Rest der Stadt.

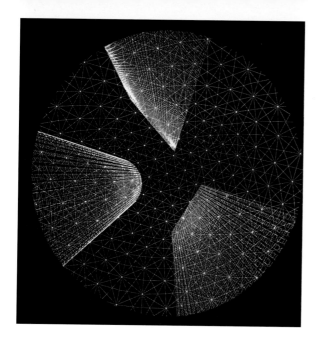

The three towers have very differentiated simple forms: square, circular, triangular; together they make up a harmonious group.

Les trois tours disposent de formes simples très différenciée: carré, cercle, triangle; ensemble elles dessinent un ensemble harmonieux.

Drei einfache aber unterschiedliche Turmformen: quadratisch, rund und dreieckig.
Zusammen ergeben sie eine harmonische Gesamtanlage.

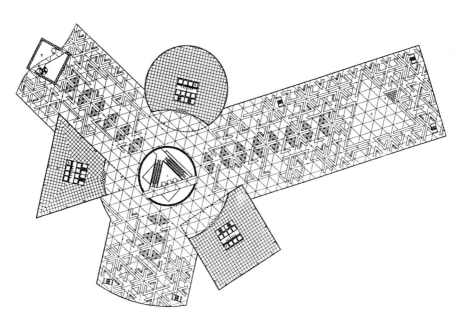

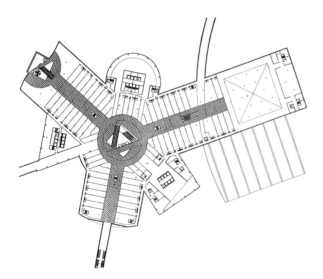

The Y-shaped base signals three directions: Jerusalem, Yaffo and the north.
It symbolizes the convergence of people united in a common objective.

La forme en «Y» de la base indique trois directions: Jérusalem, Yaffo et le nord.
Cela symbolise la confluence des gens, unis pour un objectif commun.

Die Y-Form des Grundrisses deutet in drei Richtungen: nach Jerusalem, Yaffo und in den Norden. Es symbolisiert das Aufeinandertreffen von gleichgesinnten Menschen mit einem gemeinsamen Ziel.

Shalom Center - 2nd Floor Plan - Shopping Mall
Eli Attia Architects New York

The low body presents a hexagonal
structure, the ideal container for
diverse uses. The towers present a
nuclear structure, which frees up the
rest of the ground plan.

*Le corps bas présente une structure
hexagonale, idéale pour loger des
usages divers. Les tours présentent
une structure nucléaire, ce qui libère
le reste de l'étage.*

Achteckiger Unterteil des Komplexes,
ideal für unterschiedliche Nutzung.
Die Türme präsentieren einen
kompakten Strukturkern, um sich
dann frei voneinander zu erheben.

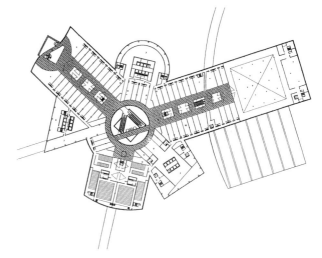

Shalom Center - 3rd Floor Plan - Shopping Mall
Eli Attia Architects New York

The blue-colored metallic curtain wall, combined with windows and skylights made of reflective blue glass, remind one of the idea of Tel Aviv as "White City".

Le mur rideau métallique blanc, combiné avec des fenêtres et des lucarnes en verre réfléchissant bleu, nous rappellent l'idée de Tel Aviv comme «Ville Blanche».

Die weiße metallische Außenhaut, kombiniert mit Fenstern und blau spiegelnden Oberlichtern aus Glas erinnern daran, daß Tel Aviv auch als „weiße Stadt" bezeichnet wird.

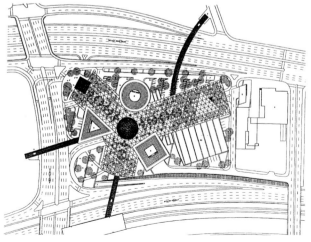

TOKYO-NARA TOWER

T.R. HAMZAH & YEANG SDN BHD

CLIENT / CLIENT / AUFTRAGGEBER: TRIENAL DE NARA

1994

TOTAL AREA / SURFACE TOTALE / GESAMTOBERFLÄCHE: 1.155.000 m²

FLOORS / PLANS / STOCKWERKE - HEIGHT / HAUTEUR / HÖHE: 210 fl / 800 m

This project is an investigation of the nature and evolution of high-rise buildings. It is the result of the application of concepts such as vertical landscaping. Part of the façade becomes a hanging garden, sustained and maintained through a spiral which wraps around the building. The spiral movement of the habitable containers generates terraces, the hanging oasis and flat community gardens every few floors.

The situation of the technological infrastructure concentrated in the culmination of the building and the layout of the materials, openings and communication cores contributes to the thermic warmth of the building.

Ce projet est une recherche sur la nature et l'évolution des gratte-ciel. Il est le résultat de l'emploi de concepts comme le paysagisme vertical. Une partie de la façade se transforme en jardin en suspension, suspendu et maintenu par une spirale qui entoure le bâtiment, le déplacement en spirale des conteneurs habitables engendre des terrasses, des oasis en suspension, des jardins communitaires plats avec une fréquence de quelques étages.

La disposition de l'infrastructure technologique concentrée sur le sommet du bâtiment et la disposition des matériaux, des ouvertures et des noyaux de communications apportent une qualité thermique au bâtiment.

Dieser Bau ist Ergebnis der Naturforschung und der Evolution von Hochhäusern. Hier werden Konzepte in Form von vertikalen Landschaften verwirklicht. Teile der Fassade verwandelt sich in hängende Gärten, die von einer das Gebäude umlaufende Spirale gehalten und getragen werden. Die spiralförmige Anordnung der bewohnbaren Bauteile ergeben in gewissen Abständen Terrassen, hängende Oasen und Gemeinschaftsgärten. Technologische Infrastrukturen finden krönenden Abschluß im oberen Teil des Turms wobei Anordnung und Beschaffenheit von Materialien, Öffnungen und zentrale Versorgungsbereiche zur hohen thermischen Qualität des Gebäudes beisteuern.

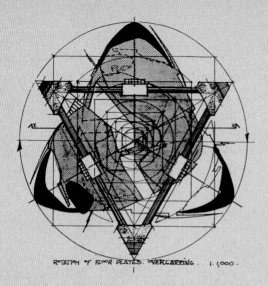

ROTATION OF FLOOR PLATES: OVERLAPPING. 1:1,000.

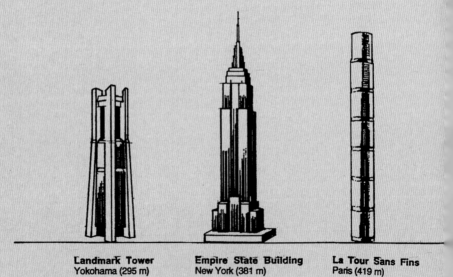

Landmark Tower
Yokohama (295 m)

Empire State Building
New York (381 m)

La Tour Sans Fins
Paris (419 m)

0   100   200

Height Comparisons

Sears Tower
Chicago (457 m)

Petronas Towers
Kuala Lumpur (450 m)

Millennium Tower
Japan (800 m)

Tokyo-Nara Tower
Tokyo-Nara (880 m)

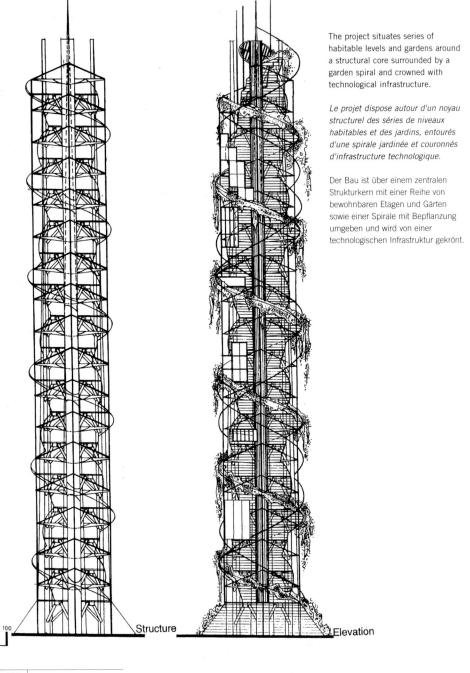

The project situates series of habitable levels and gardens around a structural core surrounded by a garden spiral and crowned with technological infrastructure.

Le projet dispose autour d'un noyau structurel des séries de niveaux habitables et des jardins, entourés d'une spirale jardinée et couronnés d'infrastructure technologique.

Der Bau ist über einem zentralen Strukturkern mit einer Reihe von bewohnbaren Etagen und Gärten sowie einer Spirale mit Bepflanzung umgeben und wird von einer technologischen Infrastruktur gekrönt.

Structure

Elevation

100

TORRE AGBAR

ATELIER JEAN NOUVEL + b 720 ARQUITECTOS

CLIENT / CLIENT / AUFTRAGGEBER: AGBAR (COMPANYIA D'AIGÜES DE BARCELONA)

2003

TOTAL AREA / SURFACE TOTALE / GESAMTOBERFLÄCHE: 47.500 m²

FLOORS / PLANS / STOCKWERKE - HEIGHT / HAUTEUR / HÖHE: 31 fl / 142 m

This building, which forms part of the urban planning operation that the city council has promoted for the year 2004, will be the tallest skyscraper to interrupt the city's silhouette. "It is not a tower, nor a skyscraper in the American sense of the term: it is a unique emergent volume in the middle of a more or less peaceful city" J. Nouvel has written to explain the meaning of the building, which aims to accentuate the symbolic and singular character of the corporate building, emphasizing through the treatment of the building's enclosures, which cancel out the concept of roof and façade underneath a single skin.

Ce bâtiment, qui appartient à l'opération urbanistique que la mairie de la ville a conçu pour 2004, sera le gratte-ciel le plus haut de la silhouette de la ville. «Il ne s'agit pas d'une tour, ni d'un gratte-ciel dans le sens américain du terme: c'est un volume émergent unique au milieu d'une ville plutôt tranquille» a écrit J. Nouvel pour expliquer le sens du bâtiment, qui désire accentuer le caractère symbolique et singulier du bâtiment corporatif, souligné par le traitement des bardages du bâtiment qui annulent le concept de toit et de façade, sous une seule peau.

Diese Gebäude ist Teil eines Bebauungsplans, den die Stadtverwaltung von Barcelona für das Jahr 2004 vorsieht. Es wird der höchste Wolkenkratzer sein, der die Stadtsilhouette unterbricht. "Es handelt sich nicht um ein Hochhaus, auch nicht um einen Wolkenkratzer im amerikanischen Sinn, sondern um ein einzigartiges Element, daß aus der Mitte einer eher ruhigen Stadt auftauchen wird", beschrieb so J. Nouvel die Bedeutung dieses Baues, der den symbolischen und singulären Charakter eines Geschäftsgebäudes betont und dabei durch die außergewöhnliche Form, Dach und Fassade aufhebt und alles unter eine einzige Haut bringt.

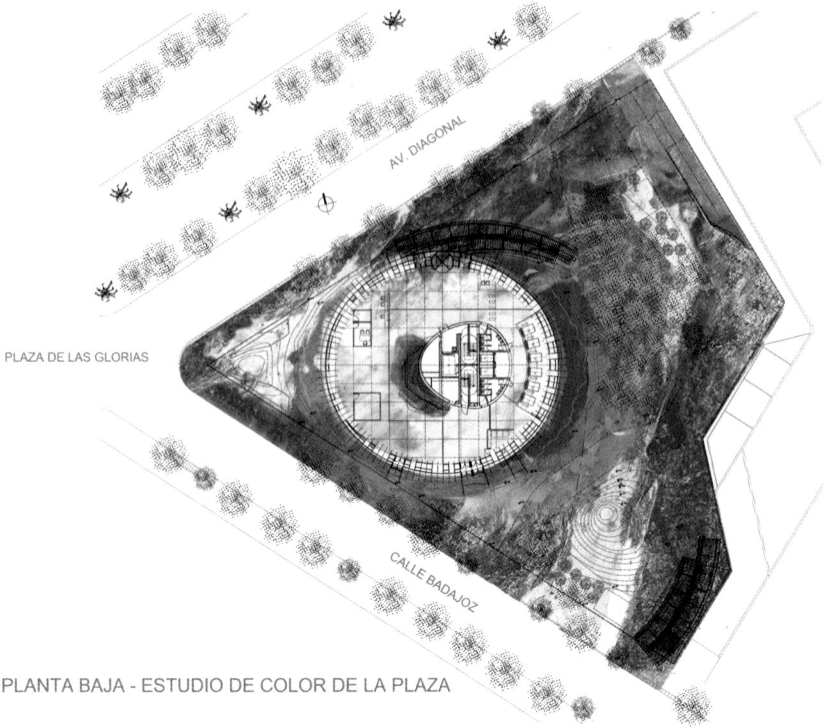

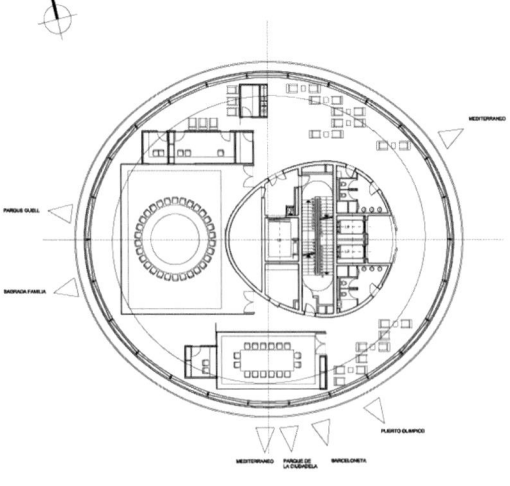

AV. DIAGONAL

PLAZA DE LAS GLORIAS

CALLE BADAJOZ

PLANTA BAJA - ESTUDIO DE COLOR DE LA PLAZA

PLANTA 26 - PLANTA DE ALTA DIRECCION

Above, siting of the tower whose base is surrounded by a very special green area, with ponds, waterfalls and a mineral area which functions as a moat which separates the building from the road.

En haut, emplacement de la tour dont la base est entourée d'une zone verte très spéciale, avec des étangs, des cascades et une zone minérale qui représente une fosse qui isole le bâtiment de la chaussée.

Oben, Lageplan des Hochhauses, umgeben von einer besonderen Grünanlage, nämlich von Wasserkaskaden und einem Steingraben, der den Bau von der Straße trennt.

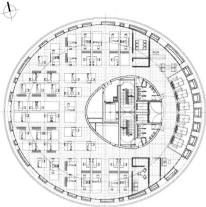

PLANTA TIPO DE OFICINAS - DISTRIBUCION LIBRE

The building can be divided into two
stretches, a concrete shaft in the
first 25 office type floors and a glass
dome in the top 6 floors for top
management which crown the
building.

*Le bâtiment peut être divisé en deux
trames, un fût en béton sur les 25
premiers étages type à bureaux et
une coupole en verre sur les 6
derniers étages destinés aux grands
directeurs, elle couronne le bâtiment.*

Das Gebäude wird sich auf zwei
Abschnitte verteilen. Ein Säulenschaft
aus Beton in den ersten 25
Büroetagen und eine Glaskuppel über
6 Stockwerke als krönender
Gebäudeabschluß, in der sich die
Direktionsetagen des Unternehmens
befinden werden.

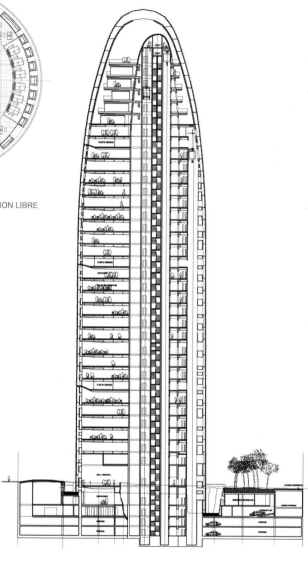

SECCION OESTE - ESTE

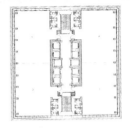

TORRE MAPFRE

ORTIZ LEON ARQUITECTOS

CLIENT / CLIENT / AUFTRAGGEBER: MAPFRE	**1992**

TOTAL AREA / SURFACE TOTALE / GESAMTOBERFLÄCHE: 70.000 m²

FLOORS / PLANS / STOCKWERKE - HEIGHT / HAUTEUR / HÖHE: 43 fl / 153,5 m

The holding of the Olympic Games in Barcelona 1992 meant a series of urban planning interventions which substantially changed the city's image. One of the most representative architectural elements of that transformation are the "Mapfre" and "Hotel de les Arts" towers in the Olympic Village, a newly created residential neighborhood where the athletes were housed during the games. The Mapfre Tower is not only a business center, its surface area is laid out in two low building used for shopping and offices. This tower is characterized by the square ground plan and the uniform treatment by means of horizontal bands on the façades.

La célébration des Jeux Olympiques de Barcelone 92 supposa une série d'interventions urbanistiques qui changèrent beaucoup l'image de la ville. Un des éléments architectoniques les plus représentatifs de cette transformation sont les tours «Mapfre» et l'«Hôtel de les Arts» à la Vila Olímpica, un quartier résidentiel nouveau où logèrent les athlètes pendant les jeux. La Torre Mapfre n'est pas seulement un centre d'affaires, sa surface est distribuée en deux bâtiments bas à usage commercial et de bureaux. Cette tour se caractérise par le plan carré et le traitement uniforme avec des franges horizontales sur les façades.

Die Ausrichtung der olympischen Sommerspiele von Barcelona 1992 erforderte eine Reihe von urbanistischen Interventionen, die das Stadtbild bedeutend verändert haben. Eines der architektonischen Veränderungen sind die Türme "Mapfre" und das "Hotel de les Arts" im olympischen Dorf, einem Neubauviertel, in dem die Athleten Unterkunft fanden. Der Mapfre–Turm ist nicht nur ein reines Geschäftshaus, sondern er beherbergt im unteren Teil in zwei Flachbauten Shoppingmeilen und Büros. Dieser Turm charakterisiert sich durch seinen quadratischen Grundriß und durch gleichmäßige horizontale Fassadenverblendungen.

The problems of image, exposure to the sun, energetic transmission, comfort, maintenance and cleaning have been basic conditioners in the design of the façade.

Les problèmes d'image, d'ensoleillement, de transmission énergétique, de confort, de maintenance et de nettoyage ont été les conditions de base de la conception de la façade.

Imagefragen, Sonneneinstrahlung, Energieübertragung, Komfort, Instandhaltung und Reinigung waren bestimmend für diesen Fassadenentwurf.

The structure is mixed, with a concrete core and highly resistant metallic perimeter pillars separated from the rigid core.

La structure est mixte, elle a un noyau en béton et des piliers métalliques périmétraux d'une grande résistance séparés du noyau rigide.

Die Mischstruktur besteht aus einem Betonkern, der wiederum von äußerst widerstandsfähigen vom Gebäudekern getrennten Stahlträgern umgeben ist.

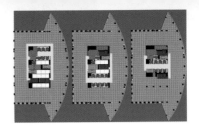

TORRE MAYOR

ZEIDLER GRINNELL PARTNERSHIP

CLIENT / CLIENT / AUFTRAGGEBER: ICA REICHMANN TORRE MAYOR	**2002**
TOTAL AREA / SURFACE TOTALE / GESAMTOBERFLÄCHE: 140.000 m²	
FLOORS / PLANS / STOCKWERKE - HEIGHT / HAUTEUR / HÖHE: 57 fl / 225 m	

This building, which will dominate the Chapultepec Park, has been designed to stand out in the skyline of the city as one of the tallest buildings. The play between the rectangular stone volumetry of the façade with its curved curtain wall will be visible and changing as one moves along the Paseo de la Reforma. The main façade breeches the curtain wall in the floors closest to the ground, creating an impressive entrance through the square. The podium, designed as two lion's claws which embrace and open the square towards the Paseo de la Reforma, was designed to give life to the entrance space, with shops and restaurants.

Ce bâtiment qui sera le sommet du Parc de Chapultepec, a été conçu pour être repéré dans le skyline de la ville, comme une des plus grandes tours. Le jeu de la volumétrie rectangulaire en pierre et la façade du mur rideau courbé seront visibles et changeants selon on avance sur le Paseo de la Reforma. La façade principale déplace le mur rideau sur les étages les plus proches au sol, cela crée une entrée impressionnante à travers la place. Le podium, conçu comme deux griffes de lion qui entourent et ouvrent la place vers le Paseo de la Reforma, fut conçu pour apporter de la vitalité à l'espace d'accès, avec des boutiques et des restaurants.

Dies wird im Park Chapultepec gelegen, eines der höchsten Gebäude an der Skyline der Stadt sein. Das Zusammenspiel zwischen dem rechteckigen Gebäudeteil und der geschwungenen Fassade wird sichtbar, je mehr man sich auf dem Paseo de la Reforma dem Gebäude nähert. Die Außenhaut der Hauptfassade zieht sich zur Bodennähe zurück und ergibt einen äußerst beeindruckenden Eingangsbereich, den man über einen Platz erreicht. Das Eingangspodium ist seitlich ähnlich wie Löwenpranken entworfen, das zupacken und den Platz zum Paseo de la Reforma öffnen. Dies wurde zur Belebung des Eingangsbereichs erdacht, in dem Geschäfte und Restaurants liegen werden.

The project concentrates the greater part of its efforts in approximating the scale of the building to the user by means of its entrance.

Le projet concentre la plupart de ses efforts sur l'approximation de l'échelle du bâtiment à l'utilisateur par son accès.

Der Bau konzentriert Hauptteil seiner Kraft auf den Eingangsbereich, um dem Benutzer auf diese Art das Gebäude eines solchen Maßstabs näher zu bringen.

The curtain wall withdraws, leaving the structure of the façade exposed, the square and the shopping center bring the building closer to the Paseo de la Reforma.

Le mur rideau est déplacé, il laisse la structure de façade exempte; la place et le centre commercial rapprochent le bâtiment du Paseo de la Reforma.

Die Außenhaut zieht sich zurück und läßt die Fassadenstruktur offenliegen. Der Platz und das Einkaufszentrum nähern das Gebäude an den Paseo de la Reforma.

The main façade repeats on the deck the breeching of the entrance, generating a skylight under which the floors are staggered.

La façade principale reprend le déplacement de l'accès sur le recouvrement, ce qui engendre une verrière sous laquelle les étages s'échelonnent.

Der stufenförmige Einzug der Hauptfassade wiederholt sich an der Decke im Eingangsinnenbereich und die offene Struktur ergibt ein Oberlicht, das die darüber aufsteigenden Etagen erkennen läßt.

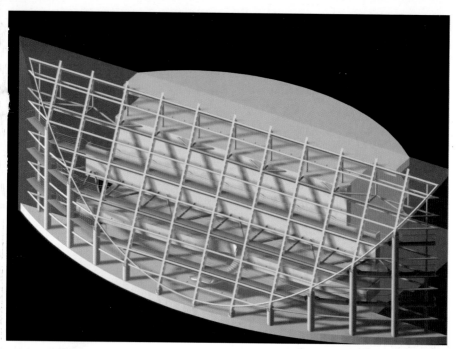

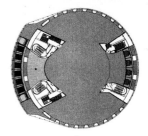

TOUR SANS FINS

ARQUITECTURES JEAN NOUVEL

CLIENT / CLIENT / AUFTRAGGEBER: SCI TOUR SANS FIN	**1989**

TOTAL AREA / SURFACE TOTALE / GESAMTOBERFLÄCHE: 91.000 m²

FLOORS / PLANS / STOCKWERKE - HEIGHT / HAUTEUR / HÖHE: 92 fl / 460,60 m

This is the winning project of a competition which proposed the construction of a building in a lot next to the Grand Arch, in La Défense, the district where the high-rise buildings of Paris are concentrated. This singular tower, which aspires to be the slenderest in the world when it is built, has been conceived from the idea of ascension and fainting. From the choice of materials for the façade (granite, stone and glass make up a gradation) to the relation width/height with which it has been designed, the idea of the project is materialized. The building responds both to the concept (Tour sans fins) and the urban context, working as a ball and socket joint which articulates the complex presided over by the Grand Arch.

Il s'agit du projet vainqueur d'un concours qui proposait la construction d'un bâtiment sur un terrain proche au Grand Arch, à La Défense, le district où se trouvent les bâtiments élevés à Paris. Cette tour singulière, qui aspire à être la plus belle du monde lorsqu'elle sera construite, a été conçue sur l'idée de l'ascension et l'évanouissement. L'élection des matériaux de façade (granite, pierre et verre composent un dégradé), mais aussi la relation largeur/hauteur de la conception, matérialisent l'idée du projet. Le bâtiment répond aussi bien au concept (Tour sans fins) qu'au contexte urbain, il fonctionne comme une rotule qui articule le complexe que préside le Grand Arch.

Dieses Projekt gewann einen Wettbewerbs für die Errichtung eines Baues auf einem Grundstück neben dem Grand Arch in La Défense, dem Pariser Stadtteil, wo Hochhäuser konzentriert stehen.
Sobald dieses einzigartige Hochhaus fertiggestellt ist, möchte es sich als das Schönste der Welt bezeichnet. Es wurde mit der Idee von Anstieg und Fall konzepiert. Von der Wahl der Außenhautmaterialien (Granit, Stein und Glas, degradierend verarbeitet) bis hin zum Verhältnis Breite/Höhe, verwirklicht sich die Projektidee. Der Bau entspricht ebenso dem Konzept des Tour Sans Fin wie auch dem urbanen Kontext und stellt ein funktionelles Glied zum Komplex dar, der vom Grand Arch präsidiert wird.

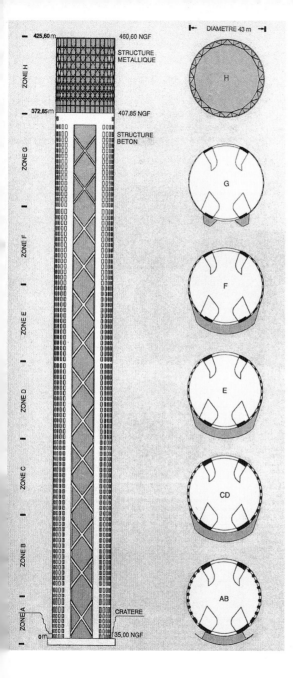

The peripheral, mixed structure frees the entire interior constructed surface area without conditioning the interior distribution. Made of perforated reinforced concrete at its base, the structure becomes lighter as it rises in height through the use of crossbeams, ending with a lightweight metallic structure at the top floors.

La structure périphérique et mixte permet de libérer toute la surface construite intérieure sans déterminer la distribution intérieure. En béton armé perforé sur la base, elle devient plus légère selon elle s'élève avec des moises transversales et s'achève comme une structure métallique légère sur les derniers étages.

Die seitliche Verlagerung der gemischten Struktur erlaubt die Umbauung der gesamten Oberfläche ohne dabei die Innendistribution zu beeinflussen. Sein Sockel besteht aus perforiertem Stahlbeton, der sich langsam auflöst sobald er auf der Höhe der Querverstrebungen anlangt, um dann in Form einer leichten Stahlstruktur in den oberen Stockwerken zu enden.

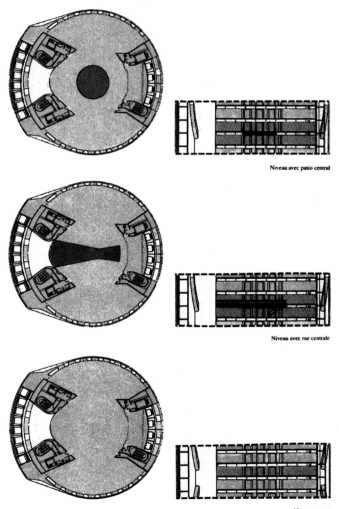

Niveau avec patio central

Niveau avec rue centrale

Niveau courant

Plan/coupe

Plateau
Noyaux
Patio central
Rue centrale
Vide sur fenêtres urbaines

LES NIVEAUX
SUPERIEURS

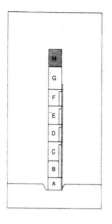

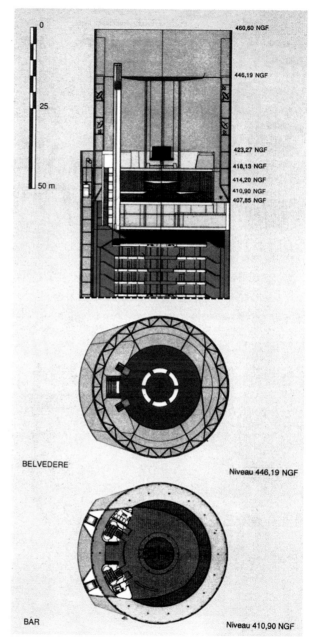

0

460,60 NGF

446,19 NGF

25

423,27 NGF
418,13 NGF
414,20 NGF
410,90 NGF
407,85 NGF

50 m

BELVEDERE

Niveau 446,19 NGF

COUPE / PLANS

- ◼ Belvédère
- ◼ Bar
- ◼ Panoramique
- ▼ Terrasse
- ◼ TMD
- ◼ Poste de sécurité avancé
- ☐ Locaux techniques
- ◼ Bureaux
- ☐ Ascenseurs publics
- ◼ Ascenseurs belvédère

BAR

Niveau 410,90 NGF

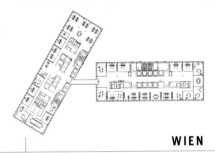

TWIN TOWER

MAXIMILIANO FUKSAS ARCHITETTO

2001

CLIENT / CLIENT / AUFTRAGGEBER: IMMOFIANZ IMMOBILIEN ANLAGEN AG WIENERGERGER BAUSTOFFINDUSTRIE AG
TOTAL AREA / SURFACE TOTALE / GESAMTOBERFLÄCHE: 139.500 m²
FLOORS / PLANS / STOCKWERKE - HEIGHT / HAUTEUR / HÖHE: 34 fl / 127 m

These glass towers united by means of a base contain offices and leisure areas. The architect's initial research was based on specifiying a solution which would enrich the skyline of the city and help to grant Wienerberg (a newly created area) a mechanism for its own identification. Articulated in a street which evokes the sinuous lines of the road ("landscaped street"), the project works from two architectural typologies (the tower and the base as two juxtaposed buildings) eluding the monotony of the complex and at the same time allowing the user a functional recognition of the whole (offices and leisure areas) in the distribution by independent elements.

Ces tours en verre jointes avec une base en tant que socle disposent de bureaux et de zones de loisirs. La recherche initiale de l'architecte a pour base concrétiser une solution qui puisse enrichir le skyline de la ville et qui permette de doter le Wienerberg (création d'une nouvelle aire) d'un mécanisme d'identification propre. Le projet, qui est articulé sur une rue qui évoque le tracé sinueux du chemin ("landscaped street"), travaille sur deux typologies architectoniques (la tour et le socle représentent deux bâtiments juxtaposés) évitant la monotonie du complexe et en même temps, permettant l'usager de reconnaître la fonction de l'ensemble (bureaux et zones de loisirs) sur la distribution par éléments indépendants.

In diesen Glastürmen, verbunden durch einen Unterbau, liegen Büros und Freizeitzentren. Anfängliche Untersuchungen des Architekten basierten auf der Suche einer Lösung zur Bereicherung der Skyline der Stadt und um dem Wienerberg (einem Neubauviertel) eine eigene Identität zu verleihen. An einer Straße errichtet, deren Straßenführung einer geschlängelten Landstraße nachempfunden ist, arbeitet das Bauprojekt mit zwei architektonischen Typologien (das Hochhaus und der Unterbau als zwei nebeneinander liegende Gebäude) mit denen man der Monotonie des einheitlichen Gebäudeblocks ausweicht, dem Benutzer aber gleichzeitig die Funktionalität zweier unabhängiger Anlagen zu erkennen gibt (Büros und Freizeitbereiche).

Located in a transition area between the density of the city and a greenbelt, the towers possess and praise the theme contained in the early sketches, the development of the urban landscape.

Elles se trouvent sur une aire de passage entre la densité de la ville et les zones vertes, les tours réunissent et exhalent aussi la thématique présente dans les premières ébauches, le développement urbanistique du paysage urbain.

In einem Übergangsbereich von der belebten Stadt in den Grüngürtel gelegen, wurden mit diesen Türmen die anfänglichen Ideen des Skizzenentwurfs zur baulichen Entwicklung der Stadtumgebung verwirklicht und klar herausgearbeitet.

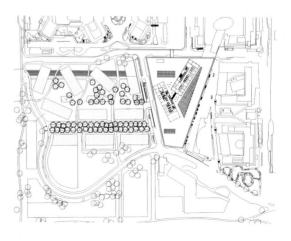

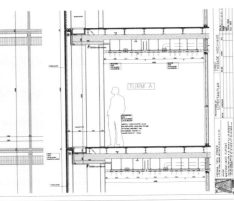

The architect researched the converging paths of art and architecture. We can see contributions of Land Art in the square set out as a "landscaped street", evoking winding country roads in the midst of vegetation.

L'architecte recherche les chemins de confluence entre art et architecture. Nous trouvons des interventions de Land Art sur la place articulée comme une "landscaped street" qui évoque les chemins ruraux, les tracés sinueux entourés de végétation.

Der Architekt fand den Weg des Zusammenspiels zwischen Kunst und Architektur. Wir finden Anwendungen der "Land Art" in einem Platz, der wie eine "landscaped street" geschwungene Feldwege von dichter Vegetation umsäumt, nachempfindet.

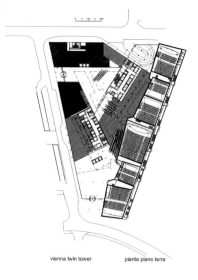

vienna twin tower   pianta secondo piano basamento
MASSIMILIANO FUKSAS ARCHITETTO

vienna twin tower   pianta piano terra

The project for the building was conventional – an office block and a shopping centre. The proposal satisfies the need with differentiating elements, the tower and the base as two juxtaposed buildings, avoiding the conventional layout. At the same time it provides a clear, functional recognition of the base and the tower.

Le programme du bâtiment était conventionnel, une tour de bureaux et un centre commercial. La proposition répond à des typologies différentes, la tour et le socle comme deux bâtiments juxtaposés, évitant le complexe conventionnel. Il permet de même une claire reconnaissance fonctionnelle entre la base et la tour.

Das Bauprogramm war eher konventionell – Büroturm und Einkaufszentrum. Zwei verschiedene Bauausführungen liegen nebeneinander – der Turm und der Unterbau – und weichem dem konventionellen Komplex aus. Außerdem ergibt sich eine klar ersichtliche funktionelle Trennung zwischen Turm und Sockel.

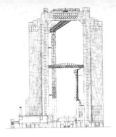

UMEDA SKY BUILDING

HIROSHI HARA ATELIER

CLIENT / CLIENT / AUFTRAGGEBER: JOHN HANCOCK MUTUAL LIFE INSURANCE CO.

1993

TOTAL AREA / SURFACE TOTALE / GESAMTOBERFLÄCHE: 260.000 m²

FLOORS / PLANS / STOCKWERKE - HEIGHT / HAUTEUR / HÖHE: 100 fl - 128 m

A skyscraper is a building which has symbolic meaning from both the economic and urban planning points of view. The promoters of this building wanted it to be an icon of Omeda City, an area in the industrial belt of Osaka. At the same time, the architects proposed it as a prototype of a building typology where the building generates a new form of urban development. This will be the city of the future where buildings like this are raised, tall towers connected by means of their upper floors via a horizontal platform.

Le gratte-ciel est un bâtiment qui est devenu un symbole, aussi bien du point de vue économique que du côté urbanistique. Les promoteurs de ce bâtiment désiraient qu'il devienne un icône de Omeda City, une surface de la périphérie de Osaka. Quant aux architectes, ils proposèrent un prototype avec une typologie édificatrice, par laquelle le bâtiment engendre une nouvelle forme de développement urbain. Celle-ci sera la ville du future, dans laquelle s'élèveront des bâtiments comme celui-ci, des grandes tours connectées par les étages supérieurs avec une plate-forme horizontale.

Der Wolkenkratzer ist ein Gebäude, das sich durchsetzen muß, um zu einem wirtschaftlichen wie auch urbanistischen Symbol zu werden. Die Promotoren beabsichtigten mit diesem Bau, in Omeda City, einem Stadtgürtel in Osaka, eine Ikone zu errichten. Gleichzeitig stellen Architekten diesen Bau als Prototyp neuzeitlicher urbaner Bebauungsart vor. Es wird die Stadt der Zukunft sein, wo sich Gebäude dieser Art – hohe Türme, die in den oberen Stockwerken durch horizontale Plattformen verbunden sind – erheben.

Siting plan of the building.
It spreads vertically, generating wide
green spaces. The glass façade
reflects everything which surrounds
it, from the sky to the ground.

Plan de l'emplacement du bâtiment,
celui-ci s'étend verticalement, ce qui
engendre des grands espaces verts.
La façade en verre réfléchit tout ce
qui l'entoure, du ciel à la terre.

Lageplan des Gebäudes.
Es erhebt sich senkrecht und bietet
ausreichend Platz für Grünflächen.
Die Glasfassade spiegelt alles vom
Himmel bis zur Erde wieder.

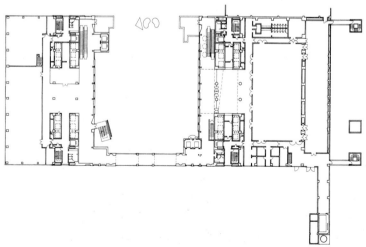

The observation platform which unites the two towers is perforated by a circle from which escalators descend down the empty central space.

La plate-forme mirador qui unit les deux tours est perforée par un cercle, de celui-ci descendent des escaliers mécaniques sur l'espace vide du centre.

Die Aussichtsplattform, die beide Türme miteinander verbindet, weist im Zentrum eine riesige kreisförmige Öffnung vor, von der Rolltreppen in dem offenen Bereich zwischen den Bauten verlaufen.

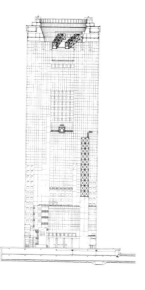
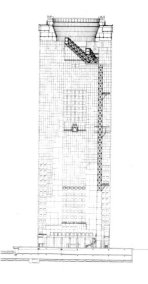

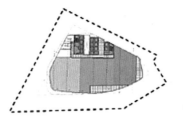
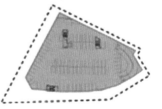

WATERFRONT HOUSE

T.R. HAMZAH & YEAN SDN BHD

CLIENT / CLIENT / AUFTRAGGEBER: WATERFRONT HOUSE SDN BHD	**2000**
TOTAL AREA / SURFACE TOTALE / GESAMTOBERFLÄCHE: 41.000 m²	
FLOORS / PLANS / STOCKWERKE - HEIGHT / HAUTEUR / HÖHE: 26 fl -130 m	

This tower, an office building of high standing which had to take maximum advantage of the possible constructed volume, was thought up by the client and the architect as an object which had to present a sustainable alternative model for the growth of the neighborhood (marked by the Petronas towers) in the heart of a city where the greatest building growth of the Asian continent of the last few years has taken place. Apart from being the company's headquarters, it is a meeting place for the clients, presenting a fresh and innovative corporate image. Apart from being a formidable contemporary object, its bioclimatic design is based on minimizing as much as possible the use of heating and air conditioning, promoting an urban culture which is sensitive to energy saving.

Cette tour, un immeuble de bureaux grand standing qui devait profiter au maximum le possible volume construit, fut conçue par le client et l'architecte comme un objet qui devait présenter un modèle respectueux alternatif pour la croissance du quartier (souligné par les tours Petronas) dans le coeur d'une ville où s'est produite la plus grande croissance, quant à la construction, du continent asiatique dans les derniers temps. Elle est le siège de la société, mais aussi un endroit de rencontre pour les clients et elle présente une image corporative fraîche et innovatrice. Sa conception bioclimatique est un objet formellement contemporain, il a, aussi, pour base la minimisation au maximum de l'utilisation du chauffage et de la climatisation, il favorise une culture urbaine sensible à l'économie d'énergie.

Dieser Turm – ein Bürogebäude des gehobenen Standards - wurde vom Bauherrn und dem Architekten als verträgliches Alternativmodel zum stetigen Wachstum des Viertels (von den Petronas-Türme überragt) im Herzen einer Stadt erdacht, in der bisher der größte Bauboom aller Zeiten auf dem asiatischen Kontinent stattfand. Neben der Funktion als Firmenhauptsitz, vermittelt es den Besuchern auch das Image eines modernen innovativen Treffpunktes. Kontemporäre Formgebung und bioklimatische Ausrichtung des Gebäudes beabsichtigen, die Nutzung von Heizung und Air-Conditioning weitestgehend zu reduzieren und möchten gleichzeitig die Idee der Energieeinsparung fördern.

The tower is located in the heart of the city next to the Petronas Towers, in an area of recent urban development. Ground floor of the building and main entrance that leads to the foyer that distributes users and the public.

La tour se trouve au coeur de la ville, près des Tours Petronas, une zone au développement urbanistique récent. Rez-de-chaussée du bâtiment et accès principal qui conduit au hall, là où sont distribués les utilisateurs et le public.

Der Turm steht im Herzen der Stadt in einem Neubauviertel neben den Petronas-Türmen. Das Erdgeschoss und der Haupteingang, der in das Vestibül führt, werden von denjenigen genutzt, die in diesem Gebäude arbeiten wie aber auch von Besuchern.

Conceptually, the building is divided in three different sections. The four-storey base houses comercial space, restaurants and bars. The displaced pillars from the perimeter of the façade result in open floors destined to office space.

Conceptuellement, le point de départ du bâtiment est disposé sur trois sections différentes. La base qui a une hauteur de quatre étages où l'on trouve des espaces commerciaux et de restauration (bars, restaurants). Les piliers déplacés par rapport au périmètre de la façade permettent des étages libres pour bureaux.

Das Gebäude verteilt sich auf drei unterschiedliche Sektionen. Im 4stöckigen Unterbau befinden sich Einkaufsmöglichkeiten und gastronomische Einrichtungen (Bars, Restaurants). Aus dem Perimeter der Fassade verlagerte Stützpfeiler ergeben ausreichend Platz für Büroräume.

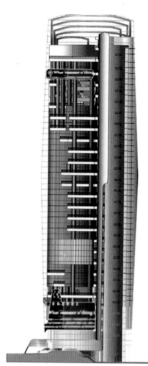

The last four floors house the company's headquarters and include a roof garden. Vegetation is a constant element throughout the entire building; it is a part of the climate control system and is psychologically a beneficial factor among the building's users.

Et les quatre derniers étages où se trouvent les bureaux centraux de la compagnie, il y a aussi un jardin sur le sommet. La végétation est une constante sur tout le bâtiment, elle appartient au système de contrôle climatique et, de même, elle agit psychologiquement en tant que facteur positif sur les usagers.

In deu letzten vier Stockwerken befinden sich die zentralbüros des Unternelmeus einschließlich eines Dachgartens. Die Vegetation ist eine Konstante im gesamten Gebäude, denn sie ist Teil des Klimakontrollsystems und zeigt außerdem einen positiven psychologischen Effekt bei den Nutzern des Hauses.

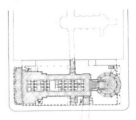

WELLS FARGO CENTER

CESAR PELLI & ASSOCIATES INC.

CLIENT / CLIENT / AUFTRAGGEBER: HINES INTERESTS LTD PARTNERSHIP & NORWEST BANK	**1989**

TOTAL AREA / SURFACE TOTALE / GESAMTOBERFLÄCHE: 188.000 m²

FLOORS / PLANS / STOCKWERKE - HEIGHT / HAUTEUR / HÖHE: 57 fl / 235,6 m

In 1982, a fire destroyed the 16-floor headquarters of the Northwestern National Bank. The new building, the Norwest Center (currently Wells Fargo), is the prototype of American skyscrapers designed to capture in their architecture the soul of the city. Its imposing presence is marked by the dominant vertical rhythm of the facade, where the Minnesota stone predominates over the glass. Starting out from a rectangular base of granite, the building ascends in a slender way by means of a light lateral breeching, thus characterizing its silhouette which is topped with a light crown of glass and marble.

En 1982 un incendie détruit le siège à 16 étages du Northwestern National Bank. Le nouveau Bâtiment, le Norwest Center (actuellement Wells Fargo), est le prototype du gratte-ciel américain conçu pour capturer quant à son architecture l'âme de la ville. Sa présence imposante est caractérisée par le rythme vertical qui domine la façade sur laquelle la pierre de Minnesota l'emporte face au verre. Le bâtiment commence par une base rectangulaire en granite, il s'élève, la forme est svelte, et décrit un léger déplacement latéral, ce qui ainsi caractérise sa silhouette qui est terminée par une couronne légère en marbre et en verre.

1982 zerstörte ein Brand den 16stöckigen Sitz der Northwestern National Bank. Der neue Bau, das Norwest Center (aktuell Wells Fargo genannt), ist der Prototyp amerikanischer Wolkenkratzer, dessen Architektur die Seele der Stadt darstellt. Seine gewaltige Präsenz drückt sich durch die ebene senkrecht aufsteigende Fassade aus Minnesotastein über Glas aus. Ein rechteckiger Unterbau aus Granit, darüber erhebt sich dieser elegante Bau mit leicht zurückgesetzten Seitenteilen, der mit einer Krone aus Marmor und Glas abschließt.

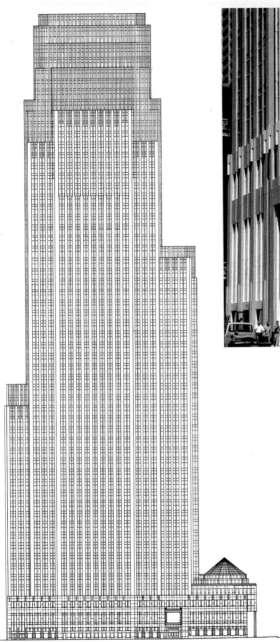

Front elevation of the building.
Despite the rectangular shape of the
lot, the vision of the building varies
according to the point of view of the
observer.

Elévation frontale du bâtiment.
Malgré la forme rectangulaire du
terrain, la vision du bâtiment varie
selon le point de vue de
l'observateur.

Aufsteigende Frontansicht. Trotz des
rechteckigen Grundstücks, variiert der
Anblick auf das Gebäude selbst je
nach Standort des Betrachters.

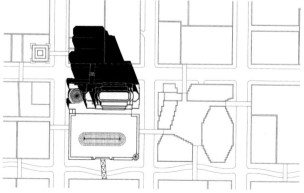

The base of the tower, which occupies more than half a block, is connected by means of a bridge to a public space designed together with the sculptor Siah Armajani.

La base de la tour, qui se situe sur plus d'un demi pâté, est connectée avec un pont sur un espace publique conçu auprès du sculpteur Siah Armajani.

Der Turmsockel belegt mehr als die Hälfte eines Häuserblocks und ist durch eine Brücke mit einen öffentlichen Platz verbunden, der gemeinsam mit dem Bildhauer Siah Armjani entworfen wurde.

WORLD FINANCIAL CENTER

CESAR PELLI & ASSOCIATES INC

CLIENT / CLIENT / AUFTRAGGEBER: OLYMPIA & YORK	**1985**
TOTAL AREA / SURFACE TOTALE / GESAMTOBERFLÄCHE: 790.000 m²	
FLOORS / PLANS / STOCKWERKE - HEIGHT / HAUTEUR / HÖHE: 34, 51 fl / 225,3 m	

This complex was built on land reclaimed from the sea, forming part of the World Trade Center of Manhattan, between the Hudson River and the West Side freeway.

On the other side, the Twin Towers contrast with the reflective façades and copper decks of the W.F.C. The two complexes form one of the most recognizable silhouettes of the city. The four office towers are connected by means of the lower floors, giving rise to a very large site with very varied uses, such as a winter garden, shopping spaces, stage and a bridge which links it with the Twin Towers.

Ce complexe qui fut construit sur des terre-pleins gagnés sur la mer, appartient au World Trade Center de Manhattan, entre le fleuve Hudson et l'autoroute du West Side.

De l'autre côté, les Twin Towers contrastent quant aux façades réfléchissantes et aux recouvrements en cuivre du W.F.C. Les deux complexes dessinent une des silhouettes les plus remarquables de la ville. Les quatre tours de bureaux sont connectées par les étages inférieurs ce qui permet une surface grande et variée, à usages tels qu'un jardin d'hiver, des espaces commerciaux, un scénario et un pont les connecte aux Twin Towers.

Dieser Komplex entstand auf einem Baugrund, der dem Meer abgerungen wurde und ist Teil des World Trade Centers, zwischen dem Hudson-River und der West Side Autobahn in Manhattan gelegen.

Auf der anderen Seiten kontrastieren die Twin Towers mit den reflektierenden Fassaden und Kupferdächern des W.F.C. Gemeinsam ergeben sie die so typische Skyline der Stadt. Sämtliche vier Wolkenkratzer sind in den unteren Bereichen durch Durchgänge miteinander verbunden. Dieser großflächige Verbindungsbereich beherbergt einen Wintergarten sowie Ladenzeilen und eine Brücke stellt die Verbindung mit den Twin Towers her.

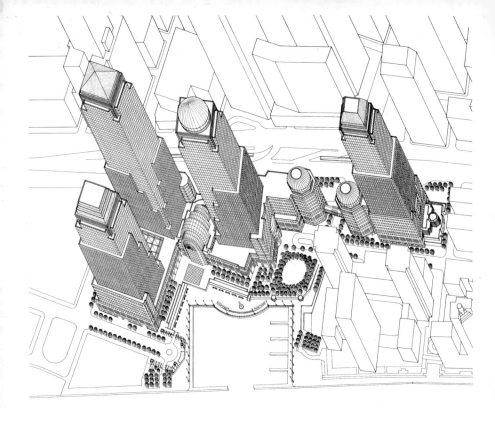

On the right, view of the great glass vault which covers the Winter Garden. On the left, boats at the Hudson River dock.

À droite, vue de la grande voûte en verre, elle recouvre le Jardin d'Hiver. À gauche, bateaux sur le quai du fleuve Hudson.

Rechts: Blick auf den großen Glasbogen, der sich über den Wintergarten spannt. Links, Schiffsanleger an der Kaimauer des Hudson Rivers.

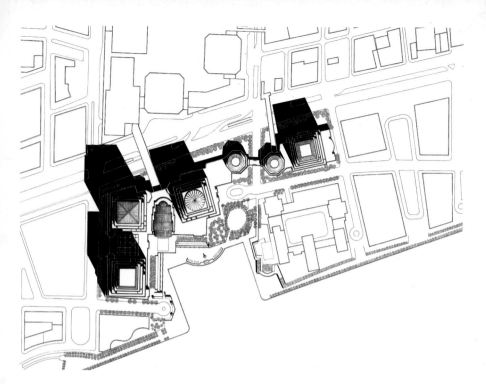

On the left, inside the Winter
Garden. Above, axonometric
projection of the group with the study
of the shadows thrown by the
buildings.

À gauche, intérieur du Jardin d'Hiver.
En haut, axonométrie de l'ensemble
avec l'étude des hombres que
projettent les bâtiments.

Links, Innenansicht des Wintergartens.
Oben, Axonomethrie des
Baukomplexes mit Schattenspiel der
Gebäude.

IN MEMORIAM

This mythical image of Manhattan has been drastically altered since the attacks of September 11th 2001, when two airplanes crashed into the two towers, causing their subsequent collapse.

Cette image mythique de Manhattan a été tout à fait modifiée après l'attentat du onze septembre 2001, lorsque deux avions choquèrent contre les deux tours, ce qui ensuite provoqua l'effondrement.

Diese legendäre Ansicht von Manhattan wurde durch das Attentat vom 11. September 2001 drastisch verändert, als zwei Flugzeuge in diese Türme flogen und diese kurz danach einstürzten.

This book could not have been produced without the collaboration given to us by the participating architects and their corresponding teams of people. We would like to take this opportunity to thank all these people for their participation and amiability:

Ce livre n'aurait pas pu être réalisé sans la collaboration que nous ont offert les architectes qui ont participé et les équipes humaines correspondantes, nous voulons ici remercier toutes ces personnes de leur participation et leur gentillesse:

Dieses Buch wäre nicht ohne die Zusammenarbeit der beteiligten Architekten und deren Mitarbeiter entstanden. Von hier aus möchten wir uns bei allen Beteiligten für ihre Zusammenarbeit und Freundlichkeit bedanken.

Alonso-Balaguer Arquitectes Associats (Pau Balaguer, Lluís Alonso)
Arquitectures Jean Nouvel (Charlotte Kruk)
Atelier Christian de Portzamparc (Gabriella Wilson)
b720 arquitectos (Fermín Vázquez, Ana Bassat)
Càtedra Gaudí (Joan Bassegoda i Nonell)
Cervera & Pioz WPA
Cesar Pelli & Associates Inc (César Pelli, James Balga, Lesley Holford)
Coop Himmel(b)lau (Ursula Haberle)
C.Y.Lee & Partners Architects/Planners (May Y.W.Chen)
Dominique Perrault Architecte (Julie Revers)
D.Lau & NG Chun Man Architects & Engineers (Liby Kwok, Shelly Tang)
Eli Attia Architect
E.Miralles & B.Tagliabue Arquitectes Associats (Mireia Fornells , Elena Rocchi)
Foster & Partners (Kate Stirling, Pippa Taylor)
Fox & Fowle Architects (Kirsten Sibilia)
Kohn Pedersen Fox Associates PC (KPF) (Gale Chaney, Elisabeth Austin)
Marc Mascort i Boix
Maximiliano Fuksas Architetto (Francesco Colarossi)
Murphy/Jahn Inc Architects (Keith H.Palmer, Lori Hladek)
Nikken Sekkei Ltd.
Ortiz Leon Arquitectos
Oscar Tusquets Blanca Arquitecturas (Oscar Tusquets, Anna Álvarez)
Pei Cobb Freed & Partners (James Blaga)
Renzo Piano Building Workshop (Stefania Canta)
Ricard Bofill Taller d'Arquitectura (Serena Vergano)
Richard Rogers Partnership (Tina Wilson)
Skidmore Owings & Merrill LLP (SOM) (Elizabeth H.Kubany, Lidia Lee Kemppainen, Kim R.D.Albrecht)
TR Hamzah & Yeang SDN BHD (Dr.Ken Yeang, Yenniu)
Zeidner Grinnell Partnership (Eberhard H.Zeidler, Rosalind Yang)
Zimmer Gunsul Frasca Partnership (Sandy Tobkin)